Discourses
Volume Four
2017

DISCOURSES:
Gateway to the Infinite
Volume Four: 2017

Yogacharya David R. Hickenbottom

Editor: Ruth M. Lamb, Ph.D

The Cross and The Lotus Publishing
Camano Island, Washington, USA

Discourses—Volume Four 2017: Gateway to the Infinite
Copyright ©2023, The Cross and The Lotus Publishing

For permission requests, contact the publisher at:
http://www.crossandlotus.com/contact.html

ISBN: 978-1-957811-03-1 (softcover)
ISBN: 978-1-957811-04-8 (eBook)

All photos courtesy of Carla Hickenbottom Portfolio
unless otherwise attributed (see page 371)

Edited by Ruth Lamb

Book design by Jan Westendorp/Kato Design and Photo (katodesignandphoto.com)

Cover design by Rob Landers, Ruth Lamb, and Jan Westendorp

Printed and bound in the USA

Published by
The Cross and The Lotus Publishing
Camano Island, Washington, USA
Website: www.crossandlotus.com

Contents

OM TAT SAT AUM

Preface

Yogacharya David, Puri, India, 2013.

Remember that you are a child of the Infinite, and in remembering this, you claim access to the realms of your greater Self.

Faith in God means that we keep our mind on Him; we think of His qualities of being all-powerful, all-conscious, everywhere present, all love, bliss, and joy. We know that He is above us, beside us, everywhere about us, and securely found within us. He is guiding us, and the events around us that lead us into His tremendous kingdom of heaven. Our faith brings us into harmony with Him, and we realize, in greater and greater measure, the truth of who and what He is, and of who and what we are. Faith such as this obliterates fear and makes us do all things in full confidence that He is ever with us, and we are ever in Him.

We must be mindful to keep ourselves in the "current" of God's will. Getting caught in the wrong current could end in staid waters of depression, dangerous whirlpools of swirling, endless desire, or running into downed trees of painful situations that rip us to shreds. Sometimes, we must paddle hard to avoid a wayward current; other times, we are easily kept in the God-current by keeping our mind on Him. Really, once we find that passageway of God-awareness, it is much, much, easier than being sub-ject to the world only.

Life, as we think of it, is the soul manifesting through the three bodies: physical, energetic, and causal. The puri-fied body and mind are perfect instruments for the tran-scendent Divine Mind and are a blessing to ourselves and this world. Go beyond the three realms, seek out contact with the ever-pure, eternal Self—not so we can get God to do what we want, but that we may be an expression of what God wants us to be.

We are not here to lead a half-dead zombie life, sleep-walking through old habits that no longer serve us. Rather, we are here to live a dynamic life filled with love, light, and wisdom—a God-realized life.

One great lesson is that, when you make a determina-tion and keep with it, especially when you invoke Divine Providence from the beginning, you attract invisible sup-port for accomplishing your positive intention. Feel that you are not alone—God, the masters, angels, and invisi-ble forces respond to your clarity and uplifting purpose. In this sense, there are no large or small goals, but only one goal, and that is the one in front of you now... Do not seek to have God on your side, but rather, know that you are on God's side through deepened meditation and intuition. Then proceed forward and be His instrument with true purpose in all things.

—YOGACHARYA DAVID

The discourses for 2017 bring us Yogacharya David listening at even deeper levels to the God-call—the inner adesh to further explore Nature's Cathedrals and to immerse in the dramatic healing power of wild spaces and nature's great gifts of rocks, mountains, forests, rivers, sunshine, rain, and stars at night. It is as if his soul sought healing, solace, and wisdom from Mother Earth's cathedrals and from the human-constructed houses of worship that he and Carla made pilgrimages to. It is as if an infinite gateway was being prepared, and that places of silence, steeped in nature's dramatic, natural, and healthy frequency, provided an impetus for healing and repairing his body, preparing him for his ongoing dharmic path.

Yogacharya David speaks:

In truth, your life is an expression of infinite nature; you are meant to live in freedom, joy, love, and light. To tune into this greater Source, you must rise above your beliefs that you are small and your problems are big. It is true that on a human level, many things can come at you, and challenges can really stretch you, but you are not a human self only. You must remember that you are a child of the Infinite, and in remembering this, you claim access to the realms of your greater Self . . . Know yourself to be a citizen of the stars—there is no limit to consciousness . . . Your life is "right-sized" for you; you need only open yourself to all God wishes to manifest through you. Let go of fear, resentment, limiting beliefs, and know that your infinite Beloved is, even right now, actively manifesting all that you need to be in His likeness and in His image.

So, any time you are feeling too cramped in your living space, feeling the pressure of life, and that you are too small for the shoes you are wearing, then instantly recall who and what you truly are—a child of the Infinite—as such, you expand to be larger than the problems and challenges you face; you walk amongst the stars and vast resources are streaming to you in order for you to live your life exactly as it has been ordered from above. In that spaciousness, breathe freedom and know that God is the solution to every problem and His ingenuity for solving problems is even greater than yours for creating them! There is plenty of room for you to breathe, live your life, and be exactly who God designed you to be.

Go boldly forward, knowing that all is in His sweet hands, shaping your soul into His likeness and image with the utmost care. For you are not different from He: He cares for you even as you love the Infinite Beloved. It is love that gives to love—and the rose blooms in the desert.

In this series of Discourses, Yogacharya David blesses us with his wisdom and his deep understanding of both the perilous and glorious nature of a spiritual climb. A climb that can take us to the highest mountain summit. There, we may experience the joy that comes from attunement with Spirit; we too can learn how to reunite soul and spirit; we can reawaken to, and reclaim, our life purpose. Let us join Yogacharya David, and climb!

Gateway to the Infinite is the fourth in a six-volume series of Discourses composed by Yogacharya David between 2013 and 2019. The volumes are as follows:

- *Discourses—Volume One: 2013–14: Living a Spiritually Rich Life*

- *Discourses—Volume Two: 2015: Re-Union of Soul and Spirit*

- *Discourses—Volume Three: 2016: A True New Birth*

- *Discourses—Volume Four: 2017: Gateway to the Infinite*

- *Discourses—Volume Five: 2018: Standing on the Threshold of Eternity*

- *Discourses—Volume Six: 2019: Writing in the Book of Life*

Regarding the use of images in this publication:

Yogacharya David put great care, creativity, time, and intention into selecting images to complement his writings in each and every posting. When preparing his Discourses for publication, we found that certain images from unknown sources or those found to be under copyright could not be included. Every effort has been made to feature replacement images as close as possible to Yogacharya David's original selections. In a few instances where no similar substitute was available, a picture of Yogacharya David or a beloved saint has been offered instead.[1] Where we have placed substitute images is designated in the caption by a double asterisk **. For example: Yogacharya David at Anandashram, 2005.** Image attribution is in the Reference section at the end of this book

OM TAT SAT AUM

---

[1]   Yogacharya David's original discourses can be found at **www.crossandlotus.com**

Introduction

Yogacharya David, Haridwar, India, 2005.

Dear Aspirant,

Whenever you begin a journey, you usually start with a destination in mind, a means of conveyance, and a map or landmarks to indicate that you are on the right path. Those of us following this path have God (Self) Realization as our Goal of goals. Our means of conveyance is God-remembrance, such as chanting God's Name, deepened meditation through Kriya Yoga, universal love and service, loving God, and discernment of Truth.

These writings often come in the early morning: a time when the day is quiet and fresh, an open page upon which to write. These thought-expressions come from an unfathomable Source, welling up from the quiet of the all-pervading Spirit. Reading these words has the power to lead you to the same Source from which they have flowed from within me.

The inspiration that fuels these writings comes to me with great power and clarity; however, mere words are incapable of holding all that is given. It is through inner attunement that the power in the words will lift you into the same Spirit that I experience in Super-consciousness, an uplifting power that is a passageway into realms divine.

Human words and thoughts are imperfect; it is only in pure Spirit that perfection is to be truly found. It is the purpose of these writings that we should rise together in the universal Spirit of God. Come, let us soar together and find truth and beauty unencumbered.

These discourses can act as markers upon your spiritual journey to make for safe and rapid progress. Unlike a scattered "hunt and peck" approach chosen by many, taking them on "wild goose chases" only to become thoroughly lost, you will receive teachings of the purest quality that speed you on the most direct path to realization. Obstacles arise that create challenges for your journey—you can find inspiration here to help you meet those challenges.

These writings contain notes from pilgrimages and journeys that also (reader alert here!) have lessons upon the path embedded in them.[2]

With deepest love and blessings on your journey,
YOGACHARYA DAVID

---

2   This Introduction comes from Yogacharya David's *Discourses 2013–14, Volume One: Living a Spiritually Rich Life.*

DISCOURSES

January 1

YOU ALL ARE THE LIGHT OF GOD

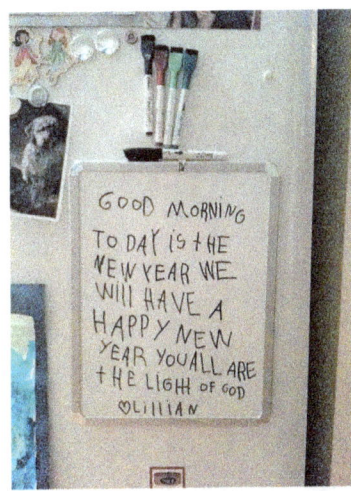

"Good morning. Today is the New Year. We will have a happy New Year. You all are the light of God."

—LILLIAN GRACE.

Little Lillian Grace's parents found this message this morning on the family fridge. What a soul in God.

Have a blessed and joyous New Year. You truly are the Light of God.

January 4

FAITH OBLITERATES FEAR

Yogacharya David on a boat on
the Ganges, Varanasi, India, 2005.**

"The only thing we have to fear is fear itself."[3] President Franklin Delano Roosevelt (FDR) said this after the Pearl Harbor attack and at the beginning of the US entry into a world war for which it was vastly unprepared. At that moment, there were many reasons to be afraid, and yet he was exactly right in his statement. Chronic fear gets us nowhere and can render us inert or direct us in absolutely the wrong direction.

---

3   United States President Franklin Delano Roosevelt stated this in his First Inaugural Address, March 4, 1933.

There are many triggers for fear, even at a time when we are not faced with such dire events as a world war. But whenever we are filled with fear (for whatever reason), it may as well be war. It is a war going on right within us. However, fear does have an opposite: faith. Many of the great warriors down through time had absolute faith in the fact that, if it is their time to die, nothing can stop it, and if it was not their time, nothing can bring death; so, either way, they could charge fearlessly into battle.

In modern life, most of us are not faced with mortal combat, but there are still battlefields of fear: money issues, sickness and disease, ostracizing loneliness, failure, looking stupid, and conflict; hence, so many battlegrounds upon which fear wages battle for possession of our hearts, minds, and souls. To avoid defeat in this war, we must look for allies that will enable us to win daily battles. Faith in fate, "If it is meant to be, then it will be," is one ally. Faith can also be placed in the support of family or friends, societies, church, or government, and when things are desperate enough, even saints, angels, and/or God.

A favorite story of mine: a young boy was separated from his parents. The parents looked everywhere for him, then finally thought that their son had returned to their car. At last, they found him sitting on the car hood. When his dad approached his son, he asked, "Were you scared?" The boy responded, "I was so scared, I prayed to God!"

Well, it has to get pretty bad before people pray to God. It is an interesting point, and it is true, many people only turn to God when things are desperate. Why is that? Many people simply don't see how useful it is to have a regular connection with God. Rather, prayer is something done at Sunday church, or in a crisis. Some may say a prayer before a meal; others have their children pray before sleep, but to think of conversing with God through the day would never occur to them, or this mode of God-conversation is thought to be just for "religious fanatics—those people."

To see God as practical, even essential———a "workhorse" in daily life—and to cultivate a faith that meets everyday needs, could be an enormous step for many. For me, it seems the most logical thing in the world. From the first thing in the morning to the last thought at night, God is part and parcel of my thoughts—of my being. Far from a "weakness," it is my strength. God is my guide, friend, comforter, solver of problems, wise counselor, an ocean of love, and peace: my all in all—the most practical thing in my life.

Faith that God is guiding and controlling me, and the events in my life, frees me to act in the moment. I need only concern myself with how He is flowing through me here and now. And, if He makes me think of some future event or something from the past, then it is His Presence that is interwoven into those thoughts as well. What of finances, health, and every other possible problem area? They are in His keeping. Now, this does not mean I do not have a role to play. Quite the opposite. I am a co-creator with God, so my part is essential. However, the responsibility for how things go is not on my shoulders; it is on His. My part is to actively attune myself to His will and follow it perfectly.

Imagine floating down a river, as we used to do with our feet pointed downstream, or floating on inner tubes, or on rafts. The current is carrying us, but we must make adjustments to keep ourselves from running aground or colliding with dangerous obstacles. Being aware of currents on the river made for the safest floats. Just so, we must be mindful to keep ourselves in the "current" of God's will. Getting caught in the wrong current could end in staid waters of depression, dangerous whirlpools of swirling, endless desires, or running into downed trees of painful situations that rip us to shreds. Sometimes, we must paddle hard to avoid a wayward current; other times, we are easily kept in the God-current by keeping our mind on Him. Really, once we find that passageway of God-awareness, it is much, much, easier than being subject to the world only.

Faith in God means that we trust, trust that whatever He brings is exactly right for us. We have faith in His guidance and wisdom and know that He is with us as a well-wisher, friend, and comforter. It does not mean that waters are always smooth and easy; but really, we do love an adventure. With God, the good ending of the adventure is always assured, but it is still an adventure.

Faith in God means that we keep our mind on Him; we think of His qualities of being all-powerful, all-conscious, everywhere present, all love, bliss, and joy. We know that He is above us, beside us, everywhere about us, and securely found within us. He is guiding us and the events around us that lead us into His tremendous kingdom of heaven. Our faith brings us into harmony with Him, and we realize, in greater and greater measure, the truth of who and what He is, and of who and what we are. Faith such as this obliterates fear and makes us do all things in full confidence that He is ever with us, and we are ever in Him.

January 5

THE MASTER'S BIRTHDAY

Beloved Master Paramhansa Yogananda.**

oday, we celebrate the birth of Paramhansa Yogananda, one of the great spiritual personalities to inhabit this world, and a personal blessing to those of us who follow this Kriya path. Master Yoganandaji wrote this 70 years ago:

> The characteristic features of Indian culture have long been a search for ultimate verities and the concomitant disciple-guru relationship. My own path led me to a Christlike sage whose beautiful life was chiseled for the ages. He was one of the great masters who are India's

sole remaining wealth. Emerging in every generation, they have bulwarked their land against the fate of Babylon and Egypt.

I find my earliest memories covering the anachronistic features of a previous incarnation. Clear recollections came to me of a distant life, a yogi amidst the Himalayan snows. These glimpses of the past, by some dimensionless link, also afforded me a glimpse of the future.

The helpless humiliations of infancy are not banished from my mind. I was resentfully conscious of not being able to walk or express myself freely. Prayerful surges arose within me as I realized my bodily impotence. My strong emotional life took silent form as words in many languages. Among the inward confusion of tongues, my ear gradually accustomed itself to the circumambient Bengali syllables of my people. The beguiling scope of an infant's mind adultly considered limited to toys and toes.

Psychological ferment and my unresponsive body brought me to many obstinate crying-spells. I recall the general family bewilderment at my distress. Happier memories, too, crowd in on me: my mother's caresses, and my first attempts at lisping phrase and toddling step. These early triumphs, usually forgotten quickly, are yet a natural basis of self-confidence.[4]

Thus begins the spiritual classic: *Autobiography of a Yogi*. Master continues his narrative with the time when he was eight, just after his healing of deadly Asiatic cholera by Lahiri Mahasaya.

Shortly after my healing through the potency of the guru's picture, I had an influential spiritual vision. Sitting

---

4   *Autobiography of a Yogi* (p. 3).

on my bed one morning, I fell into a deep reverie. "What is behind the darkness of closed eyes?" This probing thought came powerfully into my mind. An immense flash of light at once manifested to my inward gaze. Divine shapes of saints, sitting in meditation posture in mountain caves, formed like miniature cinema pictures on the large screen of radiance within my forehead.

"Who are you?" I spoke aloud.

"We are the Himalayan yogis." The celestial response is difficult to describe; my heart was thrilled.

"Ah, I long to go to the Himalayas and become like you!" The vision vanished, but the silvery beams expanded in ever-widening circles to infinity.

"What is this wondrous glow?"

"I am Iswara. I am Light." The voice was as murmuring clouds.

"I want to be one with Thee!"

Out of the slow dwindling of my divine ecstasy, I salvaged a permanent legacy of inspiration to seek God. "He is eternal, ever-new Joy!" This memory persisted long after the day of rapture.[5]

Master's intense search for God, which took him to the feet of his great guru, Sri Yukteswarji, is now immortalized in his autobiography and has become a living testament in the changed lives of those who took Master as their guru. We are indeed blessed to have this seamless connection come to us through his beloved disciple, Mother Hamilton. The traditional guru-disciple relationship has been kept intact by Master's and Mother's total dedication to realizing God, and their compassion in passing that on to

---

5   *Autobiography of a Yogi* (pp. 11–12).

spiritually thirsty souls longing for that same realization. May Master's light shine ever brighter, leading all sincere aspirants to the harbor of God-experience—eternal, ever-new Joy! Jai Guru and Happy Birthday Master!

January 12

BE AN EXPRESSION OF WHAT GOD WANTS

Mother Hamilton with David at his
ordination as a minister, March 4, 1984.**

A unique feature of water is that you can find it in every-day conditions in liquid, solid, and gaseous states. This tri-une character of water can be compared to the nature of God's creation on three different planes: solid being the material elements of this world, liquid references the fluid nature of life-energy, and gaseous is the subtle causal/idea realm.

The vast majority of people are focused on the solid-material nature of this world; some see the fluid-like movement of life-energy in and around things and people, and a few have the vision to see what cannot be seen by others, the thought-trons (Master's terminology) behind all that is—a causal realm that is much larger and more profound than all other aspects of creation. We look about us and see the crystalized life-energy of this world, but there is so much more that is not visible to the naked eye.

The three aspects of creation can be polluted just like water. Today, the residents of large cities in China carry open umbrellas when it snows; the snow, as well as the rain, is so toxic that it is a health risk to the uncovered. The material, energetic, and idea realms can also become toxic and manifest as disease and darkness of every description: an energy of darkness may form around someone depressed, the mind may become filled with wicked thoughts, or the body may suffer due to past wrong actions.

The materially minded scientist says the brain manufactures the mind and consciousness: what we think, and even who we are, is a result of firing synapses. However, the spiritual scientist sees it quite differently. While it is true that a malfunctioning brain interferes with thought processes, just as a stroke destroys memory and blocks anatomical functions, the conclusion that the brain is the source of thought and awareness is a fallacy.

Think of a computer programmer creating an operational system. If the hardware stops working due to a malfunctioning circuit, the computer will no longer be able to carry out its purpose. However, though the programmer may be frustrated by this lapse in the computer, no one is substantively harmed by the glitch. Similarly, the soul operates through the physical form of a human body, and when disease makes the body unresponsive, the consciousness of the soul remains unchanged, although it cannot continue to fully operate in the body as before.

The truth of this was demonstrated to me by my Guru. Although she was deeply affected by multiple strokes, heart attacks, and a severe case of shingles on one half of her face, and she was not able to function in the body as she had before, she was still all that she had ever been in soul and Spirit. Being disturbed by what I saw as she sat in a wheelchair, paralyzed on one side, and open sores on the other, I went home to meditate. I demanded that God explain what was happening to my beloved teacher. For some time, I focused on the breath and the ajna in deepening meditation—suddenly, I saw Mother with inner sight: she was beaming and more beautiful than I had ever seen her before. A radiant light went out from her in every direction as far as I could see. Through thought transference, she said, "Do you not know, I am now in my Light-body." And, indeed, she was, and is, a brilliant shining Light.

After that experience, I never again mistook Mother for her physical body; I knew she was so much more. She lived many years after that, and through sheer will, she regained so much of what she had lost during this terrible time. Mother, as with every one of us, is not limited to the body. We have an eternal soul—our part of God that is not born nor does it die—it cannot be burnt, drowned, or in any way changed or corrupted. No matter the choices we make, or the bad things we may have done (to ourselves or others), this pure element of divinity resides above the physical, energetic, and idea realms.

Life, as we think of it, is the soul manifesting through the three bodies: physical, energetic, and causal. The purified body and mind are perfect instruments for the transcendent Divine Mind and are a blessing to ourselves and to this world. Go beyond the three realms, seek out contact with the ever-pure, eternal Self—not so we can get God to do what we want, but that we may be an expression of what God wants us to be.

January 15

Listening and Learning

Swami Satchidanandaji holding Yogacharya David's hands lifting him
into bliss while love overwhelms his heart, Anandashram, 2007.

This is an email from Rebecca who has currently taken residence at our beloved Anandashram. I think that you, like
me, will find inspiration and interest in her experiences. This
email is used with permission. Following Rebecca's email are some
of my comments to her.

Hari Om, Dear Guruji!
Each day here is a snapshot of incredible beauty and
Joy. How blessed I am that God has allowed me to have

this time now to be intensely absorbed in communion with Him, within and without.

Some days ago, I asked Him, "Lord, what would you like me to do today?" He replied, "To listen and to learn." So, I have taken this as my theme, not for that one day only, but for this whole time here. To "listen" I am paying close attention with my "third ear," that being the medulla. I am using the technique you gave me which is to imagine it as a receptor the size of a dinner plate. One effect that has been most delightful from this exercise is that as long as I am "listening" (conscious attention at the medulla), I am not thinking—can't "talk" and listen at the same time!

And as far as learning, this place is overflowing with the highest wisdom just ripe for the picking and tasting. So much to learn, and so many humbling and empowering lessons; each day is a new unfolding of His training and teaching. On another note, I was excited this morning to have had the Darshan of a scorpion—from a respectful distance! —as he was crossing the courtyard in the early morning. A handsome creature in his own way.

And do you remember seeing giant bats in the trees? They're wonderful animals! They swoop around and make screeching sounds like monkeys do. They are fruit bats I'm told—they especially love mangos when they're in season. At first, I thought they were birds. I watch them every morning as I wait outside Centenary Hall for Swami Sannyasananda to unlock the door at 5 a.m. He never speaks to me but when he finishes opening Swamiji's room and comes out, he gestures for me to enter and smiles in such a way that it feels like it's Papa Himself who is smiling!

Thank you for your constant blessings which are being received. So necessary in order for me to use this golden opportunity for growth into complete and permanent Oneness with Him.

Om Sri Ram Jai Ram Jai Jai Ram

Your Own,

With Love and reverence: Rebecca

My Reply: Subject: RE: Listening and Learning

Hari Om my dearest One,

To listen and learn, a most perfect message. Ah, learning to listen to God, what a day that is when you open the door and really attune yourself to what God is speaking to you. And, what an attentive friend and lover God is: infinite in knowledge and wisdom, full of fun and joy, a constant life-stream coming through the medulla, a guiding light at the ajna, unfolding into infinite reaches from the crown chakra—there is nothing in the world that can compare! My heart thrills at your expansion into this heavenly realm of which there are countless mansions of experience. You may sit in simple silence with your Friend, enjoying the fullness of the moment, or He may be a volcano of inner awakening, yet you are unafraid and trusting. All is He, All is He.

I do not think I had the darshan of a scorpion, but I very much remember the fruit bats. They would swoop through the covered porches of Krishnabai and Arunachala blocks in the dark: black shapes with perfect guidance systems. They are fascinating creatures that seem to harken us back to prehistoric times.

Many, many blessings my dear child, for fulfilling all your soul's desires while there, to be in the joy of listening and learning. With loving pronams, Gurudev.

January 18

Attachment Is Being Shackled to an Idea

Bald eagle in flight, photo by Mark Hickenbottom.

We learn detachment in large and small ways throughout our days. Attachment is the ultimate cause of suffering for all humankind; thus says Buddha, Krishna, and in so many words, the great spiritual giants throughout time.

Today, when we were packed and driving down the road, a large bald eagle flew along with us when driving off of our home island: a good omen. Later, sprinkles on the windshield turned to rain and called for turning on the wipers; they did not go on. It is a small thing in life, being delayed, a change of venue for the day;

instead of driving south, it became a matter of making arrangements for repair when a new fuse did not fix the problem.

A small instance with a lesson. Attachment is being shackled to an idea of what should happen. Such a simple notion, and how anxious, fearful, lustful, angry, needy, and greedy we can become based on an idea—delusion's grip that keeps us in ignorance and suffering. The idea of leaving on a trip, days of solid preparation that evaporate into mist in an instant.

Fifteen months ago, a similar hoped-for venture was interrupted, beginning in Utah and culminating in an emergency trip home from Nevada when anemia, due to a cancerous infection, brought all travel plans to an abrupt halt (it now seems another lifetime ago). It can be anything that goes other than how we plan: loss, death, trauma, disappointment, failure, poverty, hunger, illness—so many lessons in detachment.

And how are we to be detached? We live in the world, we make plans, we have expectations, we strive to do better, to be better, to be organized, and to work hard—how are we to do all of that and not be attached? It is not an easy thing. It is one reason why yogis, mystics, and monks seek out seclusion: to make it easier to be simple, to leave behind expectations.

But even that is not a guarantee; ashrams, monasteries, and religious organizations are oftentimes battlegrounds for competing egos filled with even higher expectations of how things are supposed to be—creating even more attachment. There is a saying that helps describe this, "Wherever you go, there you are!"

The easiest way to detach is by keeping your attention on God—surrender everything at His feet. Cultivate the notion that God is in control of everything, including your thoughts, and the world around you. Feel that God is the sole reality, and if He wills it, nothing can stop a thing from happening, and if He does not, no amount of energy will change it; all is in His Keeping.

In the beginning, you base this faith on what spiritual masters tell you. Later, through direct experience, you come to the realization that God's omnipotence is a precise description of the highest reality. As you surrender all that you are to God, even positive plans and desires, and you accept that His will reigns supreme, then you are at peace.

This does not mean you do not strive, work, and fight for a good idea that God has given you. But when you face frustration and disappointment—surrender yourself to Him. This gives you the courage and strength to carry on in the face of obstacles, or the ability to accept something new, if that is what God wishes for you. You are God's faithful servant, and whether it all goes your way or not, you are focused on fulfilling His will, listening to His direction, and being a perfect instrument in His hands. This gives you perfect equanimity in good times and bad, in victory or defeat, in health or sickness—it is all He, it is all He!

Tomorrow, we will hear from the repair folks and plan to be on our way south once again. Will that plan align with tomorrow's reality? We will know by day's end. In the meantime, we plan, we work, we strive, and move toward an ideal given to us by the Infinite, and we balance this movement with total surrender to what He chooses for us—each and every moment.

January 22

CLARITY OF WILL

Hindu Goddess, Durga, fearlessly riding her tiger with a sword for cutting away delusion, a bow for shooting forth will-arrows straight and true, and a hand held in blessing—among other implements of truth and clarity.**

Master spoke a great deal about will, both the development of it through the use of affirmations and maintaining focus throughout a project, as well as uniting individual will with God's Will. We do ourselves great good to pay attention to these lessons.

Many of us undermine positive intentions by not acting with clarity of purpose in order to bring our intentions to conclusions.

All success depends upon being able to maintain focus on our goal. Self-doubt, obstacles encountered, and competing thoughts and desires rob us of initiative.

We are now headed south to Ashland, and it has been one obstacle after another. However, there has been clarity of purpose from the start—it has been God's direction to make this journey. With each problem, He has provided the means for solutions. At every turn, it has been obvious that circumstances could have been far worse. This is His play and He has tested us, tested our clarity of purpose.

Think of will as a muscle group that needs to be exercised. If you start a physical exercise program that is too difficult for where you are now, you will not keep up with it. Dreaming of climbing Mt. Everest and not even going for daily walks will not get you there. You start by getting off the couch and going for walks. Then climb hills, go on to master lower mountain peaks, and eventually you prepare yourself for the big climb. Sitting on the couch and dreaming will not get it done!

So, start with everyday goals on which to focus your will. Determine that the sun will not set without your achieving a particular goal, no matter what. Make this your daily practice and you will build will-muscle through repeated effort: the lessons you will learn!

One great lesson is that when you make a determination and keep with it, especially when you invoke Divine Providence from the beginning, you attract invisible support for accomplishing your positive intention. Feel that you are not alone—God, the Masters, angels, and invisible forces respond to your clarity and uplifting purpose. In this sense, there are no large or small goals, but only one goal, and that is the one in front of you now.

Declare with all the power of God in you that you are determined to succeed. Feel the invisible forces in and around you as support, and when you meet obstacles, as you surely will with any worthwhile goal, feel those invisible forces aid and abet you as you overcome. When self-doubt assails you, as may happen to anyone doing something great, check inside for the rightness of your cause. Do not seek to have God on your side, but rather know that you are on God's side through deepened meditation and intuition. Then proceed forward and be His instrument with true purpose in all things.

January 26

SOUTHWARD HO: FINDING THE ELIXIR OF JOY!

Dominating the view south is the magnificent Mt. Shasta:
Gateway to California in our renewed pilgrimage.

Our journey south began with a stop in Ashland to be with devotees. Time with sincere aspirants is truly an elixir of joy. Without a spiritual orientation in life, I find that life offers little in the way of lasting happiness. However, when God-experience enters the picture, then all relationships, all experiences in life, open new dimensions of deeper meaning and fulfillment.

I gave a talk to the Group there and read from Papa Ramdas:

> The path to the source of your and the world's being is
> not without. You have to go within yourself. You must go
> past your senses, mind, and intellect; you must traverse

beyond all your ideas and ideals; you must transcend all limits, conditions, and tastes, and then alone will you have the fullest vision and realization of your immortal root. This immortal root is also the root of all that exists—the visible and the invisible worlds and all beings and creatures in them.

Religion is a matter of experience. Merely by becoming a member of a church, creed, or sect, a person cannot be entitled to this experience. By reading any amount of scriptures and sacred books, he cannot obtain this experience. By the observance of rites, ceremonies, or worship, a man cannot come by this experience. Spiritual realization is a question of individual effort and struggle . . . The man of true religion, when he is on the path, is mainly concerned with his own internal struggle for liberation and peace.

A steady, persevering, and concentrated effort and struggle alone can lead the aspirant to the realization of God.[6]

This kind of aspiration that Papa speaks of is the key to having God-experience. The need to know God, is a gift of Grace combined with a keen desire of the individual. There is a simple equation that formulates a clarifying question we should ask ourselves, "Do I want God more than this world?" I may assess this question during the day as to whether I feel a greater pull to God than the things of the senses, outer accomplishments, and what others think of me.

Jesus gave us the great commandment to put God first, then, everything else (according to His will), will be added to our life. However, the human ego does this in reverse; it seeks out the

6   The Pathless Path (p. 16).

world, and then gives burnt offerings (used up life-force) to God, if anything at all.

Do you feel a passion to know God? Do you put Him first in your thoughts and desires? The equation is simple: your mind is a constant creator, and what you place your powerful mind upon is the direction your life is steered toward. It is why you get uncertain results; you swerve in this direction, then that. A steady, determined mind gets more results than a brilliant mind that cannot hold any particular course.

True genius is going straight to the Goal of goals without deviation. Make God-experience as important as breathing the air, seeking out comfort, and accomplishing whatever outer journey you have embarked upon; make Him at least as important, nay, more important in your day-to-day life and you will make rapid progress to Self-realization. You will find the fount of unending bliss and radiant light right within your own being. Be it so!

January 29

HITTING CURVEBALLS OUT OF THE PARK

Magnificent sunrise over Lake Cahuilla.

Having arrived here at Lake Cahuilla near La Quinta, Southern California, our North American Pilgrimage continues. I received a text from a family whose little one was being taken to the hospital emergency room; life can throw you some real curveballs. There are few things in life that can make us feel so helpless as when caring for a very sick child. "Oh Lord, You must see to it that this be taken care of for this child, family, and for the highest good of all." When they returned later that night from the hospital, our little one was on the road to recovery.

One of the "defaults" I now have is that in the face of difficulty, my mind immediately turns to God. "Oh Lord, You are the creator of this universe, You are of unlimited intelligence and unparalleled power. Change this situation, make it right, in accordance with the highest principles of wisdom, light, and love."

How many times in life do we have a sinking feeling in our stomach? We think that one too many things have gone wrong. That through our own doing, or simply the way life has arranged circumstances, we are in trouble—we feel alone, unable to reach out for help?

This sense of isolation is one of the great sufferings we experience in our separation from God. Each one of us has an "Achilles heel," that place of weakness that can bring us down like no other. However, there is but one panacea for all troubles: to surrender to the one, infinite Lord.

Faith in God brings about solutions to the most vexing exigencies in unexpected ways. Today, I listened to a woman describe an incident when her husband had a diabetic blackout while he was driving. He was unconscious as they were careening down the road, with no sign of the car slowing. She reached over and turned the key off and pulled it out. I protested, saying, "This is impossible to do with modern cars; they require you to bring the car to a stop, put it in park, then you can turn the engine off." She agreed, "Yes, that is right, but God did it!" And so, He did. She was then able to steer the car over and repeatedly run it into the curb to bring it to a safe stop.

Lahiri Mahasaya said although an individual's ingenuity for getting into trouble seems unending, fortunately, Divine succor is more than equally inventive for the rescue. In baseball, good batters can make contact with a curveball and turn it into a home run. There is no doubt that curveballs in life present challenges; however, they need not spell defeat. Fully concentrate on using all of your resources to rise above a situation, and demonstrate the power of divine will, and grace, on earth. To manifest God-consciousness is the reason you are here. Remain devoted to your infinite Beloved, and your Heavenly Father, Divine Mother, will make all things possible.

Stay tuned, our pilgrimage in God continues!

January 31

GLINTS OF LIGHT: MOTHER HAMILTON'S MAHASAMADHI

The great joy and fun of Mother Hamilton, 1981.

I t is the very early morning hours of the anniversary of Mother Hamilton's Mahasamadhi; my heart and soul are feeling the inspiration of what this day means. To some, it may seem an incongruity to celebrate the death of an individual, much less the passing of a beloved teacher, a Satguru. However, when we understand the true nature of what we call death, and even more a mahasamadhi, then we can truly celebrate not only the life of a great spiritual master but her actual leaving of the body as well.

In my journey to God, He has given me direct spontaneous memories of previous lives: the capacity to fully relive them just as they occurred. One such life memory included dying and what happened immediately after. In that moment of separation from the body, which came as an immense relief, I found myself in the presence of a wonderful Being of Light. Mother explained that this was my own Christ-Self—the God within me made manifest in this seemingly outer form. Together, we reviewed my life with an eye for learning, this Light-form communicated through thought-transference, conveyed insight, wisdom, and compassion.

In this review, I realized that I had lost sight of my true purpose in taking incarnation; I had become lost in the details and demands of life and did not make the spiritual progress I had originally intended when coming into that life. So many people live in fear of judgment of what God or others might think. The truth is that we each know what true success looks like, and when connected with the deepest part of ourselves, we judge ourselves with clarity and discernment. In that moment of insight, I had great self-disappointment: I had fallen short of my own goal. Right there, and then, I made an adamantine resolution to never waste a lifetime, ever again!

Great spiritual masters, such as Mother, have already learned that lesson down to the very cells of their being. Depending on the nature of their lila, the play of their lives when they choose to take incarnation, they may live a portion of their lives in ignorance. But, when the awakening comes, there is no stopping them; they are a force to be reckoned with! Mother came into this incarnation with no karma of her own, nothing that bound her to the past, a completely freed being. However, she took on the life of an ordinary person and went through many experiences living a human life. As Mother said of herself, she had experienced what any woman could go through and, therefore, had an understanding of the difficulties of living in this world.

When Mother spoke, she gave of her wisdom with the power of God burning brightly in her. She not only spoke of the highest esoteric truths, but she also brought everyday human experience into a spiritual perspective. She did not fear or shun this world, having already totally surrendered her life at the feet of God and Guru. She had gone through the death of the ego, the little self—she then embraced all creation as God's expression of Himself. This was one of the many gifts of wisdom Mother gave to us. She was a modern-day Western woman who had ascended the highest peaks of realization, and she never lost sight of the human roots of her existence.

Mother used to joke about when she would leave her body—she had such a wonderful sense of fun. She said that since people were always asking her questions, she could imagine herself on her deathbed, and someone would say, "Oh Mother, before you go, I have just one more question for you!" She also once said that sometimes her sense of humor "got the best of her," and she could imagine getting to the pearly gates and St. Peter would say, "I'm sorry, I cannot find your name on the list of those who are to come into heaven." And then a deep voice, from some distance away, would say, "Is that Mildred? It's all right, you can let her in, she made Me laugh a time or two!"

Mother lived a Christ-like life, and even as Jesus (disciples were not present when he left the body), Mother was alone when she died. In one of those moments that I would love to have back, I was driving home from work when I thought of stopping in to see Mother at the hospital. Then the thought came that my wife might like to come with me, so I went home. Soon after, I received the call that told me that Mother had left the body. Tears came, and I wondered at the strange play of God. I could have so easily been with her at the time of transition, but she had not wished it so.

Mother had said that at the time of the death of great souls, a spiritual ambiance goes out all over this world—a blessing of the light and power of God. At that moment, the masters consciously release themselves from the confines of the body, no longer carrying their heavy cross; they are now free, and the world is the recipient of their grace without limit.

Over the many years since Mother's Mahasamadhi, her life and teachings have taken on many hues, colors, and subtleties—like a multi-faceted diamond that manifests glints of light with unending variation and beauty. New truths, understanding, wisdom-thoughts, Divine Mother's love, joy, humor, and the every-thingness of God is constantly revealing itself to the attuned mind. Each revelation of Mother's immense Spirit adds to our comprehension of what a truly extraordinary God-being our Mother was, and is.

Elisabeth Haich had said to Mother, "Why do you go around thinking you are the littlest one? Do you not realize, you are greater than any master you have met, or will ever meet!" Mother was not so sure of that statement, but it speaks to what a rare and magnificent soul Mother was. Even amongst the greatest of spiritual masters, Mother stands among them—each one a shining jewel on God's necklace of spiritual splendor.

In deepest reverence, I bow at the feet of my beloved Guru. My prayer for you: that you might also receive glints of Mother's pure God-light, and thereby be lifted higher and higher, until you, like her, merge into our Infinite Beloved and know that you and your Heavenly Father-Divine Mother are ever one.

February 5

GOD'S PROMISE

Sri Yukteswarji and Sri Yoganandaji, 1935. God's
promise: between a true guru and disciple, there
are always bonds of love and divine friendship.

A spiritual life comes with a promise of a better life. Lahiri
Mahasaya said that if we make a spiritual effort now, our
future is bound to improve; so, we can now head off into
a life full of enthusiasm and high hopes.

Then something untoward happens: financial problems, relationship issues, illness, or even death. In those moments, we may
feel let down and experience a crisis of faith, feeling that all we
held to be true was a lie. The devotee may reason, "I do my part:

I proceed in faith, I meditate daily, eat the right food, love God, and now this!"

Sri Yukteswar found practical, methodical people admirable. Mother Hamilton gave people practical advice on everything from grooming to keeping an orderly house to being business-wise. Master wrote Mother a letter in which he added some wise counsel for a devotee who was an inventor, saying that the inventor needs to be practical and get a job. Practicality and daily wisdom easily mixed with esoteric wisdom of the highest order for these realized Beings.

Yet, even applying all the wisest and worldly-wise principles, there is the long arm of the law of cause and effect. Babaji said that in a previous life, while attaining high spiritual consciousness, still, Lahiri Mahasaya's karma had swept him away (he died) and that he, Babaji, had lovingly followed him in his astral life between physical death to his re-birth. Life and death still happen to highly realized souls. And, I do not know a business owner, even those following a spiritual path, who has not faced downturns, perhaps having to sell off assets, including prized personal items to keep the business afloat. Even with the healthiest diet and exercise regimen, one may become ill. If we think that leading a spiritual life makes us immune to any of life's hardships, then we may find ourselves disappointed.

The only sure result of knowing God is that we will be in His presence through thick and thin. Like marriage vows—for better, for worse, in sickness and in health—we are married to the Beloved, and in all situations, our Heavenly Father and Divine Mother promise to be at our side through it all. It is only God who is with us from our first breath to our last; it is only God who will be with us on our astral journey in between lives here on earth and for all time.

Our simple love and faith form a bond with God that cannot be broken, and while it is true that all souls have God with them, it is only His awakened ones who are conscious of His omniscient Presence—and this makes all the difference. What is it that causes the greatest suffering in this world? More than physical pain, financial downturns, or even death, it is the feeling of isolation, believing that no one knows or cares about our life. With God, we have an eternal friend, well-wisher, beloved, and confidant.

There is no doubt that God also provides a route to miracles, extraordinary events both large and small: healings, clearing the way for financial success, and every sort of amazing occurrence. I have seen them with my own eyes. A small miracle once happened to me that to this day is inexplicable. I had made a math mistake and overdrawn my checking account by over a hundred dollars. By the time I discovered my error, I knew I did not have the funds to cover the shortfall. It would result in a bounced check and further banking fees—oh dear! On that same day, I received a check from a company in New York that I had never heard of, for the amount of money I was overdrawn, plus five dollars! I never did know why that check arrived, but it saved me much embarrassment and anxiety that day, as well as the additional fees.

God creates us, He sustains us, and when it is His will, He withdraws us back into His Being. He is our well-wisher, yet there may be certain things we have to go through. It may be the result of our own doing in the moment, something from a distant, unremembered past, or from the collective karma of the world we live in.

The one thing we, as devotees and aspirants may depend upon, is that through our oneness with Him, God will be ever-present with us. We may feel His peace, love, joy, inner direction, wisdom-thoughts, comfort—all that is His. For reasons known and unknown, we may have certain things to go through, but in our faithfulness, God will never abandon nor forsake us. This is His promise.

February 9

BORREGO SPRINGS, CALIFORNIA

Full Moon rises over desert mountains just outside our door.

The desert has been beckoning to me for some time now—finally, it is here. It is easy to see why those who want to know God have sought out desert retreats: expanse, clean vibrations, quiet, and a slow-changing backdrop to support inner stillness.

We had some group gatherings during my year of silence and solitude. One participant kept saying how she yearned to be in a place of silence, but even though the rule was total silence, she kept a whispering conversation going toward me (as if a whisper qualified as silence!). Beyond the humor of it, she demonstrated how we can abstractly yearn for something, but in reality, find it quite difficult.

Inner and outer silence does a couple of things. True silence makes the consciousness expand. Whether we are viewing life across an open expanse of desert, from a high mountaintop, over a vast body of water, or from our "yogi's cave" in our home, stillness makes it easy for our mind to lose its bounds and seek out vastness. Master Mahasaya said that his great guru, Sri Ramakrishna, told him to always meditate when he was next to a body of water in order to go beyond body consciousness.

Once remembered, Spirit's domain in eternity does not easily accommodate the small confines of a human body or ego-consciousness. When we seek out the attributes of God, we yearn for freedom, peace, joy, love, and knowing who and what we truly are—pristine nature can help us realize this impulse.

There is an additional blessing to being in the desert near Borrego Springs—we are in the neighborhood where householder-yogis Rajasi and Dr. Lewis had homes. We feel our kinship with these two highly realized beings in our stay here—asking their blessings for full immersion in our Infinite Beloved.

As we reside in this place of stillness, please join me in spirit and experience the expanding purity that we feel here. Be quiet in your bi-daily sojourn of meditational bliss, and feel our gathering oneness in the blessed Divine.

February 12

The Wind Blows Where It Wishes

Fiery morning sky from the desert floor.

We continue "boondocking" near Borrego Springs. Rick and Judy and Jerry and Lois are all here nearby; we are able to spread out on these federal lands that have rustic roads and primitive campsites (really, you just pick a spot and set up camp within the defined acreage). Carla is going through some spiritual experiences in which her nervous system is *highly electrified*, so the desert expanse is perfect for us.

Out under the desert sky, a sudden breeze races through the camp, blows for some time, then, just as quickly, dies down. This repeats itself through the days and nights; it reminds me of a saying of Jesus:

Do not marvel that I said to you, "You must be born again." The wind blows where it wishes, and you hear the sound of it, but cannot tell where it comes from and where it goes. So is everyone who is born of the Spirit (John 3:7–8).

Of course, the wind has sudden surges in environments other than the desert, but on water or mountaintop, it somehow seems more understandable as to where it comes from or why. But here, in the open desert, it has more the appearance of a mystery as, to its comings and goings.

Jesus was a man of the desert. Having gone through austerities in the wilderness, he was on intimate terms with nature. In his conversation with Nicodemus, from which the above quote is excerpted, Jesus is referring to the invisible source and mysterious reasons for the habits of both wind and Spirit.

Science prides itself on observing phenomena, manufacturing theories about what it sees, designing an experiment or two, and noting if the outcomes behave according to what the theory anticipates: an admirable process for physical and psychological phenomena. However, what about Spirit that originates outside material creation? Then, the only "instrument" for measuring results is found through intuition and deep inner experience, both of whose range is beyond a telescope or a microscope—what then can physical science say about the results?

Even when dealing with unknowable origins, we can yet say, "A true understanding is that spirituality is a science." We begin with a spiritual practice, and when the experiment is carried out exactly as prescribed, the results are predictable. Perform Kriya Yoga and the spine will be spiritually charged: the light of God is seen, the sound of God is heard, the mind is purified, and consciousness expands and becomes Self-realized, or: chant God's name, think on His attributes, surrender yourself at His feet, and your mind will be purified; you will live in bliss; consciousness will rise above the mundane, and you will know God—merge with Him. Your heart, mind, and soul are the experimental labs in which these procedures are carried out, the outcome, as predicted, is the transformation of consciousness from the human to the Divine.

And yet, calling an area of study a "science" does not take away its deep sense of mystery. The astronomer may gaze upwards and identify constellations: "There is Orion's Belt, and there is Alpha Centauri, and that is the broad, bright Milky Way." However, that same astronomer may also have times of looking up at the night sky and simply be in awe, sensing the immense depth of space from which those tiny lights have traveled, the overwhelming vastness, and the incredible power of cosmic forces, both seen and unseen. In that moment of awe, is the mystical any different for the fact-driven scientist? Are we not joined in wonder, whether it is seeing a giant nebula, a tiny quark, or feeling the bliss of God?

It was ignorance and arrogance that made religious institutions square off against science, and as was perhaps predictable, science then polarized itself against religion. In fact, both are explorers and seekers of truth; both should be joined in discovering physical and metaphysical realms. No matter the factual gains of science, there will always be a mystery to this creation. On one level of experience, matter, like Spirit, will defy knowing from whence things come and whither they go.

While walking amongst desert sage, we are in wonder at the sudden gust of wind as well as the surge of bliss that delivers us into a birth of new consciousness. This type of mystery **is** knowable in the sense that you can have a direct experience of it. However, in nature, as in Spirit, there will always be that which is unknowable—the mind cannot know it all; it must simply be experienced. In this mystery of heaven and earth, we may be at ease, for it is all held in perfection by the one living God.

February 15

MASTER'S DELIGHT

Paramhansa: Supreme Swan swims in worldly waters but is unaffected
by delusion, a fresco near the entrance to Encinitas Hermitage.

We happy pilgrims set off from the desert wilds, motor around a 3,000-foot peak, and wend our way to the beautiful Pacifica shores at Encinitas—home of Master Yogananda's seaside retreat. For a long time, Master had taken trips up and down the coast of southern California, looking for just the right spot for a hermitage. It was not until he left for India that Rajasi Janakananda discovered this excellent site for Master, purchased it, and made the buildings ready for his beloved guru's return as a surprise gift.

And what a gift! Acreage upon a bluff overlooking the Pacific Ocean, charming seaside housing, and delightful gardens complete with ponds filled with koi: a peaceful setting from where Master eventually penned his spiritual classic, *Autobiography of a Yogi*. Master designed and built a lovely chapel on the cliffside, but nature broke under its weight and it had to be dismantled. God told Master that he was too attached to this beautiful ornament of worship and so took it away from him. Even on a human level, a great master has a thin veil of ignorance in order to play his or her role on earth.

We once again look upon the bright golden lotuses painted on towers of the hermitage that face the street. Entering the grounds, we are told that Master's rooms, normally open on Sunday afternoons, are now closed due to renovations. The guard standing near the gate says that some devotees were escorted into those rooms, so we might ask for permission. I do so and a sweet-natured lady enquires as to who we are, whether we are connected with the Seattle Self-Realization Fellowship (SRF) group, etc., and then goes in to make an inquiry for us. She comes back to say that none can enter, "There are no exceptions." This prevarication is not necessary; in total surrender, I acknowledge to her that, "All is in Master's keeping."

We climb the stairs through shadowy lush gardens and emerge into bright sunlit vistas of shore, waves, and ocean. Below is "Swami's Beach," a favorite for surfers, where dozens are waiting to ride that perfect wave. The eye is naturally drawn out to the distant horizon where ocean meets sky—creating Nature's altar to our infinite Creator. The intense sun makes us seek out a bench in the shade where we feel drawn to spend time with God alone.

My prayer to Master is that all in our group feel his presence as powerfully in his garden as we had in previous years experienced him in his rooms, now that those doors to that sacred site are shut. One sign of a spiritually charged environment is the ease with which one can feel God. Upon sitting down and closing my eyes, my spine straight, eyes pointed to the ajna, instantly the inner and outer expansiveness merge into blissful awareness. Time is suspended, and God and dear Param-Guru pervade the vast inner/outer experience. "Oh Master, your presence in your garden is equal to your powerfully charged rooms; your grace exceeds kindness and delivers us to your lotus feet."

Ponds filled with colorful koi.

Sometime later, my attention is once again drawn to the outer world. We stroll amongst the gardens, gaze at the large koi in the ponds, meditate under the tree that has a picture of St. Francis upon it, and although there are many people wandering through this *Garden of Eden*, there is no hurry, all speak quietly and feel the reverential awe of being in Master's kingdom.

Now that we are taking our leave, gratitude fills our hearts for Master's blessings. May this hermitage, built by Rajasi for Master with such loving thoughtfulness, fulfill its purpose and be a refuge for devotees escaping a hectic world, and always be a home for Master's delight. Jai Gurus, Jai Master!

St. Francis upon a "cross" in the Master's garden.

February 19

ONE GOD: ONE POWER

American white pelican swimming on
placid Lake Cahuilla; notice a promise of sun.

We have returned from the open desert of Borrego Springs to placid Lake Cahuilla near Palm Springs. There has been more rain in California this winter than for many years, breaking the long drought here but also causing some problems in the north with flooding. After several days of cool, cloudy, rainy weather, it shows promise this morning for the return of the sun.

A morning thought came streaming through with the sun, hammering away the walls of darkness and separation; this thought was a powerful tool for breaking duality's hold on the mind.

God, being the sole power in all the three worlds, must be behind every thought, word, and action we can conceive, and also that which is beyond what we can comprehend. The good, the bad, and the ugly must all be powered by a single source, for how can there be another when God created all there is?

"But," you may say, "there is so much in me and in the world that is not of God; there must be two powers!" In a relative, human sense, that is true, duality is by definition bipolar. However, in an absolute, divine reality, there can be only one power, one creator. Even the power for sensual attractions, to do evil, to go against the light of God, must be admitted to come from one ultimate source.

You look inside and you say, "I feel so weak, no life-energy or light at all," and yet, that powerful feeling of weakness must come from the One. You say, "I am drawn to so many temptations, those things that take me further away from God," and that too must come from God Himself, for there is no other.

On a human level, we definitely experience being on the battleground between good and evil. Each day is a test of our attraction and love for God, versus our mind's tendency for being seduced into a world of separation from the One. And here is a great secret: once we trace the power of separation back to God, really trace it (not just a half-hearted weak thought), we break the power of separateness—all that which is negative in every thought, word, or action. Darkness hates the light, and cannot co-exist with it. Once we bring the light of God into the picture as the one, true source of all, darkness must depart.

Keep your mind on God means just that, keep your attention focused on Him no matter the content of your thoughts or feelings. **There is only one power**; keep affirming this fact, feeling that all comes from Him; doing so, we purify the mind even as we practice this and cure its addiction to separateness. God is the power behind every thought, word, and action; this is the absolute truth; it cannot not be! Never let this truth go and you will be brought into His holy Presence, where no darkness or evil abides. All is He, all is He; blessed Spirit, all is He!

February 22

THE SILKEN ROAD

Travelers upon the Silk Route.**

In ancient days, there was a Silk Road route from China all the way to Italy. Silk, a symbol of refinement, and horses, a symbol of power, were highly sought after and traded, in addition to spices such as pepper (at one time, saffron was about the same cost per ounce as gold); these products made for lucrative trade between East and West.

Deep within each of us lies a route of surpassing refinement and power—a rare gift that gives savor to life. This inner route is to be found in the spine and the brain in multiple layers. These routes run north and south, from the base of the spine in the south pole to the top of the head in the north; behind the back, is west, and in front, is east. After running north starting from the base of the spine (south) to the base of the skull, the route turns east and travels through the brain to the "Star of the East," at the point between the eyebrows. Then, it turns north once again and travels to the top of the head. A circuit is created along this route and, thus, there is an exchange as life-force moves round and round.

There is both power (life-energy) and refinement (bliss) in this movement. While a value can be placed upon goods traded in days of yore on the Silk Road, the experience of God within the *Silken Road* of the spine and brain is beyond compare, and thus invaluable. This *Silken Road* is the pathway to the gold of the spirit, and in our restless search for lasting happiness, it alone is the fulfillment of our heart's desire.

As one can be a connoisseur of fine foods, drink, or music, so may one become an aficionado of blissful God-experience. There are no limits to the varied expressions of bliss and the presence of God. The *Silken Road* of the spine and brain become a never-ending variation upon a single theme; and thus, bliss is a definite experience, identifiable from every other sensory or subtle pleasure; still, this experience remains a constantly new exploration of blissful, vibrational notes.

This morning, I sit watching the sun slowly lighten darkness into a rosy aura. The Aum sings its song of many notes, the eyes close, and bliss plays along the spine. The thought of the *Silken Road* arises in my mind to describe the smooth flow of bliss in the spine and brain. The desire to share this with one and with all wells up inside me; to describe in order to awaken, to think upon others in order to convey this experience, to collapse time and space so that no barriers exist between I and Thou and His blessed children. The curse of leaving the Garden of God is lifted, the redemption of the soul is at hand, baptized in Living Waters, and barren no more—a prayer spontaneously erupts in my mind as a picture of Living Waters flowing into, and uplifting, all creation into Spirit—separation but a dream once dreamed long ago.

At one time in life, getting up from meditation would mean the end of this blissful music of the Infinite, but now all of life is varied parts of the Creator's composition—an orchestrated explosion of the Holy Ghost. Oh, stalwart brothers and sisters, followers of the *Silken Road*, know the kingdom of heaven that is only to be found within, experience the bliss supreme of life within and without as an unending symphony of His glorious presence.

February 26

MY BIRTHDAY WISH

Swami Satchidananda and Mother Hamilton: the two
greatest gifts of God in my life, Anandashram, 1977.

A birthday gives pause to view a lifetime much in the way as the turning of the New Year, only it is more personal, in that it is the first day this physical body functioned independently of my mother's womb. In part, it is a reflection: "What have I done in this journey so far?" And in part, a projection: "What do I yet want to accomplish?"

Gratitude wells up in me for what I have been given in this life: a supremely qualified Satguru, a sincere desire to make spiritual progress, kindred souls who inspire and support me in this goal, and a job to do for God to expand His Light in aspiring souls, and in the world at large.

In addition to my Guru, I also have had my second "spiritual mother," in the form of blessed Swami Satchidananda, as well as the inspiration of countless saints and realized souls, both past and present. So many gifts, so many opportunities to do the one thing that truly matters—to make spiritual progress in this lifetime. Somehow, souls of a lofty spiritual stature have found it in themselves to love me and have extended themselves to such a degree as not to be believed. There are not enough fingers and toes in this entire world upon which to count all these blessings—my heart simply flows out in humble gratitude.

This is what stands out to me thus far in this lifetime, and there are of course other things for which to feel thankfulness, but all of these seem to fall under one category: God's Grace—and it grinds me into dust thinking of the millions of kindnesses that have come my way in this life.

With this in mind, I think of the future and what should these days be filled with to give true soul satisfaction for a life well lived. Mother once asked me, "How will you pay for the air that you breathe?" Oh Mother, not an easy question to answer! What can this mudball of a body (inflated with the sacred breath of God) do that can be deemed of any worth? What a precious gift life is, and what can I possibly give in return?

I can do what my Guru asks of me, "Keep your mind on God." I can love Him, serve Him, open myself to Him totally, and completely do what He directs me to do! God and Guru ask me to teach, to minister, and to serve all striving souls; and this I do, according to His will. To serve as an example, and this I strive for with all of my heart. To surrender myself to Him, no matter what anyone else thinks (including myself!)—in short, to please Him alone—and this I do daily.

I make no claims to be a superman, to be anyone extraordinary, or to be anything other than what I am, for I strive to be transparent in what I say, do, and write to you. Somebody once wrote that either nothing is a miracle, or everything is a miracle.[7] I come down on the side of the latter. Everything **is** a miracle: every breath, the rise of the sun, the ability to move, think, and have my being, it is **all a miracle in the making!**

Perhaps one passes an age in which birthday gifts are something expected or needed. I am receiving birthday cards and messages of such love and generosity of spirit that it flattens me into a nothing. A fun gift of God came in the form of entering a State Park the other day, and when I claimed my senior discount, the Park Ranger did not believe I was of that age and "carded" me; she asked me what year I was born! She had to admit, I qualified. In addition, the one gift God gives daily and that I treasure first and foremost is His Presence—which is a constant in my life. This Presence fills my heart to overflowing to such a degree that it spontaneously flows out to you—there is no greater gift than this—it is never ending, never slackening, always increasing, and bursting the banks of every limitation. Oh, what Bliss is mine! And all I wish to do is spend my life in awakening this same gift in you, and in all.

There is nothing I love more than to see the unfolding of the lotus-life of a God-expanding soul. I know that it is not an easy journey: there are lofty peaks and dark chasms, there are fair winds at your back, and slamming storms that shudder you stem to stern, there is the guiding Eastern Star, and the Sirens who seductively call you to destruction. It is the greatest hero's journey ever told, and therefore, dangerous and uncertain, but also impregnated with Grace-filled synchronicities, tender mercies of Divine Mother, and lightning flashes of wisdom from heavenly Father. There is truly nothing more thrilling to me than to be a participant/witness in this greatest of odysseys with you.

---

7   Albert Einstein: "There are only two ways to live your life. One way as though nothing is a miracle. The other is as though everything is a miracle." www.goodreads.com

And this brings me to my birthday wish as I blow out a candle of one, standing for the One eternal Being. With this expended breath, I project my prayerful wish for you:

> That you melt in His Spirit, swim in His ocean of Bliss, for His mind to mingle in your own, and for you to see and serve Him in all creation. Oh Lord, it is You, Yourself, who has brought this birthday wish into my mind; therefore, it is Your wish and You **must** fulfill it for all your sincere lovers. For there is nothing, nothing greater in all the three worlds than to stand in Your Presence—This I wish and pray with all my heart for all of my and Your dear ones—and all who are near and dear to You!

March 1

ASH WEDNESDAY

The Resurrected Christ, stained glass,
Providence Hospital, Everett, Washington.**

Christendom marks today as Ash Wednesday, 46 days before Easter: a time of repentance, penance, and fasting (excluding Sundays, a time of feasting). The ashes of the palm branches collected the year before are blessed, anointed with the words "repent and believe."

Many Christians will take advantage of the 40 days (the time Jesus fasted in the wilderness) as a time to do, or not do, something as a spiritual discipline. Spiritual disciplines are times of great reward. Living in an era today when instant gratification is oftentimes the watchword, the rewards of not doing something in the name of sadhana (spiritual practice) are not readily known. However, it can be a wonderful time to let go of something, especially something that you now indulge in but really know is not good for you.

In years past, this has been a time of not eating sugar, not watching television, dedicating longer times to meditation, or chanting with Papa's recording of Ram Nam—it can really be anything you choose. When you dedicate yourself to this kind of practice, it has a purifying effect on you: you feel it in body, mind, and spirit. Penance for the sake of punishing yourself, for real or imagined sins, is a misguided attempt at purification. Penance done in the right spirit will leave you feeling clean, inside and out, and closer to God.

Here is something Reverend Jill sent out by email that I thought had wonderful wisdom from Sri Yoganandaji:

> As we begin the first day of Lent, a time to reflect more deeply, I wanted to share these passages from this month's Master's Lesson: "The tigers of worries and sickness and death are running after you and the only place that you can be safe is in silence. When you meet people, do not become affected by their state of consciousness. When they are singing of God, be one with them, but just as soon as they show undesirable qualities, stand aloof. Meet people with silence, eat with silence, and work with silence. God loves silence." Love to you all on this first day of the holy season.
>
> —JILL

This is a wonderful time of year as we approach Easter, recognizing the rightful death of the ego and the joyful resurrection of Christ consciousness. We can take time to read the teachings of Jesus from the Gospels, Master's commentary in *The Second Coming of Christ* (published by Amrita or SRF), and any of Mother's transcripts, or listen to her talks, especially her Easter talks.[8]

The more we explore the teachings of Jesus, the clearer it is to see that he was and is a magnificent Avatar. Uniquely, our teachings are rooted in Jesus and Krishna and find universal resonance throughout all the world's great religions and spiritual traditions. Let us use this opportunity to go deeper into silent meditation and be lifted up as on wings of angels in their peace and Divine Presence.

Discover the blissful joy of Christ Consciousness embodied in the life and teachings of Jesus and sleeping in the potential within every human being. Be blessed—dive deep and soar high!

---

8   www.crossandlotus.com

March 5

SWEET SURRENDER

Desert Bloom at Joshua Tree National Park, California.

God's will often takes you in unexpected directions, but it ends up actually fulfilling some desire of His, or making you avoid some problem you will never know about (thankfully). We had scheduled an appointment to make our car ready for towing on our journey (our North American Pradakshina). The shop forgot to order the parts and so we are now delayed a week from leaving the Palm Desert area.

As a result, we have encamped ourselves near the entrance to Joshua Tree National Park, a place we had wanted to return to from two years ago but have been unable to do so until now. So, God fulfilled His desire for us to be here through the seeming mistakes of the shop. This is the second week of delay. The other was when we were to begin and had a last-minute repair to make before leaving. The Lord, in His infinite care, makes for these delays, and through them, brings about exactly the right thing through His loving care (we avoided severe snowstorms and landslides by the first delay in January).

Surrendering to His will does not make you a non-actor. I was sure to make the owner of the company, who neglected to order the part, know that his omission had real-life consequences (for one, we will not be able to meet Rick and Judy, and Jerry and Lois in Arizona as planned). The owner was apologetic, but the parts have to be shipped and the time it takes is now out of his control.

Joshua Tree is one of our favorite places, and we have found space on Bureau of Land Management (BLM) land that has rustic roads and campsites available at no charge (always a favorite feature!). Even more than that, we are in the desert's blooming season. From the tiniest flowers flat on the ground to bushes and trees, there are buds and blossoms everywhere.

When Larry and Cate were here last week, we went to Indian Canyon for a hike through a forest-filled ravine of palm trees and a delightfully cheerful, running stream. Cate had tears well up at the beauty this desert oasis exhibited (deserts are often associated with desolation). Mother Hamilton had written about coming to Indian Canyon mid-century by jeep and spoke of the beauty she found there. In addition to the physical beauty, there is a real spiritual feeling to the place, and each time I have been there, the purity has been palpably felt in the air.

One feature of being in the desert that attracts me is the easy feeling of expansiveness. For the last few weeks, we had been in a county park, and while a very nice place to stay, it lacked this open feeling we have here. While here, God is running very strong in this form. It seems that I had a few weeks of operating more easily in the world, a welcome time for me to attend to the many tasks associated with this type of travel. However, as soon as this need is over, God comes on like a steaming locomotive—His power, His bliss, and divine Presence, take complete precedence, and He does with me what He wills. It is His Work—I am putty in His all-benevolent sculpting hands.

And while all of the beauty of His Presence is absolutely true, I also have this feeling of missing you. When God is in this mode, such as He is, it makes me indrawn, and it is even difficult to think of doing Skype or YouTube sessions with the Centers, which I hope to do in the future. It is all His Work, and He chooses what form it takes (many times, without reference to what I would prefer in a human sense!). Be that as it may, I am always happy to have Him working through me, according to what He chooses—for God and Gurus' will is always uppermost in my life. While they are in charge, I know that everything happens according to the highest good of all concerned; for that is the nature of God's will—it is, by definition, for the utmost benevolence. Therefore, we are always connected through that highest good, and the work that God does here is also done in you, for in Him there is no separation (and still, knowing that through and through, I have this feeling of missing you).

With that in mind, I send you all my love and blessings. All of what I have in God is yours, for I send out all that He gives me without reservation. May all be well, my dear ones, and most of all, may you ever be filled with the Divine Presence deep within your heart and soul.

More Desert Bloom.

March 7

HONORING MASTER PARAMHANSA YOGANANDA

Master Paramhansa Yogananda,
The Last Smile, 1952.

Today is the anniversary of the great samadhi of Paramhansa
Yogananda. Spiritual masters attain a high state of consciousness in which they transcend the limitations of the five
senses and the reasoning mind: they find themselves in states of
bliss; have visions of light beyond that which the sun, or flame,
bring to the eye; hear sounds that come from the depths of creation; and have a deep sense of knowing who and what they truly
are that transcends the short human life-cycle here on earth.
Much can be written to try and capture this high state, but none
can be the final word on it.

When an accomplished spiritual master senses that the time is right, he or she slips from the bonds of the human body for the last time and enters into the realm of light and realization as a freed being—without the necessity of returning to the earthly realm to fulfill unmet desires. For it is said that full spiritual realization answers all the heart's desires, leaving nothing for the master, except to think, do, and say, as Divine Will directs. God chooses the moment for this final ascension, a well-known path by the master who "dies daily" in Christ Consciousness.

Master chose to leave the body in a public manner, even as he had led an open life for the upliftment of all humanity. The occasion was the coming of a new ambassador from the relatively newly-freed nation of India. Master was to be a keynote speaker for the function honoring the new ambassador. After dinner, in the Biltmore Hotel conference room, Master rose to speak. He told humorous stories of first coming to America. He had heard that Native American "Indians" scalped white men, and when he saw bald men in the cities of America, he thought that "Indians" had been at their gruesome work! And when he saw signs for selling "hotdogs," he thought, "Lord, why did you bring me to a land where they eat dogs?" Through humor and instructive stories, Master touched hearts and delighted the audience with his short talk.

Then he recited part of his beautiful poem, *My India*, closing with the sentiment, "Where Ganges, woods, Himalayan caves, and men dream God—I am hallowed; my body touched that sod."[9] [10]

Then, he turned a little toward his right and his body slipped to the ground. He was gone, just like that. The ending of a life spent in service to humanity with the aim of awakening God

---

9   *Whispers from Eternity* (p. 181).

10   David's talk to the Ashland Center: *Master's Mahasamadhi*. http://www. crossandlotus.com/David/Talks/2017/20170306_DA_Skype_Master's_Mahasamadhi.mp3

Consciousness in one and in all. Master "died with his boots on." He has left his mark for all of us to follow in doing what he did, knowing what he knew, and becoming what he became; for he is the archetype of a rapidly-developing consciousness in this world.

Slights, insults, and injustices rarely stayed with Master. Even though he was subject to racist treatment and smears in person and in the public arena, he remained positive and saw the best in America and in her people. He ever kept a higher vision of individuals and nation-states. This positivity was based on an inner vision that God is the evolutionary force in nature and humanity, and that, although uneven, and at times unlovely, this force is inexorably moving toward the enlightenment of all creation.

Honoring Master is best done by emulating him. Following in his steps does not mean that we have to feign an East Indian accent or take on outward mannerisms like him. It means that we strive to know God: we honor saints and realized masters, we endeavor to live as our guru instructs us, and we serve God in all souls—even as he did! Let us think on and honor the great master today, on his Mahasamadhi Day, as on all days.

March 12

WORDLESS PRAYER

San Xavier del Bac Mission, Tucson, Arizona.**

Ｗe have packed up from our stay in the Palm Desert area and have made tracks to Arizona; first, to Phoenix, and now we are in Tucson. We are getting used to having a tow vehicle (called a "toad" by RV'rs). Thanks to Jerry and Lois, who drove it down here, we now have a car to get around in once we arrive at a destination. Our model was rated towable for only two years of its manufacturing, and ours was one of those two years—thank you, Ram!

Here in Tucson, we will revisit a vintage Catholic Church, San Xavier del Bac. Last time we were here, we enjoyed the church, widely considered the finest example of Spanish Colonial architecture in the United States. However, what we really loved was walking about a nearby hill dotted with icons that had a powerful spiritual feeling to it. We will light some candles at the prayer altar while there.

Prayer is a continual part of my life, but in recent times, it has powerfully drawn me inward. W., a long-term devotee of Mother Hamilton's, is one reason; his heart is only pumping about 30 percent of what it should, and now he is struggling with pneumonia. I have been in a powerful fight for his life, health, and total recovery.

Prayer is a very large and important topic, and oftentimes its real power is little understood. When I was a child, my mother taught me "Now I lay me down to sleep . . . ," which I said nightly. I knew I was praying to God, but I think I mostly rattled off the little poem without much thought, other than that I was asking God to keep me safe through the night. Other times, when feeling alone and in some particular trouble, I would pray to God for a resolution to my immediate problem: I wanted Him to give me friends and good grades (without any effort on my part!). Gradually, prayer wore off as I struggled to know what I believed.

It was not until I was nineteen years old and in emotional turmoil that I reached out to God due to the pain I was in. "God! I do not know if You exist, but if You do, if I have never needed You before, I need You now!" Immediately, the pain was alleviated. It felt as if thousands of pounds of crushing pressure were lifted from me. This was a turning point in my life, and it sent me on a journey of exploration into Who and What God is, and, for that matter, who and what I am.

Down through the years, I have grown in my understanding of prayer. Master Yogananda writes beautifully about the power of prayer, saying that you must put your whole self into a prayer for it to have any real effect—half-hearted appeals have no real spiritual power. Over the years, God gradually instructed me in Wordless Prayer. Wordless Prayer is more subtle than talking to God—it is vastly powerful.

In Wordless Prayer, you first feel lifted into Divine Consciousness—His bliss, His upliftment, His power; then, God turns your attention upon any particular person, situation, or part of the world, or for that matter, the whole world itself. Then, you experience all of the power, bliss, and upliftment you are feeling merge into the focus of your prayer. Time and space collapse; even barriers we call death offer no resistance; the freedom and pervasiveness of God-consciousness are the means for quickening the subject of your prayers with all that you have into Divine Union. No words are needed, only the powerful awareness of all that God is.

Wordless Prayer does not necessarily mean that you will not have any words to accompany the prayer, only that words are not necessary, and words are not the primary means of communication. Some words may spontaneously arise in your mind, reflecting what was previously wordless, but primarily, it is a direct consciousness-to-consciousness connection as God sends His power through you, His conduit. His work being done through you lifts you even more closely into Him and His kingdom—He delights in using you in this way, even as you delight in being used.

Whether with words or in Wordless Prayer, go deeper into being a conduit for God's will to quicken creation with His power, bliss, love, light, joy, and wisdom. Be a blessing to this world, for every thought you have has creative power. You must be aware as to whether your thoughts and words are healing and uplifting, or damning and giving power to what is negative (as in gossip). Wordless Prayer is a powerful way of being God's instrument and for you to be a blessing to this world.

March 16

SOUTHWEST ADVENTURES

Gila Cliff Dwellings, New Mexico.

We have had wonderful and interesting pilgrimage points in these recent days. Coinciding with the full moon, we made our way to San Xavier del Bac Mission, a Catholic Church near Tucson, Arizona, dating back to 1692. The current structure was built in the 1790s after the Apaches saw fit to burn down the original structure. However, it was the indigenous tribe, the Tohono O'odham (Desert People), who were instrumental in rebuilding the church and maintaining loyal followers, even when the church went through years of no priests in attendance.

It was our delight that a Pow Wow, a traditional dance from Nations across the Southwest, was in progress just behind the church on the day we came. This yearly event attracts dancers to display traditional dance, colorful clothing, and feathers, all there to compete in various categories of ancient ceremonies designed to keep them alive for future generations. Non-natives are welcomed; in fact, there are times in the day when all attendees are invited to join in an inter-tribal dance.

The welcoming prayer by a holy man was a fusion of traditional beliefs alongside faith in God's son, Jesus. He followed the English language prayer with one in his native tongue, which, while the words were unknown to me, I found deeply moving. It is heartening to see a spiritual tent broad enough to accommodate beliefs from different cultures—ultimately, the conclusion must be drawn that there is but one Great Spirit manifesting in endless varieties of religious expression around the globe.

There were also many shapes, colors, and sizes of dancers; in stature, some were short and round, and there was a native dancer who was northwards of seven feet tall! Ladies came in flowing, sparkling garments while moving in graceful circles, and "old bull" men brought a great sense of gravity to their dance and their beings. Multi-pitched singing was accompanied by large drums beating out the rhythm for the dancers to follow. In Native Culture, dance accompanied going on hunts, gathering a war party, a prayer for good rainfall, and an abundant harvest. Song and dance were an integral part of life for these people who have lived on this land for many thousands of years. I clearly hear the singing now as I write about this event, a haunting chant that echoes from time immemorial: the chant calls upon the Creator of us all to bring out the goodness in all endeavors.

During an intermission, we make our way to the nearby church. It is a beautiful structure that has many paintings and icons on the walls within. It continues to be an active church where mass is celebrated; candles are lit under favorite icons; some sit in prayerful attention, while others are streaming through as tourists. Carla and I each buy an "Our Lady of Guadalupe" candle. I light mine under Divine Mother's statue for W., who has been having great health challenges. Carla lights her candle for Christine—dearly departed soul, in honor of her life here with us, and now in her ongoing journey in God. There is a spiritual vibrancy here now that was not noted in our time here three years ago.

We then walk out to a hill with a cross on top and a path that circumambulates midway up. Our first stop is at a grotto that has been dedicated to Lourdes in France. This place has a definite spiritual vibrancy that is highly attractive. After some time spent here, we continue around the hill, taking in views of the verdant valley below; after years of drought, this year has brought abundant rains, which in turn have greened the hills and the valley, and have brought out smiling seasonal flowers. We feel the peace of this lovely spot dedicated to God and His saints. May the peace we feel here spread all over this earth and raise humankind's consciousness to purified heights.

After our pilgrimage to the church and the Pow Wow, we continue our journey to New Mexico. This is new territory for me, and it is exciting to be blazing new trails. We journey to Silver City in order to make our way up to the Gila (Heela) Cliff Dwellings (recommended by C.). A long drive up a very winding road finally brings us to the footbridge that begins our journey back in time. These Cliff Dwellings were built by the Mogollon (Muggy-own) People, ancestors of the Pueblos. These Dwellings were constructed circa 1275 C.E. and were inhabited for one to three generations. Located just above the Gila River, they possibly moved here because there had been a 30-year drought and the spring gives water year around.

We make our way across eleven footbridges that crisscross the creek and give us sneak peeks of the cliff dwellings above. The surrounding rocks have been beautifully sculpted into round shapes by millennia of water flow. Among these rounded shapes are larger caverns that were water-carved and make for wonderful protection from heat and cold; some of them are 20 and 30 feet tall. We climb steeply and then arrive at the first of five caves with a total of 45 rooms. It is thought that 10 to 15 families lived here.

It is not hard to imagine this being home to these families, with children's laughter echoing in the steep ravine: crops (the three sisters: beans, squash, and corn) growing down by the river and on the mesa above; a hearty group climbing up and down stairs and ladders daily for their water, crops, and game. These homes today are but skeletons after pottery trophy hunters and mindless vandals took and burned much of what was left by the families. Today, there is a peaceful feel to the place, and it is interesting to see how these structures served the purpose of protecting and nurturing families. An additional interest for Carla and me is our attraction to cave sites with yogic meditation in mind. Caves offer natural insulation from the world's constant activity and make eternity seem within easy reach.

Today, on the Ides of March, we continue on our way. It has been a time filled with outer activity, but also inner activity has been very intense. I awaken on the night of the full moon with God-activity so strong that I feel to be but a small hut with an elephant inside moving back and forth! "Oh Lord, must I remind you that this body is small? You are immense! With a touch of your finger, You make worlds tremble! If it is Your wish to break apart this 'temple not made with hands,' then so be it. But if You wish me to serve longer, then You must make me stronger, or perhaps remember to use a gentler touch. Either way, Your will be done!"

March 19

RUNES MESSAGES

City of Stones from crest of hill at City of Rocks State Park, New Mexico.

We are surrounded by 35,000,000-year-old rocks that stand as sentinels of an ancient earth where a lifetime is measured in millennia, not as humans mark it, as several dozen orbits around the sun. The land here, at the City of Rocks State Park in New Mexico, has the feel of time viewed through a wide-angle lens, not a microscope. What a brief span a human life is, barely registered as a passing gnat by these old watchers.

Having driven to this most interesting topography, we crested a small hill and looked down upon a large cluster of various shaped boulders, some creating avenues, streets, and alleys with what could easily be imagined as shops, hotels, and homes in stone; thus, the name City of Rocks. We have a site here in solitude amongst these silent monarchs of stone—no one else is close. The spirit unfolds its wings here, far from the cramped quarters of ordinary cities. Quiet pervades as the rising sun reveals a rabbit grazing nearby, a hawk soaring in circles overhead, scuttling squirrels, and other assorted friends who call this home. In amongst the rocks are rounded cactus, juniper, small oaks, local grass, and assorted desert fare.

Last night with the campfire ablaze, we sat surrounded by giant boulders—seemingly Tolkienian petrified trolls caught by an unexpected sunrise. Overall, we feel the quiet, grounded, millennial-consciousness. This comes with the backdrop in which I have been in prayerful battle. I feel spent in this tremendous exertion, and the land becomes a welcome oasis of spiritual nurturance.

Early this morning, as God has been keeping nocturnal hours, but this early a.m., my mind was filled with a past event. I know I, and I think most, have had "cringe-worthy" incidents when we have acted in ignorance, made poor decisions, and issued forth ill-chosen words or actions that would definitely not make it in our "Better Moments" videography. Well, one of those was on full display in my mind's eye when I awoke. Initially, I felt the cringe, but then an inner Voice spoke that made me know this was not for the indulgence of the ego to feel bad; rather, it was a calling of prayer for an individual. What a change that made, to move from the initial abhorrence to feeling the light, power, and flow of God blessing one and all. "Oh Lord, You remind me once again what my purpose is in life. I am not here to be self-conscious, but God-conscious. This is my lesson, again and again, until there is nothing else but You, ever-present You."

This City of Rocks is a place where stones become runes, messengers to remind us of the eternal verities: a place of awareness where you know that you have always been, you are now, and you will always be part of the Ancient One, the Source of all existence. In that Consciousness you can rest—reside in the eternal Truth of the Infinite where a human life is but a flicker—God is the ever-existent Flame of Life.

Streets of Stone.

Rock formations conjure up the image of a kneeling camel.

Natural yogi's cave.

March 25

A Sanctuary of Peace

Cathedral San Fernando altar, San Antonio, Texas.

We put on our traveling boots for a long journey from New Mexico to San Antonio, Texas. Setting the caravan on cruise control, the long miles tick away. We drive through changing desert with hills on either side, then a large flat area with low-growing mesquite and cactus, then rolling hills with oak and lush undergrowth. Originally, much of this was grassland, but as the Spanish increased their horse and cow herds, the grass disappeared; then with the lack of wildfires, the grass did not reseed—so luscious grassland became rather plain-looking mesquite bush and Gambel's quail for many hundreds of miles.

From no population to sparse ranches to farmlands, we are gradually introduced to evidence of human habitation—other than the long expanse of Highway 10, with rest stops roughly placed 100 miles apart—Texas is big! Jerry had recommended the River Walk (Paseo del Rio) in San Antonio. The River Walk has sidewalks on either side of the channeled river that is below the street level of the downtown. Restaurants and shops line the river, and quaint boats motor tourists around the circuit of waterways—designated as the "Venice of America."

After finding a camping spot a bit out of the main city, we pedal our way in on a marvelous bike path that follows the San Antonio River. We first visit the ill-fated Alamo that became a rallying cry, "Remember the Alamo!" as Texans fought Santa Anna for independence. The Alamo was a calculated slaughter, only a slave was let go to tell the tale of woe and spread panic to others who thought of joining the rebellion. However, the "take no prisoners" policy had the opposite effect on Texans, who were made even more determined—in 1839, they became an autonomous republic, and ten years later, the Republic of Texas joined the United States.

Onward, we wheel ourselves to the River Walk where we are charmed by the waterways, overpass bridges (many of which were built in the 1930s), the many shops, and restaurants. We eat lunch at the Casa Rio. It turned out to be the oldest eatery (1946) along the river. The restaurant was started by a failing hardware store owner who took over an old home and dug the mud out of the basement by hand. The vintage restaurant is still run by the family. From all the busyness of the River Walk, we emerge to street level and find the beautiful St. Joseph's Catholic Church. Upon entry, the feeling here makes it known that this is a "House of God." The artistry and colors are truly magnificent.

San Antonio River Walk.

We go in search of another church, the Cathedral of San Fernando, designated as the nation's oldest Cathedral Sanctuary, visited in 1987 by St. John Paul II. The outside of this Cathedral looks to be very old, originally built between 1738–50. Venturing into the very front through a winding, narrow hallway, we come face to face with a magnificent altar. Magnetically drawn, we sit in the first row and are immediately drawn in. The world can be interesting, lovely, even engaging, but how much more so is God! The world drops away and there is only He, blessed He. A sanctuary of peace and God's Presence in the midst of a bustling city—we are at home.

Today, we continue on our North American God-tour to Houston. He takes us to places unknown, but as our tour guide, He is infallible.

We have chanted His holy Name across many miles now, filling our hearts and this **dharmashala** on wheels with His Light, radiating the power of His Nam as we travel from coast to coast.

St. Joseph's Church, San Antonio, Texas.

March 26

SPACE AND SPIRIT

The front of Houston Space Center: Boeing 747
carrying the Space Shuttle for high-altitude testing.

These days have been filled with activity, from road travel to arriving here in Houston where we are spending time with Carla's friend and roommate from her university days. She and her husband have treated their guests with incredible hospitality and have been so welcoming.

One place I had in mind to visit while here is the Houston Space Center, the command post for NASA where engineers and managers oversaw space travel to the moon and back; it was also the training ground for the crews before flights, and their place of recovery after time spent in weightlessness.

Our hosts bundled us up in their car and drove us to the far south end of Houston where the National Aeronautics and Space

Administration (**NASA**) site is located. Now, it is more of an active museum than a working post; however, they still have equipment that trains hopefuls for the Space Station and future Mars landings; this space provides not only a look into the past, but the present and future as well. We toured the building that had a horizontal Saturn V rocket that boosted those leaving the safety of Earth to make the long trip to the moon. It is awe-inspiring to see these huge engines, each one producing **one million pounds** of thrust, providing the kind of power to take precious cargo up into orbital speed at 18,000 miles per hour.

Saturn V Engine: Each provides one million pounds of thrust.

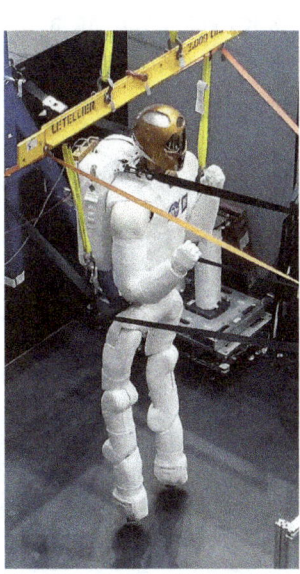

Training suit for Mars.

As a child, I remember getting up early (Pacific Standard Time) to watch the space launches, many of them lasting just minutes in orbit before making a fiery entrance out of the earth's atmosphere. Walter Cronkite interviewed scientists as we waited to see and hear those powerful liftoffs. I think much of the country sat before their television set to witness these exotic and dangerous missions. A seminal moment came while watching live feeds from the moon when Neil Armstrong pronounced that he was taking "One small step for man, one giant leap for mankind," as he was the first to set foot on the surface of an alien planetary body. It was a captivating moment for me, and for a riveted nation and world.

We also toured a building in which there is a segregated Space Station laid out on the massive floor to train astronauts for extended times in orbit. In addition, there are training areas for a Mars launch that is anticipated to occur in the 2030s. Although it is no longer used as a command-and-control center for space flights by NASA, it is a very active museum and training center for further treks into unknown frontiers of space.

Training craft for Mars.

Evidence of human evolution in intellectual and technical advances helps to prove a point that is essential to understand: a "giant leap for mankind," which going to the moon represented, did not solve the fundamental problems of human existence. As a lover of science and technology, I am also keenly aware that in themselves, material advances do not represent wisdom. These leaps in technology we have seen have certainly made things possible that would have been science fiction not long ago. But are we happier, more at peace, or living in greater harmony with our environment and with each other?

Real peace, real happiness, will not come from advances in the intellect, or through technology; rather, it will come from knowing the Self. It is through the exploration of knowing who and what we truly are that lasting happiness, peace, joy, love, harmony, and guiding wisdom manifest. Exploration of the inner space of Spirit must advance at least as rapidly as physical science, for it is only in God-awareness that we have the balance and wisdom to know what, and what not, to do next—it is the one way forward so that we may have spiritual and material advances that truly benefit one and all.

March 30

ALL OF THESE THINGS AND MORE

Opening of the Houston Rodeo.

Therefore, take no thought, saying: What shall we eat? or, What shall we drink? or, Wherewithal shall we be clothed? (For after all these things do the Gentiles seek) for your heavenly Father knoweth that ye have need of all these things. But seek first his kingdom and his righteousness, and all these things shall be added unto you (Matthew 6: 31–33).

The great Master, in these and previous verses, gives impeccable instructions for prayer, humility, and pronouncing as a fact that God knows what you need even before you articulate it. I have to say that my life has been a demonstration of this principle, as was Mother's. It has been twenty years now since

God directed me to leave my profession and to be His aspirant and minister only. Operating "without a net," I set off without any idea of how I would have food, shelter, or clothing. Since that time, I have been provided with such abundance that it is beyond belief.

Fifteen years ago, Carla joined me in this mutual quest. She had been the Personal Assistant to the third wealthiest individual in the world—with the highest pay she had ever received. Throwing her lot in with mine (and God's), she brought with her a six-year-old Ford Escort as a dowry—she has shared this life of service to God first, with wild abandon.

Cowgirl riding barrels.

It is not a formula type thing—simply leave your job and expect God to take care of you; rather, it is *living the attitude* of seva (service to Him) and knowing that as you do so, whether you are the owner of a company or an employee, He will look after all your needs. It takes a one-hundred-percent participation for this law of God to be fully enacted. When you do, then God joyfully gets busy organizing every detail of your life for your and the world's highest good.

When we have left on journeys, occasionally someone will say: "Have a good vacation." This always takes me by surprise, as I have never thought of needing or going on a vacation. He simply takes me to one place or another in order to fulfill some tasks He has assigned to me—as He is always working through me. Even though on the outside there may be few signs of the tremendous labor He performs through this form, I am witness to what He does and am cognizant of the price this form pays for the privilege of service to Him.

It has been His sweet will to burn with an inner fire each day in these three bodies—a purification rite of His choosing. Although few would necessarily notice, Carla is often highly attuned to the needs of this body, even before I am. Through her able assistance, I have been kept functioning, and she has kept this body in health when otherwise it may have very well dispersed into the vaporized atoms from which it originated.

Beyond keeping this body in operating condition, God also looks after everything needed, and seemingly more. It seems that many whims and ancient desires are also met by putting Him first. In the last couple of years, Carla has mentioned on occasion that she would like to see a rodeo; it has just been something that has been lurking in her mind, as neither she nor I had ever been to one. It had crossed my mind to one day go to a county fair and see a rodeo, but so far that had not materialized. Apparently, God was listening to her better than I, for He arranged to fulfill that desire in a masterful way.

Upon arriving in Houston to see a long-term friend of Carla's, there was some mention of a rodeo. When Carla's friend's husband heard it was a wish of Carla's to see one, he made a call and within hours it was arranged for us all to go to one of the biggest rodeos in the world, with all the top riders! Not only that, we were invited to a corporate suite with food and first-class seats all included, at no cost! Our dear hosts took us to the festivities in their luxury car, gave us a tour of the circus that was part of the fairgrounds, and we saw the blue-ribbon animals winning first in their class. We were then escorted up to the suite. Carla was given a cowgirl hat. She wore a big smile throughout the day.

Wild Wagon Race.

It is clear that when God is present, then we may enjoy the world according to His will—knowing that if He is not in residence, then it all loses its value and meaning. But, being keenly aware that this is His world, and that He manifests Himself in all forms, then we may know Him through His manifestations. Lose sight of Him, and all is lost. Know Him to be the best of this world, and we may glorify Him through His manifold expressions. Carla had her whimsical wish satisfied through following, in every area, total surrender to Him. In this way, we discover anew, that in seeking His kingdom and righteousness first, God gives all of these things (and more), to you as well. Picture below: printed in case it is difficult to read—very fun—and true!

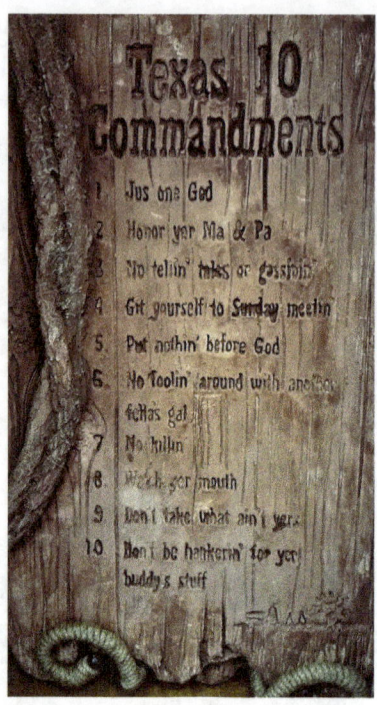

Texas 10 Commandments

1–Jus one God

2–Honor yer Ma & Pa

3–No tellin' tales or gossipin'

4–Get yourself to Sunday Meetin'

5–Put nothin' before God

6–No foolin' around with another fella's gal

7–No killin'

8–Watch yer mouth

9–Don't take what ain't yers

10–Don't be hankerin' for yer buddy's stuff

April 2

FLING AWAY DARKNESS

Our Beloved Papa, Swami Ramdas, Anandashram, India, c. 1930s.

Fling away thoughts of depression, thoughts of dark fore-
bodings, and unreasonable fears and doubts! Stand up
with a bright face and a brighter heart with the fullest
consciousness that God does all things for the best of all!

—SWAMI RAMDAS[11]

Mother distinguished a difference between a "human" perspective and a "Divine" one. From the human point of
view, life does not always go the way we would like it to;

---

11   Anandashram: *Thought for the Day.* www.anandashram.org

there are physical, family, financial, and work challenges that can cause stress and worry. However, Papa says to fling away all such thoughts, and know that, from a Divine perspective, God does everything for the best!

There is a big difference between reading and agreeing with this wisdom from this great spiritual master and actualizing it in our interior lives. Constant practice is required. Repeated times of *standing up with a bright face and a brighter heart*, impress upon the brain that it really can lift us above the problems faced in this worldly existence.

From a psychological point of view, faith that God does all for the highest good of all gives a positive emotional charge that makes us feel better in the moment—this is a product of faith. Then, through repeated experience, we find that everything works for the good "is" the literal truth. We see "behind the curtain" and know that it is not only a noble sentiment, but that God is actually working out our individual and collective karma (the law of cause and effect) to our best interest.

Jesus asked, "Which of you by worrying can add one cubit to his stature" (Matthew 6:27). Of course, we must admit that we cannot worry any problem into a remedy; rather, we can exhaust ourselves in the process with no positive results to show for it. Now, having a concern about a certain situation can be prudent—it is a question of how to resolve a problem. If clouds are building on the horizon, then we should take precautions—this is wise. But there is a line between having a concern and falling into worry. A concern comes with a focus upon taking action to improve a situation, a worry is mentally running a race with no purpose and no end. Worrying can become a habit that is mindless and destructive.

To break ourselves out of the worry habit, we must counter a negative thought with its opposite. Where worry is based on a falsehood, and that is: if we *worry about a problem*, it will improve the situation. Faith is based on a higher truth, and we come to realize that God really is working things out for a higher purpose. There is a cute line in a movie in which the character, a liar and a thief, is breaking back into a prison (that he previously had been the only one to ever break out of) in a very unusual selfless act. In his ongoing conversation with God, he says, "Well, here we are Lord, coming full circle and going back to where I never wanted to go again. I would like to think You have some higher purpose in all of this, at least it would reflect well on You if it did!" Yes! It would reflect well on God to have a higher purpose for all of His creation!

Our greatest fear is that we are alone and unseen, that our difficulties have no purpose and simply create suffering for ourselves and others. Not only Papa, but Jesus, and all the tremendously realized spiritual masters, down through time, affirm that God does have a purpose, or as some say, *God has a plan for you.* Our affirmation of this great truth brings us peace, even in our difficulties, and will, in the end, prove itself to be true. This has been shown to me in many, many situations in which He reveals to me that He is applying exactly the right remedy for the soul's evolution, even though it is difficult at the time.

An element of truth that God has shown me is a universal principle that, when applied, always leads to positive spiritual progress. Challenges in life activate us into making every effort to solve the problem. However, there will come a moment when we have exhausted our will, our resources, and come to an end of what we can humanly do. It is in that moment, if not before, that we can either give in to despair, or turn to God. When we turn to God, not just in despair, but for His will to operate directly in our lives, when we really open ourselves to Him, then we grow spiritually. Through that openness and by making a connection with Him, we strengthen our union with Him in a most intimate and powerful way. Gradually, we come to see there is not a single second that we can draw a breath, have a thought, or have a sense of our being, without an active flow of His Divine Current. From that seedling moment of turning to God when we have emptied ourselves, we will grow into the full realization of His holy Presence at all times and in all places. We see the connection then that, even in difficulties, perhaps especially in hardships, we have the opportunity to make great spiritual progress.

In whatever state of mind we begin Papa's practice, we will find it a great help to stand up with a bright face and a brighter heart with the fullest consciousness that God does all things for the best of all! Be it so for you now, and always.

Travel Note: We are currently in Pensacola, Florida, which has a claim—based on an ancient olive jar found here—to be the oldest city (founded by Europeans) in America. Carla has family here and we have spent much time with them. The weather has been beautiful, in the 80s, with only a little humidity. God is to be found in all forms. One of the great challenges is to refresh our mental screens to see family with fresh eyes, not based on the past, but seeing God evolve Himself through all forms. Then we may enjoy God in all His various aspects, and find fresh wonders peeking through old, familiar relationships. This gives new meaning to each one we meet, rather than tired-out scripts from outdated family ties.

April 7

GOD CALLING

Mickve Israel Synagogue, sanctuary
completed in 1878, Savannah, Georgia.

From Florida family visits, Pensacola beaches, and bicy-cling along its miles of fine white sands—some of the best in the world—we set sail for the last eastward leg to the Atlantic. Before reaching that direction-change point, we over-nighted at Suwannee River State Park, of the famed song, "Down upon the Suwannee River, far, far, away. That's where my heart is yearning, Home where the old folks stay." Carla and I had an enjoyable and vigorous bike trail ride along the river: we saw defensive embankments made long ago by Civil War soldiers against encroaching gunboats, Spanish moss hanging from oak trees, palm plants over seven feet tall, and exotic tropical birds calling one to another. The air was warm with more than a touch of humidity that made taking a sauna unnecessary!

The next day, we completed our eastward trek that had begun on the shores of the Pacific Ocean and completed when we reached the Atlantic Ocean. We skirted Jacksonville and changed to a northward direction. We soon reached the Georgia boundary, it being the eleventh state we had traveled in so far since leaving in January—the historical garden city of Savannah was in our sights. We arrived at Skidaway Island, home to the wealthiest populace in the country; however, we humbly situated ourselves in the State Park amongst evergreen pines and deciduous trees hanging with Spanish moss. Soon, we ventured into the city.

One of our discoveries was the location where John Wesley gave his first sermon in the New World in 1736. I grew up in the Methodist Church, and John Wesley is largely given credit for its formation—although he was never a member. Not the first or last to do so, he made some unwise moves based on passions of the heart when he moved here. Then, because of his integrity, he became a target of a powerful and ruthless "boss" of Savannah. John eventually left America and went back to England—feeling like a complete failure. Later in life, he gave permission for the breakaway colonists to form the Methodist Church—as before, all had been members of the Church of England, headed by the King of England. The previous members were now citizens of the United States of America. They could not marry or bury without sanctioned ministers, and John felt it necessary for them to form their own institution. John's brother, Charles, who wrote many of the hymns sung in the Methodist Church, never spoke to his brother again after he gave permission for the breakaway Methodist Church.

On his original trip to America, John Wesley had been on a ship that was assaulted by immense waves that ripped the main-sail, broke the mast, and poured water through the decks. Deeply afraid, he noticed a group of Moravians (a group of Czech/German Protestants who broke away from the Catholic Church one hundred years before Martin Luther). This small group sang to God without break both before and during the gale force winds. Later, Wesley asked the leader if he, the men, women, or children had been afraid during the storm; the leader replied that they were not afraid of death. In their conversations, the pastor for the Moravians asked John, "Have you the witness within yourself? Does the Spirit of God witness with your spirit that you are a child of God?" These questions made Wesley aware that there were deeper levels of God's Presence. He valued the Moravian's company for all the time he was in the colony of Georgia, and he continued keeping their company upon his return to England.

Once, while deeply depressed, John had a most significant experience during a service when he felt his "heart strangely warmed." This changed the young man from making a list of rules governing every hour of his life and being daily graded by himself, based upon a grid he created for himself, to the notion that one could achieve a state in which the love of God reigns supreme in one's heart, leading to outward holiness. He departed from the Moravians on the issue of quietism, that is, through inner stillness one could reach a perfected state. Years later, Wesley went on to be called "The best-loved man in England."

From the spot of John Wesley's first sermon, we made further pilgrimage to the beautiful Savannah Cathedral which has its roots back in 1779. (Catholics were not allowed to have congregations any earlier in Savannah due to the fear they would side with the Catholic Spanish). The current church came about in 1899 after a fire destroyed much of a previous structure. Today's Cathedral has impressive art: from its huge stained-glass windows, crafted in

Austria, to immense murals covering the soaring walls, to the 3D fourteen Stations of the Cross carved in Munich—it is truly worth a look for its art treasures. As we made our way around the fourteen stations, I was deeply touched by the drama of the Christ going through various stages of the crucifixion—not for himself, but for all humankind. These stations mark the three times Jesus fell under the weight of the cross—it seemed encouraging that even he fell, and recovered, and so might we. It was a fitting devotional during this Lent season.

Jesus fell—heart-rending depiction of the seventh
Station of the Cross at Savannah Cathedral.

However, after making a bicycle tour of several outstanding churches, it was the Jewish Synagogue that both Carla and I noticed had the most powerful spiritual feeling. We arrived after the doors had closed, but it was while standing in front of the Mickve Israel Synagogue, established in 1878—noted as the oldest congregation now practicing Reform Judaism in the United States—that we so clearly experienced its pure, uplifting vibrations. These early Jewish settlers arrived in 1733 and were mostly of Spanish-Portuguese extraction. They worshipped in various temporary quarters for many years until after the American Revolution when they were given permission to have an official place in society. It is interesting how certain houses of God can have a dulling effect, some feel all right but not very powerful, then without fanfare, you are uplifted into the One true God; such was our experience as we were rooted in front of this lovely Synagogue.

And so, we continue on our spiritual journey, chanting His Nam wherever we go, looking for His Presence in places big and small, known and obscure. Today, we were in one of the many parks in Savannah on our bicycles when a deep, vibrant voice called out, "Hello young man!" Well, you have to like being called that on occasion. I turned to see a man whose body matched the size of his lovely voice sitting on a park bench, easily weighing in at 300 pounds. With delicate hands, he was weaving palm fibers together into flower creations. He asked where I came from. I said, "Washington State." He said, "Home of Jimi Hendrix!" I affirmed he was from Tacoma. He said he met Jimi in New York—this large black man announced he was 75, though he didn't look it, and his name was Jimmy, aka James. I liked him immediately and felt a greatness of God in him. He said he didn't charge for his creations; he did it as a service, but I could donate something if I liked. We made an agreeable exchange and he said, "God bless you," and I replied with a depth of feeling in kind. Truly, here was a God-man who came in a thinly-veiled disguise—I was blessed that he had called out to me—as it was God who was doing the calling.

Palm Fiber Rose by Jimmy adorning a picture of Mother Hamilton.

April 9

WEAVING THIS WORLD INTO ONENESS

Life is leading us on a path of perfection. Spanish
moss hanging off oaks at sunset, Skidaway Island.

A recurring theme in many families is cutoffs: when a family member chooses, for one reason or another, to stop talking and seeing other family members or close friends. There are occasions when someone's self-destructive behavior or decisions in life make it dangerous or unwise to maintain contact. However, there are many other times when such cutoffs are the result of being angry with another for minor reasons. Some people and families have a history of cutting others off as a weapon of choice for showing displeasure. This is highly destructive to the individual and hurtful to others.

The counterbalancing notion to such cutoffs is to know that in the supreme consciousness of God, there can be no separation—ever. The idea of cutting others off requires a great deal of psychic energy, and ironically, that intensity demands an even closer connection—being greatly present through absence. The other irony is that the one doing the cutoff denies having full participation with the whole family, something they very often care a great deal about. This self-imposed exile limits the feeling of wholeness and therefore any sense of completeness—a tremendous price to pay.

To transcend such cutoffs, you simply acknowledge that God is, that God is in every individual, and that we are all connected through the universal Divine Consciousness. Whether someone is living or no longer in the body, whether there is physical contact or not, in God-consciousness, we are all intrinsically part of one another—to acknowledge this on a deep level removes all artificial barriers. God-consciousness is the healing balm that soothes all wounds and unifies life.

The truth is, we have all fallen short of the goal of perfection at various times during our incarnations—no one has done it perfectly all of the time. To hold some artificial notion of perfection, for ourselves or others, simply does not match reality. This is not excuse-making for bad behavior, it is just the way that creation operates. If we have all fallen short, then who of us wants to be frozen in time when we have been something less than our best? We must all be allowed to grow, change, and evolve.

Now, if there are those who exhibit behavior that is destructive, then we may, for a time, create a cutoff; for instance, we may not allow a murderer into a family home, or an abuser to be around children—in other words, set sensible limitations. But even then, the offending individuals may be in our thoughts and prayers, seeing them as the children of God as they truly are in their immortal souls. One day, they will grow into who and what they are in God, but for today, they may be kept at an arm's distance—all the while, in heart, mind, and soul, they are held in the pure light of being just as God created them from the foundations of this universe.

Let us practice seeing the best in one and all, seeing the purity of being that each one intrinsically has from his or her Creator. If an individual actively shows progress, then he or she may be given gradual access to new situations to further demonstrate improvements. If old behaviors arise, then distance may be the best feedback for learning, and at the very least, keeping those individuals from further damaging themselves, or others. Higher spiritual perception does not make one a weak doormat, willing to accept the unacceptable; nevertheless, the devotee always looks to see the higher nature deeply residing in the heart and soul of every soul from God—and where else can a soul come from, but from God?

Holding the universal vision purifies our heart, and it gives a needed boost to the one who offends against his or her own soul. Papa felt the greatest thing he could do for another was to see God in him or her. Through such persistent thoughts by others, the God-nature is awakened, and the perceiver of God's light is transformed through the continued practice of seeing God in all. Such is the power of God-aligned thoughts that this world cleaved by strife and warfare, cutoffs, and separations, may be lifted into higher Consciousness. *The Lord our God, the Lord is one!* One Being, one Consciousness, one Reality that is all-pervasive and everywhere present. Let us look past the little snubs and separations and know the unifying principle that weaves this world into a oneness of beauty and light.

April 14

EVERYWHERE EQUALLY PRESENT

Yogacharya David with rustic cross at First Union African
Baptist Church, Daufuskie Island, South Carolina.

I t has been a fascinating experience during this North American
Pilgrimage, going to some of the oldest churches and synagogues
in the country and discovering the potency of Spirit in each one.
It has also been interesting to note in this exploration of God's
great body that, even in realizing God as the indwelling Presence,
and knowing that He is with me always, there are still variations
in spiritual power in this place versus that, or in one person more
than another. So, while God is known as the eternal Self within,

and He is to be found in all creation as its Creator and Sustainer, and in truth, it is He who manifests Himself as all there is; still, the vibration of Spirit in creation comes in different hues, colors, and strength throughout His vast expression. In appearance, He seems to be *more equally present* in some places than others!

Recently, we have been to two very different churches in South Carolina, one in Charleston and another on Daufuskie Island. Charleston has historical interest to me as Fort Sumter, at the mouth of its harbor, is where a battle ensued: the first shots of the momentous Civil War. Also, across the water is Fort Moultrie. In the Revolutionary War, the fort was constructed of palmetto logs—the logs were very soft, and when the colonists were attacked by nine British warships, the logs absorbed the cannon balls, and some of the balls even bounced off the fortifications! As a result of an exchange of cannon fire, the heavily damaged British ships left—the battle created a huge uplift in the war for independence. To this day, South Carolina proudly wears the official nickname, the "Palmetto State."

While in Charleston, we made a point of visiting some of her churches. Charleston is known as the "holy city," due to the number of churches, the towering height of some of the steeples (also useful in the early days for ship navigation), and its reputation for religious tolerance during colonial times. Two beautiful spires drew us: one to Saint Michael's, another to Saint Philip's Anglican/Episcopal Churches. Both had a wonderful feeling, but Saint Philip's is really extraordinary. The church is beautifully done, and each pew section is surrounded by a wood-paneled rectangle to reflect the warmth of its inhabitants in the winter cold. The congregation first began in 1680. The church has gone through a change of location and various rebuilds as storms and wars have caused damage. George Washington once attended this church and sat in the pew, and we sensed the invisible presence of other notables.

St. Phillip's Altar.

As we sat in contemplation upon the One whose house this is, I saw that the air itself had waves of spiritual power shimmering throughout. The sound of Amen/Aum was tremendous, and individual consciousness easily merged with uplifting God-awareness. We sat for some time immersed in this temple of God. A note of interest: in each of these special places, Carla and I have been in complete agreement when we compare notes after leaving it as to its spiritual potency. The artwork and architectural details get higher marks at St. Michael's, but for purity of vibration, St. Phillip's remains heads above. On leaving St. Phillip's, there was an elderly lady sitting at the back acting as host for the many tourists. I thanked her for opening her church to us, and I commented on what a tremendous feeling we experienced there. She looked at me through cataract-clouded eyes and said, "Yes, the Holy Spirit is here!" Her physical vision may be dimmed with time, but her inner vision is bright—and I agreed with her assessment most emphatically.

Days later, we returned to Hilton Head to retrieve our car, which was in for some repairs and a new timing belt that her age and mileage required. God, as our impeccable tour guide, prompted us to take a day trip to Daufuskie Island. We boarded a passenger ferry and had a pleasant sail over to the island, then received keys to a golf cart for our transportation. Off we went to tour the island. It has had constant habitation for two thousand years, and archeologists have found human remnants there from 12,000 BC! In amongst our stops, we discovered the First Union African Baptist Church, established in 1881. Inhabitants of the island include the Gullah People, descendants of enslaved Africans who lived in relative isolation until the 1970s in the Lowcountry of Georgia and South Carolina—they also share language and culture with those who live in the Bahamas.

Behind the church is a Praise House. In front of this log cabin is a fire circle. In the evening, a fire is lit; this signals there is to be a gathering that night. Slowly, a silent group grows. A woman starts to hum a gospel tune with its musical roots going back to Africa. Others pick up the tune, adding words to a well-known gospel. As the music builds, there is a clapping of hands and soon, all are swaying and praising the Lord.

Coming around to the front of the church, we enter and find simple but elegant arrangements of bench seats and an altar, with a rustic wooden cross of two sticks from the woods gracing the wall. We sit for some time and take in the Amen/Aum, as it is tremendously loud and speaks eloquently for the spiritual feeling of the congregation. Indeed, the Holy Spirit is here—as well as St. Philip's!

"Oh Lord, what a demonstration; You are equally present, both at a church in Charleston where presidents and the famous have prayed, and here on this rural island where sons and daughters of slaves have sung and praised the one God of us all." Surely, God is not a respecter of rank, privilege, skin color, creed, or religious affiliation. Heavenly Father and Divine Mother listen to the heart and soul of the individual and those who gather in His name. Our Beloved responds in kind whenever there is a keen desire for union with the all-pervading Spirit. "Thank you, God, for once again showing us how You are everywhere, equally present in all of Your sincere lovers."

Praise House, Daufuskie Island.

We celebrate Good Friday, in which all Jerusalem sings blissful songs of praise for the coming of the Christ (Consciousness). This feeling of upliftment, and the intimacy of the Last Supper, are preludes to the most difficult time to come: the Mystical Crucifixion. Consciousness along the spine (the twelve disciples) thrills at the joyous response of Jerusalem (higher consciousness of the brain), but the all-knowing Christ is aware of what is to follow. And you, as you share in the bliss of upliftment will think, like the disciples, "This bliss will never end." However, the time of testing and purification will commence at its appointed time. With this test comes solace in the promise of the Christ, "Lo, I am with you always." And so He is, even though you may not always be conscious of this fact. Do not fear, God guides, and His direction is correct and true. Do not hold back—go on boldly—knowing that though your humanness dies when it is mystically crucified, the eternal Christ Consciousness is resurrected in you for all time.

Christ's words during the Last Supper on altar,
First Union African Baptist Church, Daufuskie Island.

April 16

EASTER'S FULFILLMENT

Easter's Promise found fulfillment in Mother Hamilton, mid-1970s.

Yesterday was a very difficult day for this body. Due to the work that God does through this body, it often experiences diverse pains and other unusual symptoms. When this happens, Carla will ask, "Do you know who this is connected to?" As, so often, it is connected with what an aspirant is going through; and by God's grace, somehow, even over great distances, God gives me a share of it. She never asks who it is, only, "Do I know?" Sometimes I know in the moment, or someone who was going through a particular experience communicates with me and that connects me to what I was experiencing. However, yesterday did not seem connected to any one individual but was more universal.

This Easter morning, it came clear from God that what I was experiencing is part of the Mystical Crucifixion on a wider plane of consciousness—I was in the midst of the two great, grinding, oppositional forces of creation. It is fascinating, it truly is, to be taken through these times and to have God as my perfect Guide. I am perfectly sensitive to the fact that there are those who would doubt such experiences; nevertheless, I can tell one and all that I am perfectly sane; I am not given to fanciful imaginations; and I am not extraordinary, but God makes it all possible through this form. It is the most interesting, challenging, and fulfilling life one can possibly live. I feel quite blessed to have God and Gurus as the sole power and guide in my life.

The scriptures take on a completely new meaning when you see that they apply to you in a most specific way. To think that Jesus, or any emissary from God, is the only one to go through such experiences and that you are to be simply drawn along on someone's coattails, without anything for you to do but have faith, is a very pale view of a spiritual life. On the other hand, to know that Jesus came to show the Way, with the intention that you are to follow every step, makes the scriptures become vital—essential to you and your life.

I remember so well; it was spring in the year 1976, and I was sitting in a meditation group in Bellingham, Washington, when suddenly there was a feeling and an interior sound of a snap! At the same time, this powerful kundalini serpent force raced from the bottom of my spine to the point between my eyebrows, the ajna. For the two previous years, I had heard Mother describe, at different times, this type of occurrence, so I had some understanding of what was happening. The ajna grew very hot and I felt an intense pressure—it was a pleasurable-pain. For about five minutes this continued without abatement, then slowly it began to lessen, but this started me into the Mystical Crucifixion—that was to last for many years.

Mother's teachings, and her active help on the outer and inner planes, were absolutely vital to my surviving these experiences and making this transformation. I look back on the many years, jobs, roles, and the work involved, all while going through these experiences; somehow, God made it possible for me to fulfill the duties required of me, although I can tell you, it was a great challenge to do so. I will also say that living in two worlds simultaneously meant I could never give myself fully to whatever work I did, so I did not always do it to my fullest satisfaction, but my employers, and customers, were usually satisfied. One of the things I proved to myself is that you can do both—with God and Gurus' grace; it is possible.

And why go to all this trouble? It is because Mother, Master, and Papa have shown the Way to the next evolutionary step for humankind. Jesus let his life serve as an example of what is possible and even more to come. To merge individual consciousness into absolute Divine Consciousness means that you have supreme bliss, a perfect knowing of who and what you truly are, and untold spiritual potential may express itself through you according to its will. In essence, you are who you have always been; all false illusions have fallen away, and you stand revealed as a perfect expression of God. You no longer crawl upon this mudball, the earth, as a worm making its way in darkness; you are now a shining spiritual being. Whatever you have been put through upon the way seems a very little cost compared to what you have become.

Material wealth and prestige come and go with the seasons of life. Youth, strength, and health can all fall by the wayside—what is permanent? The only thing lasting is your spiritual heritage that you may realize in all its fullness. God made creation with fascinating, never-ending expressions, but all have an expiry date attached. Only God can fulfill that need we all have for the inner kingdom of heaven, promised from when the foundation of this universe was created. As you celebrate this sacred experience of the resurrection of Christ Consciousness, think deeply upon its meaning and make a determination that this symbolic day will find fulfillment in you.

April 20

Meeting Roy Eugene Davis

Reverend Roy Eugene Davis with Yogacharya David.

As part of our North American Pilgrimage, I was looking forward to seeing Reverend Roy Eugene Davis, a direct disciple of Paramhansa Yogananda. When just a teenager, Roy read the *Autobiography of a Yogi* and immediately wanted to meet Master. However, he was in Florida, without funds, and Master was in California. Roy was selling door to door when a potential customer asked why he had this job. He explained that his plan was to save money and go out to California to meet this extraordinary man. She said, "If it is that important to you, just go!" And so he did, arriving at Master's doorstep practically penniless. Master made Roy a minister and gave him rare direct permission to give Kriya Initiation during his relatively short time, a couple of years, of being with Master, shortly before Master's mahasamadhi.

By prior arrangement, we arrived by 9 a.m. at his "Center for Spiritual Awareness" retreat and drove up to the Meditation Hall. Roy's car was already parked there, and when we walked up to the building, he turned the corner to greet us with an easy smile. Roy is tall, of naturally-lanky build, and at 86 years, looks in good health. He has an easy manner, is soft-spoken, and appears to be more at ease with me today than he had been at our two previous meetings.

He asked after my health and guided us into the Meditation Hall where there were marble statues of the Guru-lineage, including one of Roy at the masters' feet. He described how the craftsmen in India could sit all day chiseling and smoothing the exteriors until they became the likeness of Yoganandaji, Sri Yukteswarji, Lahiri Mahasaya, and Babaji. He said such statues are not usually done until a person is dead, but a devotee had wanted one done of him, so he had sat for photos from different angles, and they were sent to India. He also showed us a case with treasures brought back to him from India—several Ganeshas, Hanumans, a three-dimensional yatra, and other assorted statues in a newly-added wood-and-glass case.

The Hall has a wonderful, pure feeling to it, and after a full pronam to the Guru-lineage, Carla and I sat with Roy in the three chairs he had arranged. We had a wide-ranging conversation for the next two hours about Master, his work, swamis, and the current nature of the world. He first asked after our Group and the Work we do for God and Gurus. I spoke about the extraordinary aspirants and devotees we have, that we meet in small groups in homes, and that we abide by the three promises I made to my Gurudev: "Not to advertise, no organization, and to not charge for anything I do in service for God." This is different from how Master and he have operated, so he listened respectfully.

During the course of our talk, I asked him, "Looking back now from the distance of many years since being with Master, what stands out in your mind about Master? What is emblazoned in your memories?" He thought a bit, then spoke about how different Master was in person from that of his public persona. When he gave a lecture, he was the teacher; there was no doubt about that; he could be funny, tell stories, and all of that, but he was in charge. But, in private, he was softer, intimate: he often sat close to you, he leaned in close (demonstrating by leaning his head in toward an imaginary recipient), and you felt like you were the most important person in the world to him. This was a theme Roy came back to several times, how Master had no air of formality, but was open, human, and available on a personal level.

Roy spoke about how commercial hatha yoga had become. He referred to one magazine in Los Angeles that used to be quite good. Now, there were pictures of women in bikinis doing nearly impossible asanas, and advertising for clothing and accessories throughout the publication. The last time we met, the movie about Master, *Awake: The Life of Yogananda,* had just been released and Roy had expressed his displeasure over it. Today, he said that his video man had taken out the parts Roy did not like, and what was left was a 30-minute version that was just of Master—without the many commentaries from those who had no direct connection with Yoganandaji. He said he did not release this version, or I would have asked him for a copy.

We talked about our North American pilgrimage, and he asked if we planned to go to Swami Premananda's church in Washington DC (the swami has passed away but there is still a Kriya lineage there). He said that he recently uncovered a letter dated 1950 from Swami Premananda to Swami Satyananda, head of Yogoda

Satsanga Society (YSS) in India. The contents of the letter stated that "Swami Yogananda" (not Paramhansa) was going to make James J. Lynn head of SRF: Premananda told Satyananda that it would ruin YSS in India and that Satyananda should break off all connection with SRF. "Here was Master's disciple, plotting against him! Many of those who grew up with Master thought of him as Mukunda, the boy they grew up with, and not of who he truly was."

We talked much about the sad state of affairs with many of the Indian swamis, both in America and in India. However, Roy then said that Mother Hamilton had found a real one in Swami Ramdas, and she was fortunate. Like many of Master's disciples, he may find it puzzling why Mother had to go to another spiritual master in India after Master's passing. There are those who do not fully comprehend the type of experiences that Mother was to undergo while in India, and that there were no qualified masters in the organization to help Mother go through the terrific experiences of the Mystical Crucifixion after the passing of her guru and Rajasi. Mother, herself, initially had a conflict about going to India, not because she doubted Papa, but because of her loyalty to Master. It was God's will that this should happen, and it will definitely stand the test of time that both Master and Papa were destined to play essential roles in Mother's life—of this, there is no doubt. However, I do think it was a very significant comment made by Roy, and not lightly done.

Upon our leaving, I feel great love for Roy, an "uncle" in the Kriya lineage. When you look at the various scandal-ridden swamis and teachers of recent years, and others who seek to make Master their "property," it makes my appreciation grow for this God-man and the work he has done for God and Gurus. He is jnani by nature, and he tends to be understated; yet, quite open and honest. The list of those living who had close contact with

Master is rapidly dwindling, and I feel it a blessing to be with one who Master welcomed in from their first meeting, and in whom Master gave rare dispensation to initiate others into Kriya Yoga. Roy has been a boon for many thousands—may Master richly bless him and his work.

April 23

SURRENDER IS SERENITY

Upper Falls area: Babaji made his presence
known, Pisgah National Forest, North Carolina.

Continuing our pilgrimage, our caravan scrambles over 6,000-foot passes, and we cross into North Carolina on our way to see Joy and family. The change in climate is noticeable, both rising in altitude and moving northward—it is cooler and wetter, reminding us of the **Northwest** dampness. However, we are low enough in latitude that such heights display early spring, not hip-deep snow. We arrive at the Powhatan

State Park, not far from Arden, and the city of Asheville. Asheville has an interesting history as it became an especially loved place by writers Carl Sandburg, Thomas Wolfe, and F. Scott Fitzgerald, who had homes here. It is also the place of America's largest private home, the Biltmore. George Vanderbilt created this cozy little 250-room house on 8,000 acres with breathtaking gardens designed by Fredrick Olmstead.

Acting as host, Joy takes us on a wonderful drive up into the Blue Ridge Mountains in the Pisgah National Forest at over 4,000 feet in altitude for a hike to some marvelous waterfalls by the name of Skinnydip (and no, we did not). While sitting on some rocks next to the falls, I noticed an overhang next to us that reminded me of an apt yogi's cave. I fell into a reverie about Babaji—when I am in the wilderness, he often comes to mind.

Almost twenty years ago now, when at Cloud Mountain during a year of silence and solitude, I had several experiences with the great Mahayogi. In one of these, I felt him so close and beseeched him to come to me in body. In blunt language, he refused and made it known to me that I am to realize his universal nature, not limit him to a physical form. Since that time, he has occasionally come to me with his personal "signature," but expansive and universal—as well as in the perfect intimacy of thought transference.

As I look upstream at the successive waterfalls, there is a pool of water with a rocky landing beyond. The thought of Babaji is with me, and his radiant presence manifests on the rocky landing, spreading to the whole scene lying before me. The air itself scintillates with his vibration; I feel him both near and all around.

"Oh, beautiful master, you come in this superior formless-form and your supreme consciousness touches my own—thereby, I am blessed. You teach me non-attachment to form, and thereby free me of local biases, making me know that we are not material stuff, but super-existence that cannot be constrained by a simple body or location. Your very nature is universal, and through the touch of your consciousness, you make me know that I too am of universal nature. Your blessings are purity itself. I bow to you and feel myself dissolved into God's omniscient Self."

We then journey onward and enjoy more waterfalls along the way; as well, we enjoy a delicious picnic lunch Joy has brought with her. While we sit on a gravel beach by the flowing river, we watch in wonder as a ten-inch snake wiggles its way upstream and eventually disappears into some tree roots on the riverbank. As the day progresses, the experience with Babaji lingers, and God calls me inward—we return so that I might allow full sway to His magnetic current.

Truly, my life is not my own; He dictates what is to be done and not done. Whatever my, or others', expectations may be, His will reigns supreme. And, there is no place I would rather be. Through these past many days, He has periodically continued to place me between the grinding forces of universal good and evil, and at the same time, He gives me such great bliss. Most often, even when He gives me a difficult task to do, He also gives me so greatly of Himself: inner assurance, blissful joy, and a keen understanding that this is all His will.

There is a great secret in life: when you fully accept that God has you exactly where He wants you to be—it is perfect. You may judge it is not where you would like to be; however, you surrender to His will, and then you feel His Presence—this makes an enormous difference in the quality of your life. He may destroy your dreams, disturb your plans, and play with your preferences; yet, He always means well! What at first takes an effort to surrender to, eventually works itself into a knowing-understanding that His will is always best, then you no longer have to work at surrender—rather, it is now your natural state. Such surrender is the great secret to peace and serenity in all times and places. Be it ever so!

Joy Putnam and Carla Hickenbottom on a hike.

April 27

A HEALING BALM

Blue Ridge Mountains, North Carolina.

Travel Update: We are motoring along the beautiful Blue Ridge Parkway of North Carolina. It has elevations averaging 3,000 to 4,000 feet. Yesterday, we took a side trip to climb up Mount Mitchell, 6,684 feet, the highest point east of the Mississippi. We also crossed over the East's continental divide. As we roll along, we climb, then descend, only to climb once again atop a serpentine crest (the road architect said he wanted the road to look like nature had put it there). There are expanses of evergreens and deciduous forests; maples are showing bright spring colors along with early wild azaleas (the rhododendrons have yet to show), an abundance of waterfalls and lakes, and when looking out on successive rolling mountains, there is an amazing general transparent blue cast in the atmosphere. The

Blue Ridge Parkway is almost 500 miles along the backbone of the Appalachian Mountain range, with a maximum of 45 MPH speed limit—in the summer, it is the most heavily traveled of any of the national forests.

We are currently at Linville Falls State Park and will be going northward today. The Internet has been very spotty, so I am sending this from a pullout near Grandfather Mountain. We now have plans in place to fly back to the Northwest for three weeks in mid-May for medical tests: scans, probes, and prods. And, we are very much looking forward to our time together at Loon Lake as well as at local services and meditations.

I awoke this morning with God talking to me about past remembrances. A recurrent theme for many is the memories of times and places that disturb us, given they have unresolved emotional charges attached to them. We may take such memories as an opportunity for healing. We can do this by re-creating the moment of disturbance in a way that neutralizes the emotional charge and sends a message to the subconscious mind about how we would like to handle a future like-situation, if it should ever arise.

For instance, perhaps a memory takes shape in our conscious mind of a situation in which we felt embarrassment or shame. In thinking of what happened at the time, we now introduce new elements. If we were careless or thoughtless and at fault, we picture ourselves doing it all differently. Perhaps we change the scenario before the actual point of embarrassment—we see ourselves being mindful and more careful. We feel calm, methodical, and aware that, if we do not do so, things will not turn out well.

Maybe there was another time when something occurred that was outside of our control, yet the results of what happened continue to haunt us. In this case, we may recreate the situation by seeing ourselves surrounded by the Light of God—the masters are all around us, and angels of mercy hover nearby. We feel a deep, unshakable, calm within. We may see those around us also in the Light of God. Many times, people will say and do things out of their own anxiety that land very hard on us, and they do not realize the effect it has. Other times, they do know, and feel powerful in "lording it over" another. In either case, it is done in ignorance, and they will have to suffer the pain they inflict on others. Real healing comes in divine understanding, knowing that whatever we do to another, we do first to ourselves.

God meant this life to be lived in joy and light. The fact that we have wandered away from this vision of a Divine Life does not mean we are to be forsaken. Divine Mother is calling us to be awake to the fact that this creation is sacred, holy ground, and Heavenly Father wants us to know that there is a sure, unflappable, source of peace and inner assurance that transcends the thralldom of duality. The healing of the fissure between heaven and hell is as close as our next thought; simply lay the healing balm of God-remembrance upon the past, present, and anticipated future.

Wild azaleas in bloom.

April 30

CHOOSING YOUR ROAD

Yogacharya David at the base of 200-foot
Stone Mountain Falls, North Carolina.

We are drawing toward the end of our excursion along the spine of the Appalachian Mountains. When we began, we knew it would be a winding, twisting, and slow means of travel; however, the rewards have been worth the extra effort. We have been guests to tremendous vistas. It is home to countless waterfalls and streams, and wonderful little places to visit—such as Mabry Mill, which highlights the inventive mind of "Uncle Ed" Mabry—from a different era. This choice of road has been well worth the extra effort it has taken.

One thing worthy of note: there are unflattering stereotypes of the Appalachians, and of the South in general, that I have simply not found here. The people we have met have been unfailingly polite, genteel, friendly, and intelligent. There may be others who are not, but they have not been in our experience. Blowing Rock would give a run for its money to any posh, Southern California hipster spot. Other than historical displays, I have not seen any great tension or discrimination based on color of skin. There is no doubt that such things do exist here, as in all parts of the world, but on the road, there is nothing we have encountered of it in big cities or in rural spots.

Which brings to mind a related observation. Wherever I have gone, God is present, within and without. Both in temples made by humans and Cathedrals of Nature, the sound of Aum/Amen and the Light of the Infinite have been in abundance. In all places, we have found God's helping hand through timely advice, direction, a caring comment, or a friendly "How ya'll doin'?" And, of course, His Divine Presence felt within has made the Infinite Beloved a constant feature throughout our pilgrimage.

One of His helping angels came in such a timely way for such a small need. On the advice of a forest ranger, we had traveled to Elkin to find a bike trail and some much-needed internet access. We were across from the library looking for the bike trail that we had been assured was there, but we could not find it. A friendly-looking man asked if we were going on a bike ride (our bicycles in hand may have been a clue) and when I said we could not find the trail and had thought to ride off in one direction in search of it, he happily gave directions to go the opposite way! He went on to describe the trail in detail, including the exact length of each of the bridges. I observed, "You are a man who knows his bridges!" He said he should, that he helped build them. He then gave me his card and said if we became lost to give him a call. When we returned to the campground, I told the ranger about the help he gave, and she said, "Was that Dr. Bill?" I said "Yes," and she said he was instrumental in organizing the volunteers who built the beautiful bike trail with amazing bridges, and that he is a doctor known all over the state for his kindness and willingness to help! Imagine, he was there just when we needed his help—God in human form!

Papa said that when he left to go by train and foot all over India, it was because God wanted to demonstrate that He is universally present. And although I have ventured to many parts of the world, there are many areas of America yet to see. It seems that God is out to demonstrate that He truly is equally present in all places and people of America. In addition, it has given us a chance to chant His holy name wherever we go, adding our part of God to all the people and places to which we have traveled.

In life, there are certainly circumstances that we are plopped into that are beyond our control in the moment, but we also have unprecedented freedom (compared to most of recorded history). We have means of transportation unthought of by the royalty of the past; in fact, in almost all areas of life, many of us have a truly privileged existence. And, with deeper analysis, even those situations that seem beyond our control, and our liking, are the result of decisions we made countless times and from many lives. This all leads to the topic of making conscious decisions about the roads we choose to travel.

Just like we chose the slower, more difficult, Blue Ridge Parkway, so we may find that we choose a road that others may find difficult to fathom, but it is right for us. The fact that we have chosen a God-centered life makes us unique, to begin with, but even with that, there are thousands of choices we make every day that determine what road we will travel. We can live a life in which we are carried downstream by the force of what others do, or we can determine to take roads less traveled through very conscious intention. The greatest road we, or anyone, can choose, is the one that God, through His inner direction, has chosen for us. We may follow that road and its every twist and turn with the certain knowledge that it is both taking us to our ultimate destination of full realization and that the road is God Himself.

Carla at the base of Stone Mountain Falls.

May 5

To Be on God's Side

"Susan Constant," the largest of the three sailing ships that
made the five-month voyage from England to Jamestown.

We are currently encamped at Newport News City
Campground, east of Richmond, Virginia. I am sitting
amongst thickly-forested evergreens and fully-leafed
deciduous trees. What makes this place remarkable is that we
are a bike ride away from George Washington's headquarters,
and very near Yorktown: the scene of the last major battle of
the Revolutionary War, in which the British army surrendered
to American/French armies and navies, ending a six-year war.

Also, nearby, is the oldest English settlement in North America, Jamestown, and the restored capital city of colonial Williamsburg.

Colonial Williamsburg has a remarkable story. Reverend W.A.R. Goodwin became pastor of the Bruton Parish Church at the turn of the century, 1900s. The church was the original place where George Washington, Thomas Jefferson, and others worshipped when they were in the Virginia Burgess (the colonial House of Representatives). The good reverend had a vision of not only restoring the vintage church, but the entire area that includes the old capitol building and the governor's palace. Through tireless petitioning, he garnered the interest of John D. Rockefeller, who gradually committed to the restoration of the whole township.

Today, Colonial Williamsburg, the first settlement of Jamestown and Yorktown, make up the Historic Triangle of Virginia: all connected by the Colonial Parkway, which follows a route through forested trees and is exposed to both the wide James and York rivers. Colonial Williamsburg and Jamestown are both "living museums," that is, you can wander about the historic towns and character actors will tell you about the life and times they represent. Our plan has been to be here before school lets out and while the weather is mild—as a result, there have been far fewer visitors than at peak times, and the weather has been perfect, not too warm, or humid.

The Revolutionary War and the ideals that drove it have always been an interest of mine. There were many factors figuring into the daring stand of the colonists who wanted separation from England—which, incidentally, had the most formidable army and navy in the world while the colonists started with none. Primarily, it was a desire for personal freedom and the bold vision of the world's first purely representative-elected government. Ideals were set forth that were not fully embodied at the time, evidenced by the exclusion of women, slaves, and native nations from equal rights; however, those ideals have stood the test of time, and they continue to be a guiding star for a "more perfect union."

Speaking with one of the wonderful character actors playing Patrick Henry, I suggested that revolution was a bold and very risky proposition—he could have been hanged for treason. He replied, "But God is with us!" And this was very much part of the revolution, that God was with those who asserted that all men were born equal and had certain inalienable rights. The clergy was central to the revolutionary fervor, and it was felt at the time that this was a sacred cause.

"Patrick Henry" at Colonial Williamsburg:
"Give me liberty or give me death!"

There has been an imperfect implementation of these ideals. Over sixty years after the Revolution, a most terrible civil war was fought, and at the heart of the issue was slavery. It was not until 1920 that women finally gained the equal right to vote. However, the fundamental words of those revolutionary ideals have not changed, only their fuller realization (both Washington and Jefferson were uncomfortable with slavery, and both foresaw its eventual extinction).

The other genius of the time was the check and balance of a limited government. By dividing the executive, legislative, and judiciary branches, the tendency of a centralized government to garner more and more power to itself was slowed. Compare that with the disaster of the French Revolution that brought forth a single ruling body that eventually collapsed into a dictatorship, or in more recent times, the costly failure of communism without free elections or an effective Bill of Rights—this awareness helps us gain an increased appreciation for the foresight and integrity of the founding generation.

Abraham Lincoln, among others in succeeding generations, saw the creation of the United States as Divinely inspired, and its role in the world crucial to the coming of a new age of government and individual rights. However, with great wisdom, he said, "Sir, my concern is not whether God is on our side; my greatest concern is to be on God's side, for God is always right." Due to human fallibility, there may be those who doubt divine inspiration for this country, but that has always been the case with sacred ideals—as God proposes, it is up to human beings to fulfill His high ideals. Imperfect implementation does not mean that it does not come from the most perfect One; only that we need to work harder to be on God's side.

Like all great principles, they are not the property of any one person, religion, or nation—they are universal and equally true for one and for all. We can draw inspiration from the idealism and courage of those who succeeded against all odds in bringing forward a nation based on the ideals:

> We hold these truths to be self-evident, that all men are created equal by their Creator with certain inalienable

Rights, that among these are Life, Liberty, and the Pursuit of Happiness. That to secure these rights, Governments are instituted among Men, deriving their just powers from the consent of the governed.[12]

Firing of the cannon at Colonial Williamsburg, Virginia.

12   Quote from the United States *Declaration of Independence*. https://www.archives.gov.declaration

May 7

Reflections From a Battlefield

Site of Washington's Headquarters near our Yorktown campground.

The wind is rushing past as we ride our bicycles on a dirt path through thick woods and emerge into an oval glade—a sign informs us that this is the spot where General Washington had his field headquarters in the battle for Yorktown. On our way here, we rode past Civil War embankments where soldiers from the North and the South lined up against one another. The birds sing; we feel perfectly safe to pass through these hotly-contested parcels of land from another time and era. Today, we toured very expensive museums displaying acts of war. One film had special effects when viewing a 90-degree-angled screen—a sea battle was shown while a cool wind blew in the theater; bombs exploded, and "smoke" came in through vents, the seats shook underneath, and flashes of light displayed all around to make you feel you were in the midst of the action. Of course, we were perfectly safe from explosions; we were not really on rolling seas, and the concussions of bombs did not threaten to demolish the building we were in, but these effects were stunning.

And what are we to think of these intense battlefields of the past: where courage and fear run hand in hand, where germs killed many more than bullets, and metal projectiles did their terrible damage? Throughout my adult life, I have striven to peacefully resolve conflicts, whether they were of the mind, in families, neighborhoods, or in organizations—as a minister, counselor, and mediator. It has been my purpose in this life to establish peace through reason, not violence. I even go to some lengths to coax a fly to leave the indoors: after its initial wildness of finding itself trapped, a fly will often land on my arm as I escort it to outdoor freedom, or it will take my encouragement and fly out on its own.

And what of our admirable example of Mahatma Gandhi: his example of non-violent assertion of power? Was his not a more noble way to separate from England than America's violent revolution? Paramhansa Yogananda felt there was a karmic connection between America and India. Columbus was searching for India when he bumped into the inconvenient North American continent. America had a violent separation from England, while India's separation was through non-violent means—a mirror reflection? Does not India show the better way? Though the Mahatma himself promoted non-violence through word and deed, the very real threat of his fasting, at least for the British, was that there would be massive violence on the streets if he died from voluntary starvation. And then, as part of successfully quitting the British Empire, there was the awful violence that occurred on the

Pakistan/India border. This was something that, of course, deeply disturbed Mahatma Gandhi, but was not unanticipated. The point is: even with the initial peaceful means of separation, many more died in India of violence in their separation from England than in America's war of independence—it is so difficult to be a purist in these things. It is also interesting that Mahatma Gandhi's favorite scripture was the Bhagavad Gita, an exposition that takes place on a battlefield in which God, in the form of Krishna, is urging Arjuna to take up arms and fight!

Each of us is called to obey our conscience of what to do and how to do it. A hero or a villain is not defined by whether one picks up a gun or stands aside, but whether the individual adheres to the highest light he or she knows. Mother once asked me in front of a group, "If the only way to stop someone from blowing up a hundred people would be to kill him, would I do it?" In the end, I said I would kill the one perpetrator to save a hundred innocents. It is a thought experiment, but it does make one face a most difficult decision, and it helps bring out a principle. Papa, Master, and Mother were all non-violent advocates, yet none were in complete agreement with Mahatma Gandhi's absolutist view—there are times and places where self-defense, or in defense of others, violence and war may be the right solution.

As I walk these battlefields, I am sure there were those on both sides who performed right action to the best of their ability. However, I, and many millions, have been the great beneficiaries of the courage shown by those colonists who believed in the ideals of freedom, desired to have a representative government and a guarantee of individual rights. I honor those who lived up to the highest light of their times and take inspiration that I, and all of us, should be courageous in being examples manifesting the great Light of God within and without in whatever way He directs.

Just for fun! Yogacharya David in a Continental Army jacket.

May 11

GUIDING LIGHTS

George Washington statue in the Capitol
Building Rotunda, Washington, DC

I have looked forward to seeing these sites that have historical interest, as our past has always captured my imagination. I have been the fortunate recipient of excellent history teachers, and professors, and have been an avid reader of distant times brought to life—all good history teachers are good storytellers.

One of these was my eighth grade US history teacher, Mrs. H. She was not much over five feet tall, silver-haired, and a tough grader, but excellent at making the lives of others seem relevant. One day, she had a display of WWII paraphernalia laid out. My first inclination was to touch the German helmet, Japanese sword, etc. A fellow student, David R., said over my shoulder that we were not supposed to touch these articles, but that did not stop me. Suddenly, I heard a high-pitched samurai scream from behind. I turned to see this diminutive lady wearing a German helmet, holding a Japanese sword over her head, and coming in my direction! She backed me into a corner and Mrs. H. made it clear that I was not to touch these historical artifacts. She succeeded in getting my attention, eliciting laughter from everyone in the class but me.

The names of Washington, Jefferson, Madison, and Adams have long been in my memory, so to actually see Monticello, Mt. Vernon, and Washington DC has made those names take on a greater three-dimensional meaning. We had applied earlier to the office of our congressman, checking to see about tours of the Capital. One they provided was for the Capitol Building, the legislative home of the House of Representatives and the Senate. Although God kept me indrawn on Monday, Tuesday found me ready to proceed.

We took the train into the city from our Greenbelt Campground, a lovely, forested spot. Traveling through miles of tunnels, we finally emerged on "The Hill," just blocks from The Rayburn Building where our congressman has his office. Two young men, extremely knowledgeable about the history and the Capitol Building, gave Carla and me a most excellent tour for the next several hours. We made our way through a tunnel between buildings and literally made our way from the building foundations upward. We witnessed the first Supreme Courtroom, now kept as a museum, the House of Representatives room, where the Joint Session of Congress meets to hear the president and other notables address them, and the extremely impressive Rotunda—with artwork, architecture, and sculptures, all on an impressive scale. Our two guides sorted facts from urban legend and gave us an interesting commentary on notable events and places. We crossed a threshold that was the only leave-over from the old capitol that was burned to the ground in the War of 1812: the only reason it was left standing was because this was the exit for the British soldiers as they left the fiery ruins.

The next day, we ventured to Mt. Vernon, home of "the indispensable man," George Washington. His house sits on a lovely hill, overlooking the Potomac River. There are quotes from him stating that he thought it was the most perfect place in the world. He loved being a farmer and studied the developments of crop rotation, and seed production, etc. It made it poignantly clear what a sacrifice he made in being gone over six long years in a war that was against all the odds, and then another eight years as president with all the wrangling and posturing that politics brings. He had but two years of being home with his loving wife Martha before he suddenly succumbed to a bacterial infection and hypovolemia.

And how do these historical and political visitations relate to a spiritual pilgrimage—other than the sense that God is all in all? I do think that this country's origins have spiritual inspiration behind them. When we look at the number of despotic tyrannies that crowd our history books, it is a reminder of what a unique moment in time it was when guarantees of freedom were stated and put into law.

When in Colonial Williamsburg, we learned that all citizens had to pay taxes to the Anglican Church, whether they were a member or not. To be a church, you had to be approved by the government—for instance, Quakers were whipped and driven out of communities for their beliefs. These were just some reminders of what life was like before the revolution. A free thinker about religion, such as Jefferson and others of the "Enlightenment era," could be in danger of various retributions if their beliefs became public. The Western World waited for the collapse of the fledgling United States, believing that a nation could not survive without a monarch. It was tenuous at times. Would it survive at all after the revolution? But, through courage, sacrifice, and perseverance, survive it did, and the world has been its beneficiary. Master one time stated that the overall karma of America is very good—this from a man who faced some of the ugly cultural undercurrents of the times.

Today, it seems there is a rush to highlight any blemish under the guise of truth, but fact, without context, is not the truth when it is used simply as a bludgeon. If it is national pride only that arises from seeing these historical treasures, then it has value limited to those of that nation. But, when there are universal principles embodied in the formation and development of this country, then, its light can extend beyond its borders and it can be an inspiration for all: for this world still has its despotic regimes; individuals or minority communities can be persecuted for their beliefs, or way of life; and the rights of habeas corpus, and a trial by jury of one's peers, are far from universal.

Jesus affirmed the most universal law of the land:

> But when the Pharisees had heard that he had put the Sadducees to silence, they were gathered together. Then one of them, which was a lawyer, asked him a question, tempting him, and saying, "Master, which is the great commandment in the law?" Jesus said unto him, "Thou shalt love the Lord thy God with all thy heart, and with all thy soul, and with all thy mind. This is the first and great commandment. And the second is like unto it, Thou shalt love thy neighbor as thyself. On these two commandments hang all the law and the prophets" (Matthew 22:34–40).

Until this is the ubiquitous observance in all the lands, then I suppose we will need just governments and laws to enforce good behavior; however, none will ever surpass or replace this maxim as the most superior of guiding lights.

Mt. Vernon home of George and Martha Washington.

May 14

I BOW TO THE DIVINE MOTHER

Mother Hamilton, London, 1977.**

A
s we continue to tour Washington DC, we have been privy
to some remarkable sites. The Congressional Library may
not conjure up an image of someplace that is on the
"must-see" list, but that is deceptive. The art and architecture, let
alone the rare books and interesting exhibits, are more than
worth the effort (a wonderful feature of so many of these public
buildings and Smithsonian museums is that they are free of charge,
so the physical effort to get there is all that is needed). Truly, pictures do not do justice to the rotunda of the library, as the overall effect of space and art takes one's breath away. Another of the
many worthy sites is Washington's Memorial, an obelisk that was

the tallest structure in the world when built—it seems to reach all the way to the sky when looking up from its base.

Congressional Library Rotunda.

While taking the train out of Washington, we noted that the driver announced the next stop, along with a litany of added reminders. Most drivers rattle these off so slurred as not to be understood; however, this female driver had a wonderfully clear lilt—she put delight into her words. At the end of the run, she added (a day early), "And have a wonderful Mother's Day!"

On the train, we had watched a mother and child playing; they giggled and laughed in the most delightful way, making us both smile in appreciation at their loving noises. In general, it is fascinating to see all people as expressions of God, removing all false barriers of separation, rather than judging this one and that, or having a wall of defense, or a cone of indifference enshrouding them. Instead of all that, I feel an intimacy of connection that makes all a part of me, and I am a part of all. It is the most wonderful way to travel upon this earth.

These travel observations bring me back to the train driver's "Have a wonderful Mother's Day!" This morning, as I was thinking of God, the thought of Mother's Day circulated through. Mother used to say that when a mother gave birth, she went into the jaws of death in order to do so. I was breech born and the doctor was up to his elbows getting me turned. My mother was sutured afterward, for she had gone into the jaws of death and came out a little worse for the wear; she needed help for the next couple of weeks to prevent the opening of wounds. There was a time when it was common for mothers to die when giving birth; today, those odds have been greatly decreased; however, there is always risk, and there is the pain that must be gone through—for some reason, God made it a most difficult process. So much gratitude to all mothers who have paid the price, not just at birth, but for the many years of raising children and all that entails.

Washington Monument—touching the sky.

As I continued to think over Mother's Day, my mind naturally brought up my spiritual mother. A mother will draw the soul that is destined for her through her magnetism of karma, and a spiritual teacher will draw her students to her through her pure spiritual magnetism. It was for the purpose of meeting Mother that I came into this incarnation, and like a powerful magnet, Mother drew me to herself. When I first met Mother, she created an invisible umbilical cord of spiritual connection, a cord that went wherever I did.

An early reminder of this connection was demonstrated when I was in the Sahara Desert. After traveling some days through sand dunes and rocky terrain, I stood while we took a break from riding in the back of a truck. I was looking out over the dunes, and suddenly, I smelled Mother's perfume (White Lilac) so strongly that I looked around, but, of course, there was no accounting for the smell from anyone or anything around me (we had been traveling for days, without water for washing, so there was no doubt that none of us smelled nice!). With that fragrance came Mother's presence; I felt as if I was surrounded by a spiritual womb of comfort and connection.

Picture taken by Yogacharya David while riding
in a truck across the Sahara Desert, Africa, 1975.

Indeed, Mother went into the jaws of death many times in order for us to gain eternal life. Whatever a mother goes through in a human sense is multiplied many times over by what a spiritual guru goes through in order to help those striving for the highest realization. There was nothing Mother would not do to bring about the second birth of all of her spiritual children. Mother one time said that "If you worked just one-tenth as hard for your realization as I work so that you might have it, you would have God in a hurry!"

I continued to muse on this subject and thought of all the years past—having Service on Sunday guaranteed we would gather on Mother's Day. It feels strange not to be with you on this special day; however, the strong feeling comes over me of the closeness I experience whenever I closed Service by handing out roses to all the ladies, affirming, "I bow to the Divine Mother in you." I feel that same spiritual current going out from me now as I inwardly hand the rose to you, bowing to the Divine Mother. I pray, in return, that you feel honored within this divine connection. Blessings for the sacrifices made by all mothers, and may you know the absolute purity of the Divine Mother within you. Om, Amen.

I bow to the Divine Mother in you.**

May 18

KEYS IN YOUR HANDS

Ganesha: God of wisdom and remover of obstacles.

t continues to amaze me how we can be on the east coast in sun-drenched 85-degree weather, and five hours later, we have crossed three time zones, flying nearly 600 miles per hour at 30,000- feet—returning the Boeing 737/900 to where it was created—and enter into the oceanic climate zone where it is 60 degrees and cloudy.

Having been immersed in colonial history in Savannah, Virginia, and Washington DC, the thought came to me of what those early settlers would think of these transportation and technological wonders. Surely, even the most outlandish creative mind of the era could not have dreamed of such marvels. Thomas Jefferson was in awe of the first hot air balloon that lifted off from the ground while he was in France; we have been witnesses to truly amazing progress since.

Yet, biologically, the person rocketing into the stratosphere is not so different from the one riding on a horse-drawn carriage from the past—they too had hopes and dreams for happiness. A smartphone does not make a person wise—quite often, it seems it has the opposite effect (a sign we saw while on the road read something like: Go to church if you love Jesus, text while you are driving if you want to meet him now!). While the necessities of life: food, shelter, and clothing are important, they still, in and of themselves, do not have the power to make us happy. Many of the topics colonists thought about are with us still: topics of health, wealth, reputation, and happiness in relationships are defining features for our sense of well-being. Underneath all of these complicating factors competing for our attention is our essential, existential health—our spiritual happiness.

Someone with a towering intellect, substantial wealth, fame, or position, can certainly be miserable, lonely, and depressed; none of the above are guarantors for satisfaction in life. Whereas someone in the simplest of life's situations may radiate joy and be a Light unto this world. All through history, the source of real happiness has not changed: real happiness consists of aligning thought and action with one's innermost being. Proper alignment equals joy; misalignment produces suffering.

We have been given the keys to the kingdom of heavenly happiness. We have also been given the choice as to whether to use those keys or to carry on with old patterns of misery-producing habits. There is no superior being judging us on our performance; it is simply that we are a product of the choices we make in life. There are always reasons for finding fault with the world and for putting ourselves under stress: money worries, illness, feeling powerless, and not having the love and admiration of others can be voracious wolves howling in the night, stalking the halls of our dreams.

The lila between Lahiri Mahasaya and Sri Yukteswar is so instructive. Recovering from a deathly illness, Sri Yukteswar relapsed when his guru commented that though he looked better today, who knows what tomorrow might bring! Then, Sri Yukteswar rebounded when Lahiri Mahasaya next suggested that he thought he should recover; back and forth went his recovery and relapse with each alternating comment by his guru over several days. Finally, Sri Yukteswarji understood that Lahiri Mahasaya wanted him to go beyond polarized thinking—even suggestions from his beloved guru—and anchor himself directly and permanently to perfect health through God-tuned thought.

You hold the keys in your own hands for finding the eternal lightness of Being radiating in the deepest recesses of your Self. However, only if you mindfully use those keys will you find the source of eternal life. It will not come from the fabled "Fountain of Youth" associated with Herodotus, Alexander the Great, and Ponce de Leon. Living Waters come not from a hidden source in the jungles, desert, or mountains, but in the spine and brain. Those Living Waters make you know that eternal life is the true nature of your Soul, and it is discovered through intensified prayer and meditation. These vital energies may also lead to a long life and youthfulness of the body as well, but what of that if Self-realization is not attained?

Worldly cares can sap youthfulness right out of your being. God can just as easily pour Himself in and fill you with light and joy overflowing. Yes, this world alternates between highs and lows—it ever has, and it will ever be so. However, in your oneness with the Infinite, you are His evermore—knowing this is the key to lasting happiness.

It is good to be in the Pacific Northwest; it is heartwarming to see friends and to find joy in all the nooks and crannies of life here. Yesterday, I had an MRI of the brain (those magnetic forces have an interesting and somewhat invasive effect on a sensitized nervous system); other days will bring other tests, then Service on Sunday, Loon Lake next week, and a new Journal in the making: a busy schedule, all to be filled with the bliss of *Living Waters*.

May 21

UNBOUNDED LOVE

God loving God: Mother Hamilton with
118-year-old saint Bhirabai, West Bengal, India, 1968.**

We have happily returned to the Northwest. How wonderful it is to see spiritual family, to prepare for Service, and to spend time with dear Rams in human form. One outstanding feature of a spiritually awakened life is experiencing the Divine Love that flows through the heart. It was many years ago now that my heart center was first opened, but the lasting consequence has been so momentous that it never ceases to amaze and inform me.

The sudden and powerful expansion of my heart was like opening doors that had been hanging on rusty creaky hinges. Those doors did not open easily, nor without pain. But open they did, and once opened, they have remained so. Divine Love is unlike human love that is limited and oftentimes exists in a quid pro quo—*if you love me well, then, I will love you.* Nor is Prem, pure love, sentimental, which can also vacillate—running hot and cold. True Divine Love flows through the heart and is no respecter of whether someone deserves that love; it simply flows.

It has been affirmed by all the great saints down through time that *God is love, and love is God.* Jesus himself was a supreme bhakta, a lover of God and God in humanity. He demonstrated his love through his careful training of disciples, his healing of those suffering, teaching forgiveness and universal compassion, and his total surrender to his heavenly Father, even unto death. Mother oftentimes exhorted us to love God, and, at first, I did not really understand what that meant. With the opening of my heart center, I began to comprehend its meaning—in part, loving God was opening my heart to Him, allowing Divine Love full and unfettered access to the deepest recesses of my Being. As God pours His love through my heart, He loves all creation through me; He also loves me, and in that great outpouring, love comes full circle, and I love God even more greatly.

To love God is not simply a duty—something you must do. It is the greatest thing you can do for yourself and for the world! Opening your heart to God is a choice, but in the beginning, it is not an easy one. We have all been hurt and met with disappointment when it comes to loving others; however, in loving God, we have a beloved who will never hurt or betray us: He is as steady and constant as we are to Him—not that God ever turns away from us, but He will never intrude upon us if the door of our heart is closed.

Therefore, we must choose; we must allow Him to open those stubborn doors, to love the world through us, and we can let the love of God shine through our actions toward all. It is only then that we have unbounded love passing through us, that we may bathe in a vast ocean of peaceful love, making us complete—for the first time, we are truly whole.

May 25

Honors Gained

King Krishna playing the part of a humble cow herder,
picture by our dear Gargi (Lakshmi), Anandashram.

There is a saying in the world, "Having some skin in the game." That is, you are intimately connected to the outcomes of an endeavor, an active participant, not a critic sitting on the sidelines. This spiritual journey we are on is only for those who have "skin in the game." It is not for intellectual curiosity alone, although curiosity is a precursor to wonder; moreover, it is not for those who simply seek comfort, even though bliss is the greatest pleasure a soul may experience. This path, this journey, is only for those who have complete commitment, even unto death—the death of the ego.

Where does such commitment come from? In worldly endeavors, rewards sought include wealth, fame, prestige, and honors. For many who join spiritual organizations, there is the rising up in the organizational ladder, having authority, perhaps wealth and power. But we have no organization, grand buildings, or grounds; fortune is not to be made; we operate quietly and without fanfare. So, what is the motivation for our dedication and fidelity?

The outcomes we seek are not the same as the worldly, or the even more subtle, spiritual materialism that catches many an unwary soul in large organizations; outcomes can only come through the internal results of our practice. Mother designed it this way so that the traps of this world were, as much as possible, avoided. So, we are souls who are dedicated to spiritual advancement up the spine, not advancement up the organizational ladder; we seek out the "President of the universe," not to become its ruler; we have no board of directors or leaders of committees. In a worldly sense, this path is filled with costs and few benefits. And spiritually, this path is also front-loaded with costs, the cost of effort for disciplined meditation, service to humankind, and a total striving for access to higher states of consciousness; there are many costs within and without, with a promise of something greater, even if that greatness is invisible to the world.

That *something greater* is so much more than anything this world can offer; it is the *shining city upon the hill, a new Jerusalem* of divine consciousness, the eternal salvation of the soul through illumined consciousness; it is the total transformation of the individual from the human to the divine. Surely, the individual can be tempted by name and fame, but those allurements get little purchase on this path.

I think of Jesus walking the road with disciples, living simply, and begging for food from town to town. Yet even being in the company of this living avatar, being handpicked by their spiritual preceptor, his disciples got into conversations with one another about who would be the greatest among them; and I am sure there may have been thoughts of when Israel found its new king in Jesus, what position of importance they would occupy. Jesus, knowing these hidden, or not-so-hidden desires, taught them, "He that is greatest among you, shall be your servant." The servant is the opposite of a ruler, is not at the top of the organizational ladder, not the wealthiest, or most honored. Where does the ego find a place of honor as a servant?

Yet, even competition for humility can take place. I noticed one devotee at the ashram who worked every day to be last in line for the flower ceremony. Very self-consciously, this devotee always took pains to be at the end, with the idea of being humble. However, the very act of trying to be humble engendered ego. You see how tricky desire nature is?

There is a magnificent quote from Krishna:

Whoso is fixed in holiness, self-ruled,
Pure-hearted, lord of senses and of self,
Lost in the common life of all which lives —
A "Yogayukt" — he is a Saint who wends
Straightway to Brahm. Such a one is not touched
By taint of deeds. "Nought of myself I do!"
Thus will he think—who holds the truth of truths —
In seeing, hearing, touching, smelling; when
He eats, or goes, or breathes; slumbers or talks,
Holds fast or loosens, opens his eyes or shuts;
Always assured: "This is the sense-world plays
With senses." He that acts in thought of Brahm,
Detaching end from act, with act content,
The world of sense can no more stain his soul
Than waters mar th' enamelled lotus-leaf.

With life, with heart, with mind, nay, with the help
Of all five senses—letting selfhood go —
Yogins toil ever towards their souls' release.
Such votaries, renouncing fruit of deeds,
Gain endless peace.[13]

"Lost in the common life of all which lives," and "Detaching end from act, with act content, the world can no more stain his soul than waters mar th' enamelled lotus-leaf," are just some of the statements from the above quote that deserve special note.

Actually, this entire quote has long been a favorite of mine and encapsulates such great truth—truth we can spend an entire lifetime growing into, coming to realize its beauty. If there is honor to be sought on this path, it is the "honor" of being the invisible servant of God in all whom we meet, dissolving the self into the ocean of Being, merging into the vast, beginningless, endless, bliss of God, and becoming One, without a second. In this realization, how can one stand out when there is no *other*? Where can there be pride, when there is no longer a head upon which to place a crown?

---

13   Sri Edwin Arnold, translation: *The Song Celestial*. Chapter V (pp. 24–5).

June 1

A MEDITATION ON SRI YUKTESWARJI

Swami Sri Yukteswarji, portrait
at Karar Ashram, Puri, India.

We have completed a remarkable four-day retreat at Loon Lake, the focus: a meditation upon the life and teachings of the great master, Sri Yukteswarji. We took snippets from the great master's life and applied them to our own sadhana, our daily spiritual practice. One of the areas that resonated deeply was on the topic of ahimsa, harmlessness. We began with a story from the *Autobiography of a Yogi*:

It was the gentle hour of dusk. My guru was matchlessly interpreting the ancient texts. At his feet, I was in perfect peace. A rude mosquito entered the idyll and competed for my attention. As it dug a poisonous hypodermic needle into my thigh, I automatically raised an avenging hand. Reprieve from impending execution! An opportune memory came to me of one of Patanjali's yoga aphorisms—that on *ahimsa* (harmlessness).

"Why didn't you finish the job?"

"Master! Do you advocate taking life?"

"No; but the deathblow already had been struck in your mind."

"I don't understand."

"Patanjali's meaning was the removal of *desire* to kill." Sri Yukteswar had found my mental process an open book. "This world is inconveniently arranged for a literal practice of *ahimsa*. Man may be compelled to exterminate harmful creatures. He is not under similar compulsion to feel anger or animosity. All forms of life have equal right to the air of *maya*. The saint who uncovers the secret of creation will be in harmony with its countless bewildering expressions. All men may approach that understanding who curb the inner passion for destruction.

"Guruji, should one offer himself a sacrifice rather than kill a wild beast?

"No; man's body is precious. It has the highest evolutionary value because of unique brain and spinal centers. These enable the advanced devotee to fully grasp and express the loftiest aspects of divinity. No lower form is so equipped. It is true that one incurs the debt of a minor sin if he is forced to kill an animal or any living thing. But the *Vedas* teach that wanton loss of a human body is a serious transgression against the karmic law."[14]

We took time to find that place inside where we would do no harm, nor would we wish harm towards another or ourselves. In the heat of the moment, when in an intense interaction, can you maintain an attitude of not wanting to strike out physically, verbally, or even in thought? Ahimsa can only come when we are established in an unshakable calm, even to the point of spiritual evolution where every thought, word, and action is saturated with the inward flow of God-consciousness.[15]

When going deeper into the life of any great spiritual master, we think on that one, meditate upon him or her, and we may,

---

14   (pp. 111–112).

15   Editor's Note: Sri Yukteswar added to these special teachings in his writing. He discusses the five states of the human heart: dark, propelled, steady, devoted, and clean. "By these different states of the heart, man is classified, and his evolutionary status determined . . . In the dark state of the heart, man misconceives; he thinks that this gross material portion of the creation is the only real substance in existence, and that there is nothing besides." With the propelled heart, "man becomes a little enlightened; he compares his experiences relating to the material creation, gathered in his wakeful state, with his experiences in dream, and understanding the latter to be just ideas, begins to entertain doubts as to the substantial existence of the former. His heart then becomes propelled to learn the real nature of the universe and, struggling to clear his doubts, seeks for evidence to determine what is truth." Here, individuals seek the company of like-minded seekers. Advancing toward deeper understandings, and withdrawing from the programs of the material world, individuals start to understand that they are more than what is apparent on the surface. This leads to the experience of being "twice-born," causing the heart to become steady; hence, a steady heart. Next, as individuals develop, they comprehend darkness and ignorance in a new way and now make choices for truth, light, and love, qualifying for the devoted heart status. This Godward path takes individuals to the clean heart state of repentance, refusal of ignorance, and to a purity of heart such that they can comprehend the Spiritual Light, the real Substance of the universe...the spiritual portion of creation. Gloriously, from this state of clean heart, Spiritual Light is manifest, and the heart can rise above Darkness and enter the "Kingdom of God, that is, the creation of Light." Sri Yukteswar. *The Holy Science* (pp. 77–85).

somehow, touch the fabric of his or her being. The presence and grace of *the great lion of Bengal,* Sri Yukteswarji, were experienced by retreatants; some had deep transformative experiences. We are blessed by having this great God-man as part of our para-param guru lineage—as a fully realized master, he easily transcends time/space barriers, and even the shut-door of death is no obstacle to devotee and master when in deep inner communion with God.

June 4

THE GREAT PROMISE

Sacred Lotus: The Promise of Everlasting Life.**

There are innumerable times a day when a sense of isolation can be triggered—a feeling of being separated from our true Self. Triggers may be: a pain in our body; another day in which we must go to work; stress of financial burdens; loneliness; anger about how life is putting demands on us; fear that we will not be successful; there are so many ways to be triggered, both large and small. Each of us lives a private life in our own mind and body, and at times, this existence can be termed a hell, and at other times, it is a quiet desperation of unhappiness.

Life can just as easily take a sunny turn: some happy thought, news, or a favorite song comes to mind. These alternating moods of happy and sad, security and fear, accomplishment and failure, are the changing tides of everyday life, moving back and forth on a continuum of highs and lows. This is reality for the vast majority of humanity. However, as an aspirant upon the path, we aim for something quite different; we seek to be established in a state of mind that provides protection against those never-ending dual forces of attraction and repulsion that compete for attention.

Krishna tells us the way to this freedom in God in the Gita:

Abandoning egotism, force, arrogance
desire, wrath and possessions;
selfless and peaceful,
one is fit to be one with God.

At one with God, of serene self,
neither grieving nor desiring,
regarding all beings alike,
one attains supreme devotion to Me.

By devotion one knows Me in truth,
what and who I am;
then having known Me in truth,
one enters into Me at once.

Performing all actions,
taking refuge in Me;
by My grace one reaches
the eternal indestructible abode.

Renouncing mentally all actions to Me,
regarding Me as the supreme,

resorting to the Yoga of discrimination,
have your thought always on Me.

Thinking of Me,
you will transcend all difficulties by My grace,
but if from egotism, you will not listen,
then you will perish.[16]

There is a lot said in these few verses, but one may draw progressive lessons from them. Taking the focus of our mind from those things that separate us from our oneness with God, we are then ignited with love for Him. Through that love, we experience His presence, and He enters into us, and us into Him. Doing all actions as service to God, feeling that God is all in all, we destroy all thoughts that represent separation and keep our mind on Him continually. We are then lifted up beyond the dual forces of creation and merge into oneness (yoga union) with God. If we ignore these teachings, we will sink back into the old ego-self and die to our eternal Self; our spiritual journey is all undone.

Let us discriminate between what uplifts, purifies, brings closeness to God, and what separates us from oneness with Him: let us serve God in all we do and in all whom we meet; love God more than the things of this world; deeply meditate upon the supreme Being, our true Self, and we will free ourselves from the thralldom of suffering created through the ignorance of not knowing our eternal God-self.

It is a tremendous promise, but one that has been backed up by countless saints and realized masters down through all time. One such confirmation comes from I John 4:26:

---

16   Wade Hatcher, *The Complete Bhagavad Gita and the Bible.* Chapter 18 (pp. 245–246).

We have known and believed
the love that God has for us.
God is love,
and whoever dwells in love,
dwells in God, and God in them.

Another comes from Paul in Romans 6:22–23:

But having become free from sin
and servants of God,
you have your fruit of holiness,
and in the end, everlasting life.
The gift of God is eternal life
Through Jesus Christ our Lord.

The promise has been made; it has been verified by realized masters through the ages, and now it is our time on the field of endeavor to fulfill that promise.

June 11

WISDOM QUOTIENT

Sri Ramakrishna: Lover of God and Wise Teacher.

The IQ (intelligence quotient) is a measurement of a person's reasoning ability, often equated with the notion: *if you are intelligent and educated, then you are wise.* However, there are many types of intelligence; reasoning ability and recall of a large knowledge base are just two of them. In addition to reasoning intelligence, there is an emotional quotient, a socialization quotient, a wisdom quotient, and a God quotient.

The emotional quotient is having full access to a wide range of feelings and the ability to process them as they arise; the socialization quotient is measured by the ability to connect with others, display empathy, and be a follower or a leader depending on circumstances; the wisdom quotient is knowing what is true, and discerning right action; and the God quotient is the faculty for experiencing higher Consciousness, and helping others to do the same.

Although all of these types of intelligence are important (though many have not been studied, scientifically), the wisdom quotient has been of particular interest to me, as it is essential for real success in all other fields. Wisdom and discernment are sometimes associated with a high IQ—the smartest person in the room will have the right answers in all areas of life. However, while this may be true for answering standardized test questionnaires, it is hardly proof for finding one's way through life's many bewildering situations, its vagaries, seemingly unsolvable problems, and moral dilemmas. For knowing what is true, and for deciding right action, discerning wisdom is the most important faculty available for any individual and can be quite independent of one being a brainiac.

A study of three men who may be the three most prominent individuals in the American Revolution reveals much about discernment. Washington, Jefferson, and Adams were all highly intelligent and successful individuals. Adams and Jefferson were both brilliant, and, in all likelihood, would outscore Washington on an IQ test, and perhaps Jefferson would top all three. However, both Jefferson and Adams could not have played the role Washington did, nor did they display the consistent right decision-making ability that made Washington's handling of the American Revolution not just an overthrow of a government, but an opportunity to birth a true revolution of ideas and, subsequently, a successful democratic republic—Washington was the one *indispensable man*.

Learning discrimination came early in Washington's life. For self-study, he copied *Rules of Civility* (mostly based on a Jesuit writing from 1595), whose first rule, of 110, was respect for others. Such early adherence to right behavior built a foundation for true discernment later in life, not based on rules alone but on a sense of knowing right action based on intuition—access to what the great yogi Milarepa called inborn *Dharma Essence*. Learning rules of good behavior is a first step, but it should lead to a search for truth that is only to be found within, and while the reasoning mind may be helpful in this pursuit, its acquirement requires a more subtle faculty, a direct apprehension of truth through intuition leading to right action—ultimately coming from the Divine Mind.

Washington was not the most brilliant tactician or strategic military general of his time, but he knew that holding together his army on the field was absolutely needed, not a desperate all-or-nothing battle—as lesser generals were urging. Also, as a general, he did not afterward proclaim himself dictator/king, as some urged him to do, but voluntarily disbanded the army he had led successfully, and at great expense, built up over the previous six years. President Washington demonstrated selfless integrity as he performed all the duties of the office—without a template and while doing everything for the first time. As the first head of a constitutional Republic, he did something absolutely unique—up until that moment in history: Washington voluntarily stepped down from power without giving it over to an heir: he turned all over to a new democratically-elected president.

I use Washington as an example because he is prominent, showed the right temperament, and performed right action as Virginia's representative, as a military general, and as the first president—all done with the least education of any president, yet, he was universally accorded absolute respect from all who knew him. Washington had wisdom and discernment that had escaped others around him, who I am sure would score higher on an IQ test; his actions demonstrate the superiority of the wisdom quotient.

Another example is found halfway around the world in the person of Ramakrishna Paramhansa, a saint held in high repute for his realization of God. Ramakrishna received very scant education, but nevertheless pursued God-realization with his whole might. His words were recorded, most notably in *The Gospel of Sri Ramakrishna*, by Master Mahasaya. Without reading or writing skills, Ramakrishna etched for the ages a remarkable wisdom from stories of his own life experiences, as well as via Indian tales that he brought into relevant context through his talks with devotees. His ability to bring out great truth, earned through his intense spiritual practice, is wisdom on parade, and in truth, is today, regarded as scripture. Ramakrishna puts to shame pundits and those well-known and much more accomplished in the world of his day—and his light continues to shine.

Some seem to have discernment from the very beginning, despite all other factors in life. Ramakrishna, Anandamayi Ma, Meher Baba, and other greatly realized masters were thought to be mentally defective when young because they were attuned to a higher Reality the world simply did not see. Yet, because their words and life activities are based in higher truth, their lives have only gained strength through time, even as the great masters: Jesus, Buddha, and Krishna.

We do not need to denigrate the value of education or a high IQ to acknowledge the superior value of true wisdom. Let us seek out wisdom as a vital complement to all other life skills—in the beginning, this may well be based on reason, then, later, from inner attunement and communion with the greater Self. In a reciprocal manner, right action leads us into greater attunement with higher consciousness; higher consciousness then becomes a direct guide for right action—as long as the individual remains mindful of both right action and inner attunement, the growth of both make for a seamless life of wisdom and intuitively-guided right action.

George Washington Quotes:

"While we are contending for our own liberty, we should be very cautious not to violate the rights of conscience in others, ever considering that God alone is the judge of the hearts of men, and to him only in this case they are answerable."[17]

"The ways of Providence being inscrutable, and the justice of it not to be scanned by the shallow eye of humanity, nor to be counteracted by the utmost efforts of human power or wisdom, resignation, and as far as the strength of our reason and religion can carry us, a cheerful acquiescence to the Divine Will, is what we are to aim."[18]

George Washington at Verplanck's Point,
painting by John Trumbull, 1790.

---

17   From a letter to Benedict Arnold, September 14, 1775. www.mountvernon.org

18   From a letter to Colonel Bassett, April 20, 1772. www.mountvernon.org

June 15

THE NATIONAL CATHEDRAL

The National Cathedral, Washington DC

Washington DC sports a large gothic-style Episcopal church dedicated to St. Peter and St. Paul, commonly referred to as "The National Cathedral." It was the main item on our list of places to go in DC upon our return from the Northwest after the Loon Lake Retreat and the positive results from the medical tests.

The cathedral is an immense building (6th largest cathedral in the world), covered in Indiana limestone. The building of it began in 1907 and was completed in 1990. An earthquake damaged it in 2011, from which it is still recovering. It is truly impressive; when entering the church, one sees huge columns reaching up to support pointed arches high overhead; starting with the nave, the church stretches out in front of you for a tenth of a mile. There is a nice overall feeling in the cathedral.

After completing a guided tour, we went down under to prowl the crypts and explore the four chapels below the main floor. We meandered our way to the Bethlehem Chapel, and immediately felt a spiritual vibrancy and a loud Aum/Amen resonating. We sat to meditate and soon a small service began (communion). That morning, a man nearby had repeatedly fired a rifle, wounding a congressman, several congressional aides, and some police officers. Prayers were said for them, followed by a nice short talk by a retired Episcopal minister—she spoke of accepting the will of God in all situations. It turned out that this chapel deep under the church (just below the high altar), had the cornerstone of the church under its altar (Teddy Roosevelt attended the laying of this stone), and it was the first completed section of the church in 1912; a service has been held here almost every day since.

We then sat in the pews and attended a talk pertaining to the large organ. The minster described the placement of ten thousand pipes and demonstrated its various sounds, from a high piccolo sound to a deep base (a pipe which could accommodate seven people standing inside it). He then played Ode to Joy, and then a longer piece. It was a magnificent demonstration. Sitting with eyes closed, I reflected on the remarkable difference between live and recorded music, whether a symphonic orchestra, or this magnificent organ.

I had wanted to have the darshan of this National House of Prayer, as designated by Congress, and it was more than I expected. We topped off the tour by ascending to the Pilgrim Observation Gallery, seven stories up with a 360-degree view of Washington DC, including the Washington Monument seen from this highest point in the district. It seemed significant to be here on this day of attack on the congressman (by a politically-motivated gunman).

Though we may differ in ideas, we have a history of peaceful political transitions, and the rule of law, and the freedom to speak our minds. Let us not become so overheated that intolerance and hate supersede peaceful ways of expressing our differences. Wise or ignorant, freedom of thought is a fundamental right from our Creator—as He proves by giving us minds that will never perfectly agree one with another. God's will **is** supreme, let us trust in Him to guide this world in all its ways for the highest good of all. The universal cathedral of God occurs when the love of God, by whatever name (or no name) He or She is called, is broad enough to include all humankind and is made manifest here on earth as the universal vision in which all are known to be various expressions of the one Supreme Spirit.

The National Cathedral's
Virgin Mary Altar.

Lincoln Kneeling in Prayer,
located in the National Cathedral.

June 18

Pilgrimage and My Brother Mark

Candle offering on the Ganges, Varanasi,
photo by Mark Hickenbottom.

When pilgrims begin their journey, they many times envision going to a holy place and getting the benefits from a holy site or saint. However, a larger view of a pilgrimage is that, from its very conception in the mind of the aspirant, everything that happens—including oppositional forces of every kind—is all part of the sacred journey.

The first foray into this North American Pilgrimage was seemingly interrupted by illness; various mechanical problems needed solving, and a family crisis delayed us another week—all are part and parcel of this pilgrimage, not simply interruptions. This past week, on June 15, my brother Mark passed away. This is a new dimension for this pilgrimage, and with it, there is sorrow, reflection, and surrender to God.

Sorrow comes at the loss of my brother. He has been a fixture in my life since my birth, and he will be missed. As an aspirant, one may wonder at the role of emotions—do realized masters have them? We know that from the lives of Jesus, Master, and Mother, emotions played a definite role. The real question is not whether one has emotions—as long as we live in bodies, there will be emotions. The central aspect is whether the emotions put us into a mood: do they separate us from God? Emotions can be a sign of attachment, and if that is the case, then it will be difficult to allow them to move through; we will be immersed in them, or block them. However, if we feel that it is God who is expressing Himself as the emotion itself, and we are the witness as it comes through us, then we maintain detachment and it has no hold on us; we seamlessly continue our connection with our pure Self.

Besides sorrow, Mark's passing has also made me reflect on his life, my life with him, and the lessons that I draw from it. Mark has been a great teacher for me in this life. There were very few things we agreed upon, and this made me be clearer in my own thoughts—as, in the past, I was someone who wanted to please others, sometimes at the sacrifice of staying true to myself. He made me stronger, and for that I thank him. Mark could be fearless in expressing himself; this too was a valuable lesson for me.

Surrender comes in the form of giving Mark up to God. Although he did not profess a faith in the sacredness of life, I hold it for him—he is a divine soul in God. He did not see the supreme Light beyond worldly preoccupations; I behold the eternal light in him. In my surrender of him to the Infinite, I see his eternal soul ever in God. With inner vision, I see his life proceeding and finding happiness and joy—not joy from a world that disappointed him—but peace from the ever-shining Light of his perfect Self. This is how I see him now. This is how I know him to be always.

I am including these written snapshot memories of Mark I wrote on the day of his passing. He did not want a service or memorial, so I have written these down in honor of his life:

> Today, June 15, 2017, my brother Mark has passed away. A few of you have met Mark; some have heard stories about him, and it is with sorrow that I tell you he has quit this mortal coil.
>
> Family members play a special role in our lives, as they have been with us longer than most acquaintances—with us through every stage of life. It seems that life gears us up to know its temporary nature when, in the usual order, grandparents depart, eventually parents, and then siblings. Each passing reminds us to value the time we have, for we will all reach an expiry date in these human incarnations.
>
> Mark has had a lasting influence on my life. When young, he alternated between taking out his childhood aggression on his little brother, and then ignoring me. This was interspersed with times of fun. Like looking through a picture album—snatches of memory erupt on my mental screen.
>
> We used to talk in B-Balk when youths. The rule was to replace the first letter of every word with the letters B. Bes, Bou, Ban, Bearn, Bo, Balk, Bhis, Bay, Boo! We also shared great fun in getting the latest Mad magazine; 25 cents—cheap! Other times, we fought: getting back at him, I once threw a hammer from one yard to another, and the claw hit him on his bare foot—I got into trouble for that one! Or, the time I hit him over the head with the cast of my broken arm when defending myself!
>
> Mark had a brilliant mind, filled with more trivia and historical facts than most could ever retain. He could go through the *Trivial Pursuit* cards, one after another with

very few misses. Though he was not inspired to finish a university degree, much of Mark's education came from reading, for he consistently consumed books. Pure history, historical fiction, and fiction were his appetites. War and spy books were consistent favorites: Le Carre and Clancy for fiction, and World War II was a favorite target for history.

He traveled through Europe and Africa in the early 1970s. When in Africa, he became ill with malaria. Wasted to a skeletal form, the consulate contacted my parents, asking them to fly him home (he was also robbed while there). He was to have ongoing bouts of malaria and digestive problems for years to come. Nevertheless, world travel continued to be a passion. However, later he could afford to travel with less risk to his life and health.

He rode bicycles long distances—on one such trip, he ended up in New Mexico, and while there, he ended up in the hospital with another bout of illness. He flew back to Seattle and lived with me for the next year. Toward the end of that time, he asked what I thought he should do for a living. He had been a Volvo mechanic but never wanted to be greasy again. I suggested that he could combine his love for travel with work by becoming an electrician—thinking he could travel the world plying his trade in construction projects overseas. He was a brilliant student, and before he completed trade school, Stanford University hired him.

Mark became an avid tennis player. He was team captain for Stanford University professors who played competitively (he was uniquely situated to be captain as he was above university politics). He enjoyed telling some of the top professors in the world that they could not play in the tournament because they missed too many practices. He also delighted in telling stories about professors he dealt with; he, armed with the power of being a blue-collar journeyman.

One professor called Mark in after he had started an experiment. They were not getting a "clean electricity" flow, which was affecting their results. Mark analyzed their system and said: "You need to shut it all down; I will have to rework your wiring or you will never get reliable results." The professor protested. This experiment had been going on for months; so much money had been invested in it, and he responded: "I can't just shut it down!" Mark informed the professor that he should have called him in before he started the experiment, but it would have to be shut down now if he wanted valid outcomes. A few days later, Mark received the call, "Come shut it down!"

Whatever Mark did, he did all the way, and when he was finished with it, he would say: "Why would anyone waste their time doing that!"

He taught me a valuable lesson when I was a young adult. Even at a fairly young age, Mark was a contrarian and a curmudgeon who fearlessly said what he thought. A few times, I would echo some thought he had expressed on a previous occasion; however, being a contrarian, Mark would take the opposite point of view! In this way, he taught me to be my own person. I would never win his approval by parroting something he had said. Down through the years there were, in fact, very few things we ever agreed upon.

However, if Mark respected someone, he could (rarely) subject himself to their criticism. When I received a digital camera as a wedding present, he said he would never have such a thing, and that using film was the only way to go. He was a serious amateur photographer. Granted, early digital cameras could not compete with film cameras. However, later, he switched over to digital-only, having to discard his very expensive lenses. He studied under a professional photographer who gave classes. On one such occasion, Mark traveled to Florida, shot pictures in the early morning, worked on them digitally in the afternoon, then gathered together with the class where each picture presented was dissected. The teacher would ask, "Who thinks this is a good picture?" Some poor soul would venture to say he thought it was, then the teacher would go over it point by point, stating what was wrong with it. Walking through town one day, Mark and I stopped in front of a photography studio with large pictures in the front window. He said he couldn't believe they used that wedding photo in the front window. When I asked what was wrong with it and said it looked okay to me, he gave an excellent analysis of details I had not noticed, but once pointed out, they were obvious flaws. I then wondered, as well, why would the photographer use that photo?

Mark traveled all over the world on photography tours. From Madagascar to China, Alaska to Venice, India to quaint Maine coastal towns—he gathered an impressive array of photographs from places that took his fancy. In the process of showing his photos, he told stories about his adventures. Mark could be an inventive storyteller, and if he had a captive audience, and a captive audience is the only one he would spend his time on, the stories could grow and grow. One aunt, in particular, would express amazement at his recounting some adventure, and the more amazed she got, the grander the story became. It was entertaining to watch him work his listener; there were many a story that took on greater dimensions as I heard them repeated through the years.

Mark spent much time and effort putting together beautiful family tree portraits. He intermixed family pictures and history with larger world events consistent with the times. In typical Mark fashion in giving gifts, he put together expensive family history books and gave them to family members. His gift-giving would mostly come in unpredictable ways and would always be very nice. It was not unusual for me to not hear from Mark for long periods of time, then very occasionally, he would send me an expensive gift. Once I had not heard from Mark for over a year, and one day, he sent an automated bread maker—without explanation, it just arrived in the mail. He gave generously, but he gave on his terms, one never knew from where or when. The family history books ended with our grandparents' generation. I asked about our parents; he said, no, he would never include them. Later on, he did. The family history project ended up having a healing effect on him.

Mark had a difficult relationship with our father, and in truth, there were painful events in his growing-up years. Soon after our father's passing, Mark moved back to our hometown, went to work for brother Jerry in the family business, and spent time with our mother. In a sense, he came full circle; it was the last of his working years, and a significant time. However, our father and Mark did share definite traits. In a pattern much in the mindset of our father, Mark planned out every detail in the event of his death.

He was anti-religious and had contempt for much of the world. However, when meeting him, you would most likely like him, there were few who did not. However, his approval, if it came at all, could be fleeting. He and I had gone through years when he had not spoken to me (never an overt argument), and other times, we got along as if no time had gone by at all. Relationships seemed to sour more times than not with Mark: a mystery for one who could win the approbation of others so easily.

One gift Mark gave, one that has been a gift for many of us, is the work he put into the DVD: *Mother Hamilton: A Divine Life*.[19] Mark spent many hours with me, and many more on his own, working and reworking the details for this centenary DVD celebration of Mother's life. Even though Mark evinced no interest in the subject matter, he spent countless hours with Mother's pictures, history, music, and my commentary. It was a selfless service, and as always, he would accept no compensation for it. He helped others with their family histories, as well as on other projects he found interesting; he spent many hours at a community history museum, documenting pictures and putting together a DVD history. He never had a thought for compensation, but some Oohs and Aahs were always much appreciated.

Mark did not want a memorial service of any kind and asked that his ashes be spread into the Pacific Ocean. I have always been struck by obituaries in which a life is summed up in a picture and a few paragraphs—it seems so inadequate. And, of course, it is. These snapshots of my memories seemed to be a way for me to convey a little of the uniqueness of Mark's life.

Each life is important, at least to the person who lived it, not to mention all the lives that one touched. Each life is sacred, and whether Mark would like to hear it or not, so is his.

---

19   www.crossandlotus.com

His sojourn in this life is now ended, may God bless him and keep him, and reveal ever-new wonders of our heavenly Father's house, which has many mansions, enough even to entice a lovable contrarian and curmudgeon.

Eagle in Alaska, picture by Mark Hickenbottom.

Mark when he was in Alaska to take
pictures of eagles—as he said: "Chilly!"

June 21

Summer Solstice

Aarti on the Ganges in Varanasi, India, photo by Mark Hickenbottom.

Sri Yukteswarji spoke of the special significance of the solstice and equinox as times when a tide of cosmic uplift facilitates a transformation of consciousness to the sensitively attuned. Summer Solstice was a time in which Sri Yukteswarji had food, kirtan, and gave a talk on the value of deepening Kriya practice.

We have often gathered at this time of year, in which potlucks, meditation, and spiritual talks make for a festive and holy gathering. I feel an especial pang of distance on this day, and in my inner Mind, I see us gathered together in spiritual kindredness, happiness, and bliss. Let us spend some deepened time with God today, feeling the closeness of divine fellowship that links us without consideration of distance, or even time. All blessings to you.

I thank all those who have sent sweet and loving messages regarding the passing of my brother, Mark. What wonderful souls, those whose compassion is awakened for the sorrow of another. Please know that every note, every thought, and prayer is keenly appreciated. There are two notes I would like to highlight, as they pertained to Mark's photography, a subject he dearly cared about. One from John, a retired Center Leader from Victoria and a professional photographer, conveys great sensitivity to Mark's artistry and provides a glimpse into his soul:

> Dear David,
>
> I am so sorry to learn of your brother's death. You have temporarily lost a great love and a great teacher. Mother gave me a prayer for someone else. I have sent it to you before but would like to send it again for Mark: Divine Indwelling Presence My part of God You see to it for me that Mark rises above any actions he may have done And goes to the ever-loving arms of the Father.
>
> Even the two photos you have included show that Mark had a tremendous sense of the great mystery. The first shows a brief light floating on the dark sea of eternity (a floating candle on the Ganges); the second shows life suspended (crucified) in space (eagle in Alaska). Many take photos where they only record subject matter—often this is appropriate, but Mark felt more when he pressed that shutter. He felt a sense of timelessness and silence, a sense that others search all their lives for and never know.
>
> Dianne and I wish you all the best. God gave you a great gift in Mark; you have been so fortunate. Love, John

And this email from Briana that, by wishing me a happy Father's Day, as several other loving notes also conveyed, reminded me I did not wish all fathers a very happy Father's Day, a day of recognition well deserved for all dedicated fathers around this world.

> Dearest Beloved Guru,
>
> My heart goes out to you deeply for the passing of your brother. It is strange how, even though I never met him, he blessed my life too. I have the very first card you ever gave me with the picture Mark took of the Golden Buddha at the foot of my altar and I meditate in front of it every day. I pray that his soul finds true fulfillment in God alone, forevermore! I honor you today, my precious spiritual father, and manifestation of my beloved Father of all fathers. You have captured my heart entirely, and I love you with every part and parcel of my being. Whatever measures are needed, O dearest Guruji, take me with you into the Infinite! I am God's and yours alone. Ever at Thy feet in love and gratitude, Briana

Buddha, Sarnath, India, photo by Mark Hickenbottom.

Madagascar chameleon, photo by Mark Hickenbottom.

June 24

GETTYSBURG: AN EXPERIENCE

Gettysburg Battlefield National Park, Pennsylvania.

W e traveled north through the beautiful Maryland countryside and broke across the Pennsylvania border in a very different manner from what General Lee's army did 150 years before. The year, 1863: it was hot and muggy and approaching the month of July. The American Civil War is raging, battle casualties range in the tens of thousands in a day or two. The war is a test of wills between state rights to secede versus federal authority to maintain the union—and the war is far from over.

Lee's idea is to build on the South's recent successful battles and strike hard into the North, destroying the Army of the Potomac, then attack Philadelphia, Baltimore, or even Washington DC. Such a blow will further demoralize a war-weary North, forcing them into a negotiated peace—allowing the South to become a new nation, to maintain and expand its valued slave population, and its way of life. This goal is a very likely outcome if Lee and his army are successful. Using the Blue Ridge Mountains to screen his advance of 70,000-plus men, and a handful of women disguised as men, he races northward as fast as marching soldiers in the murderous heat can. They are in high spirits, feeling that their general has a golden touch: a subtle, but real, collective energy that Napoleon called "moral force"—a confidence, or what today in sports might be called "momentum," or being on a "winning streak."

A Federal cavalry unit spots Lee's advance men and sets up a line of defense just north of the small hamlet of Gettysburg: a hub with ten spokes of roads spreading out in all directions, making this a vital strategic spot. It is to be a three-day battle that has the highest casualty rates of the war—over 50,000—for an already deadly war, the stakes cannot be higher. Three days earlier, Lincoln relieved the commanding general of the Army of the Potomac for incompetence and placed a reluctant General Meade at its head. The North had been pummeled in several battles and the spirit of the soldiers had suffered. Nevertheless, they rush in great numbers to meet the newly arrived Confederates—a tremendous battle ensues. Though not unanticipated by Lee, neither side could have planned for the battle to occur precisely at this time, or in this place.

General Meade was the right man; he proved it time and again by making correct decisions—from the formations of his corps in a fishhook appearance that stretched Lee's army, to the speed of Federal troops who responded to the fluid conditions that occur in any battle. A brand-new General Meade out-generalled the leading general of the South, and the Gettysburg battle sent the Army of Northern Virginia back home with tremendous losses of men and supplies; both of which it could not easily replace. This was a change in fortune for the North and a pivotal point in the war. Gettysburg coincided with a brilliant victory by another Northern general, U.S. Grant, with the taking of Vicksburg and the surrender of a Confederate army of 30,000 soldiers on the fourth of July.

We arrive at Gettysburg, which is now a National Park. Its peaceful countryside betrays nothing of the three-day battle that exploded with 160,000 troops over these fields 150 years ago. President Lincoln, a great soul in God, was convinced, as many of the founding fathers were, that the United States Republic was an experiment that could be a model for governments around the globe in years to come. Its ability to survive the election of a president who did not win a majority of votes, and whom half the country deeply mistrusted, is essential to this vision. The United States had to continue in order to lead the way, not only for itself, but for the good of the world. It was divine Providence that Lincoln felt was at work here, and the union had to stay united—not be fractured into smaller nation-states. This belief raised the stakes beyond the moment of simple politics, power, or force; it made it a spiritual mission that superseded the lives of individuals, including the president himself. Although Lincoln abhorred slavery, it was not his intention when he took office to do away with it; rather, for the sake of maintaining the union, it continued to exist in southern states, and, hopefully, it would one day die out due to its inherent inefficiency. It is only when the great cost of lives and resources mounted in the war that he resolved that slavery would not continue. This was celebrated by some and decried by many others in the north for various reasons. However, the stage was being set for the repugnant stain of owning a human being to be abolished forever.

We spend a full day touring the vast field of battle, larger than what you can see from any one vantage point. We have an excellent tour by a retired career military officer who once taught military strategy and has been involved in the NASA program; he is eminently qualified to talk about this battle. He also spent years walking these fields, imagining the foot soldier enduring the noise, confusion, fear, pain, and exhilaration of battle. He wants us to immerse ourselves as well, not as casual visitors, but as far as possible to be participants in those events. He relates personal stories and speaks of the terrific sounds that haunted men's lives forty years after the battle.

Imagine the sights and smells as the battle rages all around: sulfurous smoke stinging and blinding the eyes; cannon shell exploding overhead, with fragments zinging all around; mini bullets sounding like angry bees zipping by; comrades dropping; hearing screams of agony; pushing forward or defending against an onslaught; surrounded by calm minds focused on the business at hand or panic filling another's eyes; standing shoulder to shoulder; officers calling out commands; not knowing what is going on, who is winning or losing; asking when will help arrive; hearing rumors, mostly wrong, spreading like wildfire; all the while, experiencing the fog and confusion of battle all around. The men ask themselves: "Will I go home? Will that be my amputated limb left on a pile stacked like cordwood? Will I be brave or will I run?"

In the midst of this time of battle, there are extraordinary acts of courage and compassion. As the first day of battle is engaged, a caring officer helps a mother and two young children move from their home that happens to be in the middle of this quickly-evolving battlefield. Exhausted, with too few men to defend the army's left flank on Little Top Hill, an officer and all his soldiers are out of ammunition—he leads his men in a frontal bayonet charge that carries the field. Countless heroes on both sides. A desperate battle that can hinge on the seemingly smallest of factors decides who will win and who will die. It is a tour and a day to remember.

After this guided tour on the field, we move through the museum and then follow a CD voice tour (Bruce and Janice have loaned us) as we drive from site to site, following the historian's description of the action where the battles actually ensued. It is all interesting, engaging, and exhausting. Not exhausting just because of the physical demands of the day, but due to emotionally and spiritually engaging with the horrors and sufferings, the heroism and selfless sacrifice that are, to this day, poignant beyond words. It is a feeling that continues to cling to us.

As President Lincoln said a year and a half later in his second inaugural address (below), describing the karmic consequence of slavery by a nation that allowed it, even embraced it, in con-tradiction to its own *Declaration*: that *All men are created equal.* Obviously, all men are not created of equal physical strength, intelligence, or moral fiber. However, all of humankind is equal in the sight of God; all deserve respect, dignity, and the *unalienable Rights of life, liberty and the pursuit of happiness.*[20] Lincoln said:

> Fondly do we hope, fervently do we pray, that this mighty scourge of war may speedily pass away. Yet, if God wills that it continue until all the wealth piled by the bonds-man's two hundred and fifty years of unrequited toil shall be sunk, and until every drop of blood drawn with the lash shall be paid by another drawn with the sword, as was said three thousand years ago, so still it must be said, the judgments of the Lord are true and righteous altogether.[21]

The day after this experiential tour of the battlefield, we had a very different kind of experience. Previously, when driving north through Maryland, we saw signage that alerted us to the fact that Emmitsburg had been home to a Catholic saint—the first

---

20   *Declaration of Independence.* https://www.archives.gov.declaration

21   President Abraham Lincoln's Second Inaugural Address, March 4, 1865, Washington, DC www.nps.gov

canonized American. In anticipation, we were thrilled to think of having the darshan of the Samadhi Basilica of this first recognized Catholic saint of America—but the description of our time with her will have to wait for another posting . . .

Gettysburg Monument to those who fought for what they believed in.

June 24

MOTHER SETON

Saint Seton.**

Rural northern Maryland was the unlikely home of a remarkable daughter of God, Elizabeth Ann (nee Bayley) Seton, the first canonized American saint of the Catholic Church. Born two years before the American Revolution, daughter of a wealthy and socially connected doctor in New York, wife of a wealthy shipping magnate, mother of five, widow, and convert from the Episcopal Church (grandfather was rector of St. Andrews) to the Catholic faith after the passing of her husband while they were in Italy.

From early, on Elizabeth had an ongoing connection with God as demonstrated by her remembrance of a day when she was fourteen years old:

> . . . found an outlet in a meadow; and a chestnut tree with several young ones growing around it, found rich moss under it and a warm sun. Here, then, was a sweet bed—the air still a clear blue vault above, the numberless sounds of spring melody and joy, the sweet clovers and wildflowers I had got by the way, and a heart as inno- cent as human heart could be, filled even with enthusi- astic love to God and admiration of His works . . . God was my Father, my all. I prayed, sang hymns, cried, laughed, talking to myself of how far He could place me above all sorrow. Then I laid still to enjoy the heavenly peace that came over my soul; and I am sure, in the two hours so enjoyed, grew ten years in the spiritual life . . . The wintry storms of time shall be over and the unclouded spring enjoyed forever.[22]

This was a special memory, but her conversations with, and faith in, God, were a constant in her life. Every loss, every sorrow, found consolation in her connection with her Lord.

During the last days of her husband's life, when he was suffer- ing from TB,[23] imprisoned in an Italian quarantine area with no heat, and locked in a cell because they had just disembarked from a ship that left New York when it had an epidemic of Yellow Fever. Through this time, she drew her strength and comfort from God, for she had no other succor:

---

22   Seton, Elizabeth Bayley. See Collected Writings, Volume One (pp. 264, 268, 292) for all quotes in this Discourse.

23   Tuberculosis.

Well, I was alone; dear indulgent Father! Could I be alone while clinging fast to Thee in continual prayer or thanksgiving, prayer for him and joy, wonder and delight to feel assured that what I had so fondly hoped and confidently asserted really proved in the hour of trial to be more than I could hope, more than I could conceive? That my God could and would bear me through the most severe trials with that strength, confidence and affiance which, if every circumstance of the case was considered, seemed more than a human being would expect or hope? But His consolations, who shall speak of them? How can utterance be given to that which only his spirit can feel?

After the death of her husband, and while still the guest of a wealthy Italian family, friends of her husband, and now her friends as well, she was taken with the eucharist ceremony. It differed from the Protestant conception of communion in that the wafer and wine are actually converted into the body and blood of the living Christ. Elizabeth struggled with the idea, but God seemed intent on opening up this reality to her sincere search for Him:

February 24.
How happy we would be if we believed what these good souls believe . . . When they carry the Blessed Sacrament under my window, while I feel the full loneliness and sadness of my case, I cannot stop the tears at the thought... The other day in a moment of excessive distress, I fell on my knees without thinking, when the Blessed Sacrament passed by, and cried out in an agony to God to bless me, if He was really there, that my soul desired only Him.

On her return to New York, the family did not take well to Elizabeth's conversion. In part, it was due to family history. They were Huguenots, protestants persecuted by the majority Catholic population of France. This fact had precipitated their move to the religious freedom of the colonies. Also, at the time in New York, being Catholic was associated with poor Irish immigrants, and there was discrimination and even violence against the Irish and their priests. The Seton family became even more enraged when Elizabeth's 15-year-old sister-in-law converted as well.

As a result of their withdrawal of support, Elizabeth and her children went from socialites to living in impoverishment, from connections in society to being shunned, from the protection of a powerful family to being on their own. One source of support was her husband's previous business associates from Italy who directed their bank to advance Elizabeth funds, which she only drew upon when they were absolutely needed for her family. She attempted to start a school but was torpedoed by the Seton family and the minister of the Episcopal Church, Elizabeth's prior spiritual advisor.

Her plight was seen, however, by those in the Catholic hierarchy, and she was offered a position in Baltimore, and so, she moved her family there. She was asked to lead a group inspired by the Daughters of Charity, an order from France that was connected with the work of St. Vincent De Paul. She took vows and brought her children and two sisters-in-law with her. She became Mother Seton, head of the order of the Sisters of Charity: providing education and service to those in need was their mission. The school and growing list of sisters were given a home and acreage in Emmitsburg, Maryland. Several of her daughters succumbed to TB, and so eventually did Elizabeth at age 46. She created a network of sisters in education, care for orphans, and those in need.

We visited the magnificent Basilica where her bones are kept, and were given a tour of the grounds which included her first schoolhouse and the "white house," built later to accommodate the growing number of sisters and students. She promoted the novel idea of free education for those who could not afford it. There was no effort to convert Protestant students; all were treated equally. She was also not in favor of corporal punishment; she disciplined with love. Mother Seton had a special veneration for St. Joseph. Saint Seton was canonized in 1975.

Visiting the Basilica a day after Gettysburg, we felt a spiritual baptism that washed away the suffering we had continued to feel from those battlegrounds and their history. It is easy to think of Mother Seton and Mother Hamilton as kindred spirits. Both were married, loved their children, both had TB (Mother Hamilton's TB was healed by her guru, Swami Yogananda), both disciplined with love, had very strong wills, bucked their family's intense desires that they remain in their own church, and both were strong women who pioneered new pathways to God. It was a blessing to have Mother Seton's darshan.

Carla on Mother Seton: The Power of a Saint:

> Going to see where a saint lived and worked is a highlight for me on this pilgrimage. I just happened to see a bill-board that advertised the "Seton Basilica and home of a saint," and, of course, what else could be better than to go and visit? After a tour of the grounds and Mother Seton's home and teaching areas, we hurried up to the basilica before it closed. I was awed by the magnificent Light-filled space. The physical beauty was inspiriting; it was one of the loveliest churches I have ever seen. A volunteer said that Mother Seton was buried along the far side of the church, and that there was a relic (a bone) of hers that was on the altar. It reminded me of Anandashram and the special opportunity to touch Papa's bones on the altar there.
>
> I walked over and touched the wooden carving that held her bones and immediately felt a very powerful

spiritual charge. It was a delightful and surprising gift after hearing about her life and all the wonderful things she had done. The information they provided was interesting, but it felt more like reading a biography. Yet, when I touched the altar, I was clearly shown that this was a great God-woman. I sat for as long as they allowed (too short, but God arranged it perfectly) and just melted into that powerful feeling of love and bliss.

It felt like a huge spiritual waterfall of healing that continues to fill me with such gratitude to God, Gurus, and Saints. You never know how, when, and where God will direct you so that His Grace and love can be seen, and most of all, felt and experienced!

Shrine and relics of Mother Seton.

National Shrine of Saint Elizabeth Ann Seton.

June 29

The Amish Way of Life

Lancaster County Amish: horse and buggy.

Driving down the roads of Lancaster County, Pennsylvania, there is a dark, covered buggy pulled by a single horse. A bearded man staring ahead is holding the reins, and a mother with her children are in the tiny compartment behind. It could be a scene from the seventeen or eighteen hundreds, but this is modern-day America, with cars, trucks, and semis competing for the same road. We are in Amish country—as we see another, and yet another, buggy making its way down the busy roads.

At a time when the emphasis in modern culture is on the latest upgrade, the Amish have chosen the opposite way. Striving for humility drives their decision-making process. Far from wanting to stand out from the crowd, the Amish want to blend into their community. They have embraced a few changes since their coming to America: use of propane, diesel engine/generators, tractors to use the power-take-off capacity to operate processing equipment (not for use in the fields), and occasionally cell phones for business (never in the home). These innovations are often in response to the demands of the world around them, and I am sure each has been considered from every possible side before being adopted by the local district. Some use of modernity has been in response to the law of the land. For instance, power is needed for milking machines which are required, so an electric generator is used, but power is never taken from the grid. A carefully-considered interaction with the English (anyone not Amish is referred to as English) means a truck can deliver goods to an Amish home loaded with lumber or propane, but an Amish would not own or operate such a truck. An Amish may work as a carpenter for an English, but it is preferable to work at home, on the farm, or in a cottage industry.

Far from diminishing in numbers, today, over 90 percent of young Amish choose this traditional life. The Amish are part of the Anabaptist movement; baptism only occurs when an individual can make a conscious choice. Between the ages of 16 and twenty-something, during which time they can freely mix with the outside culture so that they can make an informed choice, a young woman or man can then choose to be baptized. Baptism means entering the community as an adult and marrying only another Amish. If one chooses not to be baptized, then he or she may continue to have contact with the family and community. Many of those who do not continue as Amish become Mennonites, who have similar beliefs but are more liberal in dress and lifestyle. In the past 20 years, the Amish population has doubled, from 100,000 to over 250,000 nationwide. The estimate is that in another twenty years, the Amish population will double its number again, currently about 31,000 in Lancaster County; it is not unusual for a family to have seven or more children. If an adult chooses baptism, then, later, leaves the community, they risk being *shunned*. There is no communication or support, with the idea that the wayward soul will come back—baptism and marriage are considered to be commitments for life, although remarriage is encouraged if there is a death of a spouse.

Three key teachings of the Amish: the rejection of pride or arrogance (Hockmut), cultivation of humility (Demut), and calmness (Gelassenheit). To promote these values, they dress simply and wear a single color (no plaids); black, gray, and purple are common colors. The men wear beards but no mustache—mustaches were once a source of pride for men. Modern day conveniences, such as electricity, cars, trucks, or cameras are eschewed due to the probability of competition and pride, or that they take time and focus away from the family and community (no Air Jordans or $150 jeans for the kids). You have to carefully consider going to the store if you are being pulled by a horse, versus jumping into your car. The idea is to be more grounded in the earth through farming or a cottage craft.

The Amish originated in Switzerland (German speaking Swiss) in 1683, founded by Jakob Ammann. (The name Amish is a derivative of Ammann.) Due to persecution in Switzerland and Germany, they moved to Pennsylvania, where William Penn, a Quaker, practiced tolerance for all religions. It is theorized that when asked where they were from, they responded Deutschland (Germany), and it was thought they were saying Dutchland; so, they became associated with Holland (not true) and it has stuck, (much like the First Nations in North America are stuck with being Indians, even though it has been well known from early on that they are not from India). At home, and amongst themselves, the Amish speak a dialect of German. Over time, that dialect has changed to such a degree that a native German cannot understand an Amish. English is learned by children when they go to school.

All the Amish we have met, mostly men and women vendors selling goods, have been friendly, not standoffish. They speak very good, accented English, and are, overall, a very handsome group of people. Parking lots regularly have signs for hitching posts for horses, even at Costco. They have large family gardens, but also buy goods from local stores. They are not particularly focused on modern-day health food standards: they use pesticides on crops, grow tobacco for a cash crop, and a favorite recipe is *Amish Peanut Butter*: peanut butter and marshmallow combined! Only a third of them are now full-time farmers; others have branched out to cottage industries—too many people for farming to support. The Amish are famous for making furniture, and other crafts of high quality. Schooling is in their own one-room school, which ends at grade eight. Then, for boys, it is on to unpaid apprenticeships.

Church is every other week, held at a family location. There are districts within the community; an average district will be about 80 adults, plus children. Service begins at 8:30 with a short talk, slow singing (an average song lasts about 15 minutes), followed by silence, then a longer talk. After Service, there is food; this is an important part of any Amish gathering. Community norms are enforced: no drinking, no drugs, and no smoking. They will use modern hospitals, but do not have health insurance and they do not collect social security. Older adults live at home with the family. They pay taxes, but do not use the schools or other government services. They are pacifists, so no military service. If someone is in trouble, if a house or barn burns down, the community bands together to meet the emergency and skilled labor shows up to rebuild.

A tragic and touching story came about in 2006 that tells much of how the Amish live their values. A deranged man came into an Amish schoolhouse and shot ten girls, killing five, and seriously wounding the others; then, he killed himself. The Amish put into practice forgiveness when they respectfully came to the killer's funeral after attending the funerals of their own girls. Not long afterward, the Amish community gave money to the killer's family, his wife and three children who were now without a husband and father. One can only imagine the shock and horror of a close community when a local man kills their children, and what it would take to then be mindful enough to think of the needs of a sudden widow and the children of the murderer. It is quite a thing to do.

As we travel in the county today, we are mindful that the Amish do not care to have their photographs taken; no graven images of God (little figurines of the Amish by a local artist have blank faces)—it may also turn into a source of pride. I am sure that every compromise with the society they live in is very carefully debated—each district to some degree sets their own rules; so, you do see variations. Carla mentioned during our time here that it has felt peaceful. And it is true. After a week of being here, longer than we had initially thought to stay, and contending with all the usual traffic, seeing the box stores and outlet malls, there is even a "Dutch" amusement park nearby, but underneath it all, there is a quiet vibration that makes this a special place.

A young Amish man is drawn to our campground by a single horse. His buggy, with his wife and children tucked in behind, has a small, attached trailer. He is sweet natured, selling canned "chow chow," delicious pickled mixed vegetables and fresh lemonade. He has a whole miniature store in his wagon. He stops and very quickly a crowd is around him buying his goods. What root beer he sells in quart jars, fabulous! Pickled beets, the best I have ever had. We see him a couple of times over the days we are here. He is soft spoken, his wife, demure, in the back; one of the kids, a small boy, has his bare foot up over the top of the tailgate of the buggy, and while the word quaint naturally comes to mind, they are not trying to be quaint—they are simply living their faith.

It does provide an interesting counterpoint to our constant movement on this pilgrimage, our vehicles, and our use of electronic gadgetry as I am writing these words on an electronic tablet that I will send out on the world wide web. And while I do not choose their lifestyle (the closest I would have come is when I was in silence and seclusion for a year); nevertheless, I find there is an appeal to living so close to the earth absent of our many modern conveniences that often come with hidden costs derailing us from simplicity. One takeaway is that we can choose simplicity in our daily life. Perhaps walk to someplace close by or ride a bike (Amish do not ride bikes, but foot-powered scooters), take time away from electronics—find ways to be a little Amish, to be simpler in day-to-day living.

Street sign in Lancaster
County, Pennsylvania.

July 2

INTO THE CHAMBER OF THE INFINITE ETERNAL

Papa, Swami Ramdas, radiating
blissful joy during early sadhana days.

Travel Note: We have migrated north of Boston to a wooded campground near Concord, where in April of 1775, British troops marched to take a stash of guns from the colonists. The colonial militia here were known as Minutemen (the militia could be ready for action in one minute). The militia resisted the British troops, and it was the first shot of what became a revolutionary war: the "shot that was heard round the world." We had not planned to come to Concord, but Ram herded us here quite unexpectedly. And I might say, we are delighted to be here. This is not only a historical revolutionary site, but also the home of Ralph Waldo Emerson (a fully realized sage), another Transcendentalist, Henry David Thoreau (Walden Pond is nearby), Nathaniel Hawthorne, Bronson Alcott, and Louisa May Alcott. Concord was originally known as Musketaquid, an Algonquian name for a grassy plain, a prayag where the Sudbury and Assabet rivers join. Ram is ever kind in his direction for His pilgrims as they wander without any fast plans—only by His direction.

The *World Is God* is the title of one of Swami Ramdas' books, a description of his travel around the world and finding his beloved Ram wherever he went, in whomever he met, including his first meeting with Mother Hamilton in Seattle. For Papa, Swami Ramdas, during his sadhana days, the world had taken on a wonderful transformation in which he came to see that the world truly is God. He describes his awakening to this great Reality in this way:

In this cave, he lived for nearly a month in deep meditation on Ram (God). This was the first time he was taken by Ram into solitude for His Bhajan. Now, he felt the most blissful sensations since he could here hold undisturbed communion with Ram. He was actually rolling in a sea of indescribable happiness. To fix the mind on that fountain of bliss—Ram means to experience pure joy! Once, during the day, when he was lost in the madness of Ram's meditation, he came out of the cave and found a man standing a little away from the mouth of the cave. Unconsciously, he ran up to him and locked him up in a fast embrace. This action on the part of Ramdas thoroughly frightened the friend who thought that it was a mad man who was behaving in this manner and so was afraid of harm from him. It was true, he was mad—yes, he was mad of Ram, but it was a harmless madness, which the visitor realized later. The irresistible attraction felt by him towards this friend was due to the perception of Ram in him. "O Ram, Thou art come, Thou art come!"—with this thought Ramdas had run up to him. At times, he would feel driven to clasp in his arms the very trees and plants growing in the vicinity of the cave. Ram was attracting him from all directions. Oh, the mad and loving attraction of Ram! O Ram, Thou art Love, Light, and Bliss. Thus passed his days in that cave.[24]

Such a transformation of experiencing God as pure joy, and seeing Him in all creation, is not unique to Papa, or just a favored few, but to all who strive for this universal vision.

We read in the Bible that we are all made up of God-stuff! Then God said, "Let Us make man in Our image, according to Our likeness" (Genesis 1:26). Our Soul is in inseparable union with God as His likeness—this union is pure bliss, unalloyed joy, a conscious realization of our oneness with the infinite, eternal Reality. We do spiritual practice in order to re-member, and bring back together that which is seemingly separate. The ultimate truth is that humankind is, and ever has been, an expression of God; we are made in His image. However, we have a veil of ignorance, drawn like a curtain, that makes us believe we are forever separate.

Union, yoga with God, is our natural state, and our spiritual practice brings to conscious awareness this pre-existing fact. During my sadhana, I was taken through a state of awakening in which such divine love flowed through my heart; this, combined with the experience of being immersed in an ocean of love that permeated all the world. Divinity was in the plants, trees, the air I breathed, and in the ground upon which I stood.

---

24   *In Quest of God*, Chapter X (pp. 33–34). This and a number of ashram books are now available for download at no cost at www.anandashram.org

As I write this, the thin bubble of individuality dissolves and consciousness spreads out in all directions, the sound of Aum reverberates throughout, creation trembles with the power of the Holy Ghost, and nature's blueprints stand revealed as thought-creations of an infinitely wise and loving Creator. Beyond this creation is pure Spirit, unadorned, unchangeable-ever as it has been—beautiful beyond words, perfect, pure, and pristine. These three aspects of God, creation, thought-forms of the Creator, and changeless Spirit beyond duality is the trinity—One as three and three in One—Father, Son, and Holy Ghost. For, the same perfection permeates all three, making them one, whole and complete. God loves to express Himself, and thus gives rise to the idea of seeming separateness but only so that the pure Spirit may enjoy the play, the lila—and for no other reason. But enough talk! I am dissolving once again into that chamber of the infinite and eternal—let us plunge together into the sea of Pure Being, Consciousness, and Bliss—it is what an aspirant must do, so why wait another moment?

Ralph Waldo Emerson, 1857,
a fully realized American sage.

July 4

DECLARE FREEDOM

Independence Hall, Philadelphia.

Today, July 4th, we are in Freeport, Maine. This is a special day in the United States. It was the day the Declaration of Independence was adopted, signed by those with the knowledge that it could be a death sentence. The Congress had actually voted for independence on the second of July, and it was after this day John Adams wrote to his wife Abigail:

> The second day of July, 1776, will be the most memorable epoch in the history of America. I am apt to believe that it will be celebrated by succeeding generations as the great anniversary festival. It ought to be commemorated as the day of deliverance, by solemn acts of devotion to

God Almighty. It ought to be solemnized with pomp and parade, with shows, games, sports, guns, bells, bonfires, and illuminations, from one end of this continent to the other, from this time forward forever more.[25]

He was off by two days, as the declaration was finalized and read out to the public on the fourth, but he was amazingly prescient about the celebrations, and his advocation for this to be a day of devotion to God Almighty indicates he believed it to be a spiritual revolution just as the vast majority of those involved with the revolution believed it to be.

If it was a war over only property, money (taxes), and personal pride, then it could not rise up to the caliber of being called spiritual. However, we know from the speeches and writings of those participants that the spiritual was foremost in their minds—Divine Providence was the author of this movement—it was to be far more than a political movement; it was to be a spiritual revolution.

Part of this North American Pilgrimage has been our standing upon some of the historical sites where pivotal actions and words created the spiritual foundations of America. We traveled to Philadelphia and Independence Hall where the rights of citizens were debated. It was in this very place that the final dissolution of a parliament and king (who were tone deaf to the petitions from its distant citizens) resulted in the colonists declaring independence.

If it is national pride only that spurs me on, then it would be relevant only to those of the United States. However, these actions and thoughts carry a more universal meaning. The urge for freedom of thought and action, the rule of law, a check and

---

25   Excerpt from John Adams' letter to his wife Abigail on July 3, 1776. www.nps.gov

balance among governmental entities to prevent abuse; the affirmation that fundamental rights are derived from God and not the caprice of a king, despot, or even an elected government; that citizens elect their leaders and may depose them if they misbehave or abuse their power; that there are certain fundamentals that may not be tampered with, combined with a flexibility for change in law—these were revolutionary ideas at the time—never been tried before—many, most, around the world thought it would fail—and it was a revolution of basic rights and protections that a large portion of humanity still do not have today.

We recently stood at the North Bridge near Concord, where Ralph Waldo Emerson wrote some years after the fact in the poem, *Concord Hymn*:

> By the rude bridge that arched the flood,
> Their flag to April's breeze unfurled,
> Here once the embattled farmers stood,
> And fired the shot heard round the world.[26]

A citizen's militia called Minutemen: they could be ready in a minute, were ordered to fire back at British Regular Troops who had come to confiscate their guns. This order led to the first act of resistance ordered by a militia commander. This first shot was a shot heard round the world, affirming the rights of colonial Englishmen, and ultimately, all humanity. Emerson's grandfather's house was but 300 feet from North Bridge; the Reverend Emerson was an advocate for the rights of individuals, the revolution, and became chaplain to the Continental Army—he died of camp fever while with the army. From their house, the Reverend Emerson and family watched as the British Regulars marched

---

26   Emerson, Ralph Waldo, *Poems*.

across the bridge, heard the gunfire of the opposing sides, and watched as the Regulars left as a scattered group heading back to Concord.

Some of America's great writers lived in the vicinity of the North Bridge; one of those was Henry David Thoreau. Thoreau brought the revolutionary ideals to the next level when he wrote:

> Do we call this the land of the free? What is it to be free of King George and continue to be slaves of King Prejudice? What is it to be born free and not to live free? What is the value of any political freedom, but as a means to moral freedom?[27]

Moral freedom, spiritual freedom, must then be the natural consequence of the great gift of liberty gained through self-government and from those who sacrificed so much. To squander our freedom on licentious behavior that results in a tyranny of bad habits shows disrespect for our Creator who has endowed us with a far-ranging freedom of Soul.

We can all declare our freedom from ignorance, from the maya of delusion, from separation from our oneness with Divinity. Then we must act upon that declaration of freedom, to break the chains of king-attachment. We truly are endowed with the gift of ultimate freedom from our Infinite Beloved; however, we have bound ourselves to endless rapacious desires which make us a captive soul.

Yes—declare freedom! Let us *soar on wings like eagles* and experience the soul's joy born of deepened meditation and love of God.

---

27 Excerpt from *Life Without Principle*, derived from the lecture, "What Shall it Profit?" December 6, 1855.

The *Minuteman* near North Bridge, Concord (pictured above); this is an early sculpture by Daniel Chester French. He also sculpted Abraham Lincoln placed at Lincoln Memorial. We were told by a lady out for her walk across North Bridge that French had lived nearby and was encouraged to sculpt by May Alcott after she saw him carving vegetables!

July 9

BEHOLD THE LIGHT: GURU PURNIMA DAY

Our Light in the darkness: Dearest
Beloved Gurudev Mother Hamilton.

Guru Purnima falls on the full moon in July—a day for honoring one's guru. Sage Vyasa is the author of some of India's greatest scriptures and was the first to be honored on this day. Also, on this day in history, Shiva gave the cream of his teachings to seven sages who had the capacity to receive it, and it is the anniversary of when the Buddha gave his first sermon for spiritual emancipation at Deer Park in Sarnath, Varanasi, India.

The term "guru" has been bandied about much in the West: we have *wall-street gurus*; if individuals are specialists in any area, they may be called a guru in their field. In India, a professor or any teacher may have this broad distinction of being one's guru. "Gu" means darkness; "ru" means light, and so "guru" is interpreted to mean the remover of darkness; therefore, a guru may be anyone who enlightens you, lifting you out of ignorance.

In addition to this generic usage, there is the specialized knowledge of Self-realization; one who imparts wisdom or knowledge in this area is known as a guru, and the meaning now takes on greater gravitas. Just as you might go beyond undergraduate university classes to a master's or doctorate degree, one is given a special advisor in graduate school who guides the advanced student into higher, more specific, knowledge. When this occurs spiritually, and the aspirant is ready for the *last mile* of God-realization, then a Sat Guru comes into the devotee's life.

A Sat Guru has become a spiritual master him or herself, or else he or she could not guide another. One may have many teachers in life. However, God sends a specific teacher to take one all the way to Himself. Here in the West, we pride ourselves on individuality, but in the area of Self-realization, the true guru is absolutely needed to guide one with surety and has the power to awaken an aspirant with his or her own superconscious—to impart a spiritual seed that matures into fruition of full realization.

I have taken university classes in which the intelligence the professor conveyed, not only in words, but also through who he or she was, caused something to excite the life-energy in the brain: one could feel new territory being opened up as if one was an explorer just setting foot in newly-found lands. The occasional professor who inspires students like this serves the mind of the student as a guru. The spiritual guru does this and much more for the awakening soul.

When I first met my Gurudev, Mother Hamilton, she transmitted a spiritual power that lifted me far beyond what anything or anyone had done before. She taught me the methods for liberating my soul from the darkness of separation; she was the example in thought, word, and deed of what I was striving for in my own life. She did not ask, nor would it have been useful, for me to become a carbon copy of herself—she wanted me to stand on my own two feet. Yet, I was in need of learning the fundamental principles she taught; more than that, I gradually attuned myself to her superconscious mind. This is the kind of power and subtlety that requires a true guru. For, if ego is in charge of the guru, how can following such a one enable anyone to transcend ego? A guru can only be an open door to God-realization if they have that realization themselves—not just to occasionally have a spiritual experience, but to be a real guru, one needs to be established in oneness with God. This is a rarity in this world—a fully realized soul.

When I look up the ladder of our guru-lineage, I am in awe of what I see. My own dear Mother, Master—Paramhansa Yogananda, Sri Yukteswarji, Lahiri Mahasaya, Babaji, and Jesus—it is a blindingly blessed lineage of realized Beings that have gone before us to blaze an unmistakable path to the Infinite. Mother was also the recipient of another fully realized Being, Papa Ramdas. And for me, Swami Satchidanandaji played a pivotal role in helping me to realize God. What gratitude comes to me when thinking of these divinely illumined souls: it humbles me to dust.

The supreme master, Jesus, was the example for all of us to follow:

> So when He had washed their feet, taken His garments, and sat down again, He said to them, "Do you know what I have done to you? You call Me Teacher and Lord, and you say well, for so I am. If I then, your Lord and Teacher, have washed your feet, you also ought to wash one another's feet. For I have given you an example, that you should do as I have done to you. Most assuredly, I say to you, a servant is not greater than his master; nor is he who is sent

greater than he who sent him. If you know these things, blessed are you if you do them (John 13:12–17).

We are not here to rise up in hierarchies, to attain name and fame for ego's sake—we are here to serve one another. We are the products of humble servants of God. In order to honor them on this special Guru Purnima Day, we may emulate those who have gone before us to the full. Even as Babaji demonstrated for Lahiri Mahasaya:

> No sooner had I passed the ascetic than my astounded eye fell on Babaji. He was kneeling in front of a matted-haired anchorite.
>
> "Guruji!" I hastened to his side. "Sir, what are you doing here?"
>
> "I am washing the feet of this renunciate, and then I shall clean his cooking utensils." Babaji smiled at me like a little child; I knew he was intimating that he wanted me to criticize no one, but to see the Lord as residing equally in all body-temples, whether of superior or inferior men. The great guru added, "By serving wise and ignorant sadhus, I am learning the greatest of virtues, pleasing to God above all others—humility."[28]

We may not be prompted to literally wash the feet of others, not because we are afraid of what they would think, or due to our own pride: God does not need us to be so literal. However, we may look to serve others with equal humility and surrender, just as Jesus, or Babaji.

We have been given a gift beyond measure in having such living examples of greatness in our guru-lineage and via other saints

---

28   *Autobiography of a Yogi* (p. 310).

from around the world. We have been given the very highest methods for realizing God and we have been shown examples of who and what we should be in God. We need these examples, and along the way, we need encouragement. We may find both in the exchange between our beloved Param Para-Gurus, Babaji, and Lahiri Mahasaya:

> "Angelic guru, as you have already favored mankind by resurrecting the lost Kriya art, will you not increase that benefit by relaxing the strict requirements for discipleship?" I gazed beseechingly at Babaji. "I pray that you permit me to communicate Kriya to all seekers, even though at first they cannot vow themselves to complete inner renunciation. The tortured men and women of the world, pursued by the threefold suffering, need special encouragement. They may never attempt the road to freedom if Kriya initiation be withheld from them."
>
> "Be it so. The divine wish has been expressed through you." With these simple words, the merciful guru banished the rigorous safeguards that for ages had hidden Kriya from the world. "Give Kriya freely to all who humbly ask for help."
>
> After a silence, Babaji added, "Repeat to each of your disciples this majestic promise from the Bhagavad Gita: 'Swalpamasya dharmasya, trayata mahato bhoyat' (Even a little bit of the practice of this religion will save you from dire fears and colossal sufferings)."[29]

What we have done to deserve such grace from these truly great spiritual masters one cannot say. It is said that grace, by definition, is undeserved. Perhaps that is true. Surely the love and

---

29 *Autobiography of a Yogi* (p. 307).

constancy I received from my Guru was more than I could give to her at the time; therefore, we would have to say that all she gave to me was definitely undeserved. The greatest gift we can give our beautiful lineage, along with the inspiration and grace we have received from so many saints the world over, is to strive with all of our hearts, strength, minds, and souls to attain that most blessed state of consciousness wherein we know that we are no longer separate individuals living in darkness, but that we have boldly stepped into the light, and we find the same light radiating in us that is so clearly seen in our guru-lineage. This is the greatest way to honor Guru Purnima Day.

May the great blessings of God and Gurus on this special day ever grace you with a deep-seated desire to realize God, and, in that, fulfill their greatest wish for you, that you know God, and become immersed in the infinite Divine Consciousness—now, and always. Have a blessed day.

Full moon of Guru Purnima Day, tree of life and birds of heaven.**

July 13

CONFIRMED MAINE-IACS

Divine Mother's purity at Acadia National Park.

We have been traveling along the coast of Maine, upon the recommendation of many travelers who we have met along the way. We are pleased to say we have become Maine-iacs—lovers of Maine. This northeastern state is comparable to Washington State in latitude; however, Acadia National Park (a bit south in latitude from Salem Oregon) accumulated 71 inches of snow this year and became terribly cold. The Northwest, on the other hand, has the inflow of the Japanese Currents, much as England has the Gulf Currents, which bring moist, warm air. However, we are here at a different time of year (by design!). New England has now shaken off a record-cold year that lasted late into the season and has put on her summer clothes. Temperatures with highs in the 70s and 80s, combined with coastal breezes, make this an ideal time to be here.

The coastal villages are around every corner, with charming harbors and homes that bespeak the wonderful design of the seventeen, eighteen, and early nineteen hundreds. From Cape Cod to Victorian and Georgian designs, these houses are immaculate—clustering around the harbors known for their lobsters. We have driven, hiked, and biked along the coast and enjoyed every moment. John Rockefeller obviously enjoyed this area: on Mt. Desert Island, he bought half an island that is within walking distance at low tide. There, he built 75 miles of carriage roads on the big island—all for public use. Rockefeller knew all the names of the workmen. They were of a quality that would make ancient Roman builders proud. Those carriage roads are now bike and walking paths, and the bridges, made of granite blocks from the island, are designed to match the needs of the environment.

Rockefeller Carriage Bridge.

We found several spots that are Nature's Cathedrals. One spot we discovered when riding our bikes; we felt we could stay there and never leave. We explored a river running under one of those magnificent bridges. Just upstream, there was a series of small waterfalls—the feeling was one of purity itself. Such is Nature's design that She gives us of Herself in all Her original state in naturally sacred spots. When we are attuned to the inner Quiet, then the resonance of Spirit easily transfers itself to the open heart—God is everywhere speaking His truth, love, and kindness. However, it is only those who have "eyes to see, and ears to hear" that such wonders reveal themselves. It is not difficult to perceive this sacred essence; it only takes a keen desire to know Spirit—within and without—giving up prejudice or presupposition, and standing in wonderment and awe in one's own prime simplicity, leads to such receptivity. Such willingness is not hard, but seems to be rare for some unfathomable reason—for being blind and deaf to this miracle is a banishment that is hard for the soul to endure. Attunement to God cannot be made up for by the constant bombardment on the brain by playing music, watching television, drinking alcohol, or taking drugs, all these things leaving the soul even more thirsty for the Living Waters of pure Spirit.

Later that same day, Carla decided that for Guru Purnima Day, she wanted to do something special for me. She arranged for us to take a sail out on the bay for the afternoon. The weather could not have been more perfect: a sunny mid-eighties with 10 miles-an-hour winds. Perhaps due to my Pisces sign, the water has always had a salubrious effect—this day was no exception. It was another wonder-filled day. There is no day that God does not have this body under some tremendous stress throughout the day in doing work for Him; however, this seemed to be an exception to the rule, and it was pure joy. I thought of you, those who were having Service, those who sent loving notes, those who silently sat in meditation with inner attunement, and all felt close, near, and dear to me on this most special of days.

This is a tremendous life God has given us. Surely, there are times when life tests us hard, straining us to the limit of human endurance. There are other times when things seem to go so smoothly—both can be tests of our loyalty to God. Do we forget Him? Do emotions becloud our judgment and obscure Him? When life is hard, do we seek out His power, wisdom, and comfort, or do we feel sorry for ourselves and have a pity party of one? Or, if things go wonderfully smoothly, do we bow in wonder and awe at what He has brought about? Or do we feel we can do without God—ego thinks: "I am the clever one; I am riding high and do not need attunement with anything, or anyone, much less with God?"

Just as in marriage: in good times and bad, sickness and in health, in prosperity or adversity, beloved, I am ever yours. That is our vow, our commitment, and we keep it unconditionally in our marriage with God. He is our eternal Beloved, and though He might be able to do without us, we could not exist for even a nano-second without Him.

I have loved Maine because I have found God there, even as I have found Him in all the places I have traveled—for He is in me, and I am in Him, and He is all in all. Even though He is equally present everywhere, He seems to be more equally present in some places and people than others. He has certainly outdone Himself in revealing Himself in our tour of Maine, making us firm Maine-iacs.

Travel Note: We have traveled north through Maine and entered Canada, and we are currently camped near Quebec City. Our internet is very limited here; we had a plan for having a device that will give us good coverage while here, but it has not yet arrived. As a result, I do not have the ability to receive or send emails or texts, but both may be possible soon. Also, neither Carla nor I will have phone coverage for the time we are in Canada for the next month or more. Feel free to contact me by email, and I will get back to you as soon as I can. Pronams, David

A beautiful dragonfly on a sacred stream.

July 16

OUR VISIT WITH THE HOLY FAMILY

Montreal Notre-Dame.

I have been looking forward to our time in Quebec City and Montreal in order to pilgrimage to the holy sites of St. Anne's Basilica, Montreal's Notre-Dame, and Brother Andre's Saint Joseph's Oratory (prayer) Basilica. Our first stop outside of Quebec City is Saint Anne's, holy mother of Mary. We drove to a little village that sprouted an immense Basilica out of the ground. It has two bell towers and is a remarkable work of architectural art. In fact, we have been treated to the most beautiful Basilicas across North America; they simply, from an architectural and artistic point of view, must rank amongst the world's great treasures. St. Anne's is not only beautiful inside and out, but it radiates a blessing of a holy site, worthy of pilgrimage.

It is interesting to consider Anne, mother of Mary. Said to have immaculately conceived the holy Mother, she is a personage of great spiritual worth. As Jesus' grandmother, she must have held his little body in her arms; being spiritually sensitive, there could be no doubt that she felt something wonderful holding this incarnation of God. It has been said that the Essenes prepared for this birth for generations, each successive generation making themselves spiritually pure, developing the potential to bring a perfect incarnation into earthly existence. Who could have known what those spiritual seeds would become, seeds that were planted in an obscure part of the world—not in the worldly capital of Rome, nor in the intellectual capital of Alexandria, but in a village of no account, to a humble family.

St. Anne holding baby Mary.

In the caste system of Judaism of the time, Mary and Joseph would have been from similar family backgrounds: Joseph was a carpenter— respectable, but hardly of a higher caste. Anne, then, would have been from a respectable family, and she bore in her body a pure spiritual being who was destined to be the mother of a great savior. Surely, she is venerable herself, and has been the inspiration for this great Basilica. We stayed for Mass, which was half French and half English. The priest spoke very lovingly of sacrifice. The woman who led the singing sang as with the voice of angels. As we left, the sun was setting, but a glow kept growing inside of us from this sacred visit.

After spending a day in old Quebec City, where my high school French from so many years ago was not of any use at all, we caravanned on to Montreal. Having seen the pictures of the Basilica of Notre-Dame, dedicated to Mary, mother of Jesus, I was curious to see what could only be described as wondrous pictures of unearthly beauty inside the Basilica. We drove to the center of the city and found the Basilica there amongst narrow streets that could have come from a European set design. Upon walking in, I was even more wonderstruck by being there in person. The color of Mary is a beautiful deep blue; this is contrasted with the 23-karat-gold-leaf stars on the ceiling. The neo-gothic wooden structure has intricately painted columns, gold statuary, master paintings, and unusual wood carvings that appear to be a city in profile in the front; it all combines to transport one more to a heavenly, astral world than to this material one. The building's architect was American-Irish and Protestant—for this very French Catholic Basilica! The guide was relieved to tell us though, that at the end of his life, the architect converted to Catholicism—all God's fun! This is a very fitting house of worship dedicated to the divine mother of Jesus, and it carries a beautiful vibration; still, it is a tourist center, complete with a cover charge.

In the afternoon, we traveled across town to Brother Andre's Basilica. Unlike many cathedrals later turned Basilica, by decree of the Pope, this church was designated as a Basilica from its first foundation stone. Brother Andre was orphaned at a young age and taken in by a priest named Andre, whose name he later adopted when he took vows. After traveling to the States for work after the American Civil War, he returned to Montreal and desired to become a monk. He was uneducated, could barely spell his name, and it was a question of how he could serve. It was decided he couldn't cause too much trouble being the door-man of the Montreal Notre-Dame College, checking in students and visitors. With a lifelong dedication to St. Joseph, father of Jesus, Andre amazed local people because those whom he prayed for were healed. More people came for his divine healing, so he moved his ministry to a nearby train station to avoid crowds at the college. He used the money he collected for giving haircuts, $300.00 in all, to build a little chapel on the hill to carry on his work for God.

Dear Brother Andre, a little man with a big heart.

A local doctor, perhaps jealous of his prerogatives, protested that an uneducated Andre should not be healing people of their maladies; he didn't have the right background! One of Andre's superiors asked if Andre would stop this work if asked; he was assured that Andre had taken vows of obedience and would. The director said the work could continue for the present. Crutches abound in the little chapel that was also a home for this little man (five feet tall) with a big heart. What a wonderful feeling there was at the altar in this small chapel. Upstairs, we saw his apartment just as he had kept it. The largest Basilica in North America now towers over the little chapel, and it also sports the no-longer-needed crutches from those healed. The interior of the Basilica is modern, not to my liking, but Saint Brother Andre had nothing to do with that. However, the feeling in the little chapel, and the chapel deep under the Basilica, is very wonderful.

St. Joseph holding baby Jesus.

We feel so blessed to have come to these holy sites, each dedicated to a family member of Jesus. In truth, it was for this purpose we have come at all. In all these places, we prayed deeply to the Holy family of Jesus for those who are having physical problems, among those are M. with tumors, D. for dangerous bone spurs in the neck, B. for stroke symptoms and tumors, W. for heart problems, and others held in my heart who are all in definite need. All three of these sites are charged spiritual centers—the prayers made there were deep and sincere.

Oh Lord, you see to it that the highest good of all is fulfilled. You are the miraculous, healing power that regenerates a cut into repaired skin, brain damage into renewed wholeness, a weakened heart becoming a vigorous pump once again; so many conditions, and You are the sole source of healing in little things and large. You are the immense power that explodes as this universe; You are the regenerative ability for rapid, complete, and most perfect healing, You make what many call miracles without a pause or difficulty. Oh, my most beloved One, miracles abound all about us every day when the sun rises and in the blush of an unfolding flower—exercise Your ability to bring about healing for those who suffer, comfort for those in need, and most of all, offer Your supreme bliss for Your awakened souls who desire You above all other things. We pray in the name of Your Infinite Self, the masters Jesus and Babaji, Lahiri Mahasaya, Sri Yukteswarji, Master, Mother, and realized masters and saints around this world who You use to carry out Your will here on earth. Be it so—Aum Amen.

Yogacharya David lighting candles for our dear ones in need.

July 22

ONLY YOU

Mackinac Island, Natural Arch with aqua blue water.

We have left the eastern cities and toured west, even dipping into the States for a campground in Sault (pronounced Sue) Ste. Marie. While there, we thought to take an excursion to Mackinac (pronounced Mackinaw) Island. Today the island is reached by a 15-minute ferry; the island has no motor transportation. It is bicycle, ped power, or horse-drawn carriage only. We brought our bikes and took the 8.2-mile ride along the stunning coastline. We also sprang for a posh lunch at the classic Grand Hotel, where the movie *Somewhere in Time* was filmed.[30]

One thing of note about the island: we consistently felt a quiet calm there, even though it is a tourist destination. Even the lunch we enjoyed in a room of a thousand diners seemed tranquil. As we rode around the island, there were signs outlining the history of the island, the story being told with one sign every mile or so. This island was called Michidimackinac (Land of the Great Turtle) by the Ojibwa and Odawa People and is considered sacred—the turtle has a mystical meaning. The waters on the great Lake Huron were a wonderful color of aqua to deep blue, the sun shining—a perfect day.

Continuing back up into Canada, we traveled to Thunder Bay along the coast of Lake Superior (the Ojibwas called it Gitche Gumee: The Shining-Big-Sea water). It is wonderful to chant Ram Nam as we move along the highway, over some rough patches of pavement, and some smooth; there is a lot of summertime road work in this area where winters are rough on all the infrastructure. There have been wonderful vistas of the great lakes along the way. Nature's Cathedrals are in great abundance here, and what stands out is that God is present in all the places we have traveled, seen in all people—enough to represent all the races and many of the nations of the world.

> Oh Lord, You are the all in all. You have taken Your pilgrims upon this journey so that we might know that Your Spirit is to be found in all places, and all people. This vast creation is Your playground, and while it can be rough play; nevertheless, You are ever-present—a Guide, Comforter, and Protector for Your devotees. Certainly, life can take a deleterious turn from a human standpoint,

---

30   *Somewhere in Time.* Universal Pictures, directed by Jeannot Szwarc.

but when seen correctly, it is only You, only You. Oh Beloved, take the scales from our eyes, unstop our ears, and open our hearts so that we may see only You, hear only You, love only You.

Carla riding the tranquil roads of Mackinac; no motor vehicles allowed.

July 24

BABAJI REMEMBRANCE DAY

Illustration of the great Mahavatar Babaji.**

"Whenever anyone utters with reverence the name of Babaji," Lahiri Mahasaya said, "that devotee attracts an instant spiritual blessing."[31]

We pay special tribute to Babaji on July 25th as the co-founder of our Guru-lineage. Master Yogananda said that it was Jesus who requested Babaji to send someone armed with the science of yoga (union with God) to the West to re-awaken original Christianity. In the early formative

---

31   *Autobiography of a Yogi* (p. 293).

years of Jesus' ministry, and that of his disciples, it was well acknowledged that God and the kingdom of heaven were to be found within. Over the years, succeeding religious institutions were granted enormous worldly power, and due to the influence of the Kali Yuga, a formula developed in which acceptance of a creed was thought sufficient to be saved.

To be born again is far more than an intellectual agreement to a certain dogma, being sprinkled with, or dunked in, water, and even more than an initiatory experience such as feeling the power of the Holy Ghost in a Spirit-filled church. Follow in the steps of Jesus as he is baptized by his guru from a previous life, during which he sees the power of the Holy Ghost descending, he then goes out to the wilderness where he is tested. In fact, there are many steps to be taken that eventually lead to the hill of Golgotha, the hill of the skull.

We learn that the spiritual journey of many steps leads to our *skull*, our own brain, where the Holy Ghost, Christ Consciousness, and God the Father are all to be found through actual experience. This interior experience of the Mystical Crucifixion has been known by saints and realized masters around the world, yet the world at large is either indifferent to divine pursuits, or it is drawn to the idea of belief through simple faith, sans the inner experience of following the Christ all the way to the resurrection of Divine Consciousness.

Great masters such as Jesus and Babaji are ever anxious that all should enjoy the inner kingdom of heaven, so Jesus asked Babaji to send the liberating methods of Kriya Yoga to the West. Babaji had his great disciple, Lahiri Mahasaya, through whom he had already started a spiritual revolution in India via diksha—initiation into Kriya Yoga—a technique of breath and mind control that awakens the spine and brain to the higher frequencies of innate divinity. Lahiri Mahasaya had a very advanced disciple in Priya Nath Karar, later Swami Sri Yukteswarji, who perceived the underlying truth behind both the *Bhagavad Gita* and Biblical scriptures.

Babaji then guided young Mukunda, later to be called Swami Yogananda, to his guru Sri Yukteswarji, where he was grounded in the insights of both Lahiri Mahasaya and Sri Yukteswarji with regard to the scriptures, both East and West. Of course, the work could not be carried on through intellectual conversion only, but Yoganandaji walked in the steps of realization, even as Jesus and Babaji, and discovered directly the great truths that all saints perceive in the vision of God.

Babaji prompted Yoganandaji to travel to, and then live in, America so he could introduce the science of Kriya Yoga. Babaji felt the desire of certain devotees in the West, and he considered that they were ready for these teachings—his intuitive compassion reached across time and space. He knew that such souls as Rajasi Janakananda (James J. Lynn), Sister Gyanamata, Mother Hamilton, and others would take advantage of these teachings—a few bringing them to full fruition.

It would be Mother Hamilton, Paramhansa Yogananda's great disciple, who would be destined to experience and further elucidate original Christianity and the inner meanings of the Mystical Crucifixion based on her own experiences. Babaji's awareness stretched further down through time. He knew that succeeding generations of disciples would also find those who would go the whole way to full God-realization. Of course, he also knew that there would be a tendency to institutionalize these teachings, and much would be lost along the way. But, implicit, is the opportunity for truly realized souls to keep the flame of realization alive, and that, in time, it may grow beyond into a cultural revolution as we have already witnessed through the influence of *Autobiography of a Yogi*. May these teachings bloom fields of realized souls scattered across the globe.

Babaji has ever been interested in the long-term evolutionary needs of the world, and it is for this reason only that he has maintained a physical body for so long. He continues his influence primarily through the inner attunement of advanced devotees. It can be a tricky thing to say that Babaji said this, or appeared here or there, as the ego-mind is at work until it is completely transcended and can cause delusions. There have been many books written about Babaji since Master penned his spiritual classic, *Autobiography of a Yogi*. However, due discrimination must be used in this regard. Just as in social circles, there may be name-dropping to enhance one's own status, so those with a spiritual interest will drop names to lend a halo of credibility to the incredible. Going to God is not a circus—it is attained by dedicated souls sincerely making an effort to change their lives and attune themselves to the highest Light. We all enjoy tales of the remarkable; however, God-realization is much closer to home: know God-realization to be right in the heart and the soul of the seeker.

I am prompted to relate a remarkable experience I had with Babaji. It occurred when I had first left my profession and Phyllis had generously offered me a cottage on Hornby Island. Late one night, I was walking in Helliwell Park. Suddenly, I was enveloped in a powerful spiritual field. I felt my footsteps guided as I made my way through the dark woods onto a small beach on the ocean side. The night sky and stars seemed to grow close, or I seemed to grow large, and it felt that I could reach out and touch the twinkling lights. The thought, "Babaji could come down to me as one of those lights," came to my mind. However, Babaji has never acceded to my desire for outward remarkability; he only draws my mind inward. Just then, I saw the wonderful inner five-pointed star radiantly glowing. Entering the vast ocean of Spirit, I swam in God's ocean of Bliss. Through my open eyes, I saw that it was

Babaji as Spirit permeating all creation. Through his Grace, I pierced the personal and entered the impersonal—I describe here in words what cannot be described, but it seems right to do so, anyway.

On this day of Babaji Remembrance, it is good to think on him and to read about him in the *Autobiography*; and better than all is to be inwardly attuned to him and open to his Grace. Of course, we seek out God Omnipresent beyond form, and on the way up, we are inspired by realized masters and saints, and rightfully so. Going beyond all form, we find God is all-pervasive, everywhere present. In the universal vision, we find His voice being spoken through all: a child, someone in ignorance, and most lovingly through His perfected ones. Babaji's words soaked in love and bliss are an encouragement to all to rise above the thralldom of everyday concerns—know the Supreme One, the One who is ever-present within you.

Travel Update: We have continued our westward march and find ourselves encamped at a pretty spot just outside Winnipeg, Manitoba, named Birds Hill Campground. Well-known Canadian writer Gabrielle Roy (1909–1983) called Birds Hill, near where she grew up, her most sacred memory of Manitoba. It has a wonderful feeling here. We are taking a day's rest after several days of uninterrupted travel. As soon as we arrived here, God took me upstairs and has largely kept me there. In writing about Babaji today, he seemed so close, guiding my choice of words, and making his will known to my receptive mind. Tomorrow, the 25th, we will caravan further west and will be in thought of Babaji and of you.

A picture of Babaji along with a framed
photo of Yogacharya David and Carla in India

July 30

MEDICINE HAT: A TIMELESS STORY

The Medicine Hat legend on a wall relief
at City Hall in Medicine Hat, Alberta.

After some long continuous travel days, we arrived in the Province of Alberta. We are encamped in a peaceful coulee: a wide ravine with a river running through it in the city of Medicine Hat. It has been warm, and now with the low humidity of the interior, it is a reminder of the summers where I grew up.

The name Medicine Hat has a very interesting origin. The Blackfoot Nation tells of an event that happened a long time ago. It was a bitter winter with starvation howling at the door. The

Council of Elders gathered to discuss the matter. They decided a brave young man should be sent to a special place known as the "breathing hole," an opening in the ice of the Saskatchewan River where the Great Spirit was known to be present. After many days of arduous travel, the young man finally arrived there. He made camp and settled into fasting and prayer in order to summon the spirits. After his intense prayer, the Great Spirit appeared as a serpent. The serpent told the young man to spend the night on a small island (Strathcona). He was told, "In the morning when the sun lights the cut-banks, go to the base of the great cliffs and there you will find a bag containing medicines and a saamis" (holy bonnet). It was a hat to be worn only during battle. It would ensure victory. Aided by the saamis, the young man found food to save his starving people—he became a great Medicine Man.

This story has many interesting symbols, and I see in it a tale that contains tremendous inner meaning for the mystic. For the seeker of truth, the dark winter and starvation is the darkness of ignorance—not having joy and enlightenment which feeds the soul. The Council of Elders means inner direction, and the young warrior represents a newly-formed intention. The breathing hole is pranayama, a breathing exercise done in prayer and meditation. Pranayam kriya breaths and deepened meditation awaken the Great Spirit in the form of a serpent—the transformational kundalini force in the spine. The rising of the serpent force makes it possible to see the morning light—the great light seen in the ajna, or the point between the eyebrows. The "bag of medicines" is the powerful spiritual uplifting energies coursing through the body and healing it of spiritual sickness—ignorance. The bonnet of feathers or a hat, is the consciousness lifted up to the top of the head, or what in yoga is called the sahaswara, the thousand-petalled lotus (such "hats" are used to symbolize uplifted consciousness such, as the tall hat of the pope, or the crown worn by a king). This medicine hat, given by the serpent, assures the warrior victory, assures that the spiritual aspirant will have the power to overcome the ignorance of separation from the Great Spirit in the "battle" of spiritual practice. All the people are then fed by the continuous flow of dynamic spiritual energy and consciousness flowing throughout the entire system—feeding all the people. Thus, I find encoded in this ancient story a clear trail leading to spiritual illumination for a Medicine Man, or a spiritual adept.

Truth is universal, and it is fascinating and inspiring to know that it is, and has been, available to those who sincerely seek it in all parts of the world. Stories around the globe are adapted to the physical and social environment of the aspirant, but Truth is one.

A Ram Nam Note: as we have circumambulated this remarkable North American Continent, we have chanted God's Name as part of this spiritual pilgrimage. While moving down the road, I feel the spiritual aura radiating out through the power of the name (Nam) as a gift from the Infinite—awakening and resonating with the Divine vibration underlying all creation. God alone knows the full purpose of our pilgrimage, but the power of God's Name is definitely a part of it. Since my earliest days with Mother, in fact, the first time I met her, she instilled in me the holy mantra "Om Sri Ram Jai Ram Jai Jai Ram." She received this chant directly from Papa Ramdas and it is imbued with an all-powerful uplifting Grace. Not only did Papa use the chant to gain full realization of God, but others have done so before and after him with God's name ever being chanted. The transformed consciousness of those who attain spiritual heights through the Nam further surcharges it with ever greater and greater power to help others do the same. Imagine the vibration of many devotees chanting this holy mantra in full devotion towards the Infinite—helping to raise the consciousness of this world and all its inhabitants. The Lord knows this world is in need of upliftment, and though we may be in disparate places, we are all in union with our infinite Beloved through chanting and harmonizing with His Holy Nam.

Mother and Father Hamilton with
Papa at Anandashram, India, c. 1957.

August 10

BANFF

My mystic mountain friend in morning reverie.

Our pilgrimage has brought us west to the Canadian Rockies, rugged stones piled ten-thousand-plus feet high: peaks standing amongst the clouds, rivers ribboning through valleys, lakes mirroring the peaks, and sky above. Banff and Lake Louise deserve to be known as reputed beauties and the area is famous for its outdoor life. We have picked up Carla's sister and eleven-year-old grandnephew who have flown in from Georgia for a week in these glorious mountains.

As part of nature's outdoor cathedrals, it is one thing to admire its many beauties, but what stands out to me are a couple of peaks that soar above us and share their great presence each morning and throughout the day. It has been my experience that mountains, trees, rivers, lakes, and the land itself, emanate life-energy consciousness—there is no such place that is lifeless.

Particular places bear greater vibrational weight; they radiate more life, and have a presence that is undeniable.

While out in nature, a hunter will see game as something to shoot; a lumberjack will measure trees to topple; a photographer will frame an image to capture; a loner will find space to breathe; and, a mystic will be receptive to the inner life of nature's wonders.

One peak, I see it every morning and I feel its power and majesty—it has become a friend. In the life of a mountain, measured in multi-millions of years, my time with it is less than a blink; yet, we sit in silent communion one with another. It is wonderful to commune with nature and not only see its beauty but sense its spirit as well: pitch-dark ravens, black-billed magpies with florescent green tail feathers, and Columbian ground squirrels come to visit daily and scamper under feet.

Throughout the world and down through time, we find that each race and ethnicity has its own particular genius. Many of the native tribes of North America have a close relationship with nature, perceiving spirits in various animals, while sensing the overarching Great Spirit—both immanent and transcendent. To perceive the Great Spirit as all-pervasive is an astounding gift for any who knows how. Although we use the gifts of nature for food, habitation, and depend on it for life itself, it deepens our life-experience to see nature as more than something to exploit, kill, or tame. The creation of large national parks as a means of keeping portions of the earth in a more natural state is a remarkable idea that has found fruition here and in many other places around the continent. After seeing so much of Europe and the East Coast lose its pristine forests and natural settings, there was a determined effort to preserve a substantial amount of land in the West—keeping it fresh for future generations. We are all the beneficiaries of this marvelous idea, and Banff National Park stands out as a wonderful example of this principle. May generations to come find they can rest in, enjoy, and find spiritual nurturance from pristine nature—cathedrals made of stone, tall trees, flowing rivers, and cool lakes.

Morning Thoughts on Pilgrimage and Choices: We will soon be making our way west and south, completing our pilgrimage of these past seven months. What will come next? God knows. Each day of this pilgrimage brings its wonders and its challenges; in that sense, it is no different than any other time of life. Travel has not left the time I would like for working on Mother's writings, and this work I feel is coming closer as we make the transition to being home-based without wheels underneath—at least for a while! Even though we have traveled this pilgrimage without an itinerary, it is little different from how my journey in life has been in general. It is a matter of what God wishes from moment to moment.

You may say, "Well, I do not have that freedom." In a sense, that may be true. But in another way of thinking, we are the sum total of all that we have done, and that has led to this moment in life—it is to here that our choices have brought us. In that sense, you too choose to be where you are, doing what you are doing, and being who you wish to be. Some may think, "This is not the life I would like," but is it not true that in any journey you make, there are times you regret the road you are on? Deep analysis of your situation reveals that your life is the sum total of choices that you have made. Perhaps some of those decisions are from a very distant past, but ultimately, this life is perfectly designed for you. Within the context of your life, you may choose happiness or unhappiness, to act in harmony or disharmony, to put your mind on God, or on the delusion of this world.

You know what I would have for you: to be happy, harmonious, and filled with the light and the bliss of God. The question always is, "What do you choose?"

❊   ❊   ❊

Travel Note: It proved unexpectedly quite difficult to get an internet connection while in Canada, so I was not able to send this out last week. Currently, we have entered back into the States. We are pointing our noses back toward Camano Island—should be there by Monday. All through Canada, we were pressing forward to meet Carla's sister and grandnephew on time, so we are taking a few days next to the Methow River, enjoying not being in motion—it feels very restorative. We are also getting caught up on email and various tasks easily done here, but not before. So it is with great joy that I am able to connect with you once again and get caught up on our North American Pilgrimage.

A Columbian ground squirrel who came
out of his hole each morning to sit by my feet.

August 13

TWISP, FOREST FIRES, W., AND COME TO ME!

Methow: a river valley of peace.

While in Banff, at Lake Louise and heading west and south, we have been party to an abundance of smoky skies; depending on the winds, sometimes thick with smoke, sometimes clear blue skies. It is said that this is the worst year for forest fires in over half a century. Going down a canyon road, we drive by a hill with multiple fires on the hill next to us; helicopters are flying overhead with large dangling buckets of water doing their appointed tasks to dampen the spreading flames; additionally, we see brave, hardworking forest firefighters, with smoke-blackened faces, taking a break next to the road.

A forest on fire.

Up at Williams Lake, D. is performing seva (even while their own home may be threatened) by issuing vouchers to those who escaped from fast-running fires, leaving their threatened homes, some with nothing but the clothes on their backs. For the forest's sake, it can be beneficial for the lightning-induced fires to burn what they will, renewing the forest in its wake—surprisingly few animals have been killed in a forest fire as they flee or find shelter. But it is a hard thing for those who have homes and property in the forest to lose all according to the whims of Agni—God of fire—that consumes one tree and leaves another next to it untouched. Our hearts and prayers go out to those affected by the fires and for the safety of the firefighters.

As we motor further south, the smoke-filtered skies go with us—stretching across British Columbia, Washington, and Oregon. From Osoyoos through the Okanogan and finally to Twisp, to one degree or another, the gray residue of the burning forest continues. Just 20 miles away from Winthrop/Twisp, there is a fire growing in a wilderness area and we see the residue flowing in, then thinning to blue skies, only to darken once again, depending on the wind's direction.

Such is this creation that preservation and destruction are intricate parts of the whole. When a little girl asked Meher Baba,

"Why are there wars?" He asked her in return, "Why do you make stinky?" Wars are not necessary to life, but when humankind lives out of harmony with natural and spiritual law, then wars are a predictable outcome. In a golden age when natural and spiritual law are observed and lived, then many things out of balance will be brought into harmony. When a creation becomes attuned to higher thought and vibrational living, then a material world may simply transmute into pure spiritual Being—such things are possible and do happen. However, we are far from such harmony today—though we cannot discount that, like a rising flood, God's power can sweep over this earth and make it new. How my heart yearns for such upliftment for one and all.

The constant rolling of wheels underneath us for the past weeks is currently silent. The river flows by and the earth hums quietly, bringing peace to earth's flowing currents. It is time to restore before making the last part of the journey. God has me in His all-powerful, blissful grip and is whispering to me, "Tell one and all to enter into their silent caves of meditation and feel My uplifting power. I yearn to give My devotees all they need to fulfill their heart's desires, for it is in My power to do so. Tell all, 'Come to me!'"

Update: While we are here in the Methow Valley, W. breathed his last breath. His heart had been pumping less and less life-giving blood. W. talked of living to 120, but his years fell short of that goal. W. has been a wonderful example of someone staying focused on the guru through these past 65 years. He often said that Mother was the greatest person he had ever met, and he never wavered in his faith in her. He has been generous to this work, giving regularly and generously. In the early 1980s, I was injured at work and off work for a year while I went back to school to finish my degree. One day, W. came by with two large boxes of canned vegetables in thoughtful support at the time—I know he and his wife have helped others as well. In kirtans, W. sang with all his heart; he gave bone-crushing hugs and always had some witticism to offer, or a time-tested saying at the ready, and he wished everyone well. I know that he is with Mother Hamilton, and Mother is with him—a joy-filled, heart-filled reunion. I will miss him. It resounds in my mind his wish to all, as he smiles his smile, "Have a cheery day!"

August 20

TRANSITIONS: ALL IS WELL

Rainbows in the Desert of Utah.

ndings and beginnings always dovetail from one to another—a birth leads to an end, and a closure opens a new door. When we began this North American Pilgrimage, we had a skeletal plan as to the course of our circumambulation of the continent. We were directed by God to seek out Nature's Cathedrals, be led to places of saints and holy sites, look upon all people and situations as expressions of God, and explore the spiritual roots of the creation of this great American experiment proclaiming the rights of the individual and the audacious idea of popularly-elected leaders.

A great wealth of this North American continent is in her natural wonders. Pristine landscapes hold special meaning for each one: for the sightseer, it is the rugged beauty of the magnificent outdoors; for an artist, it is a canvas of inspiration; for the mystic, it is a profound feeling-vibration of a place carrying unveiled depths of realization—these being unrivaled by any other experience. Our journey included: Utah's Bryce and Zion Canyons; Nevada's Valley of Fire; South Dakota's Black Hills; Montana's Yellowstone and Glacier National Park; Wyoming's Grand Tetons; California's Redwoods and Joshua Tree National Parks, Palm Canyon, and Borrego Springs Desert; New Mexico's Gila Cliff Dwellings; Florida's Suwanee River; Georgia's Skidaway Island and Tallulah Falls; South Carolina's James Island; North Carolina, and north, on the Blue Ridge Parkway; DC's Greenbelt National Park; Maine's Acadia National Park, Pemaquid Point Lighthouse, and Bass Harbor; Michigan's Mackinac Island, and Alberta Canada's, Glacier, Banff, and Lake Louise National Parks. Though this reads on this page as a simple list, each of these places holds an experience for us—highlights in the body of God—genuine spiritual upliftment was felt at these wonderful Natural Cathedrals.

Besides these Natural Cathedrals, we were privileged to have the darshan of human cathedrals and places of worship: Idaho's Old Mission; Utah's Mormon Tabernacle; Master's retreat in Encinitas; Tucson's Native Pow Wow and Mission San Xavier del Bac and San Antonio's St. Joseph Church; Savannah's St. John the Divine Cathedral and the Congregation Mickve Israel Synagogue; Daufuskie Island's First Union African Baptist Church; The National Cathedral; Quebec City's St. Anne's Basilica; and Montreal's St. Mary's and Brother (Saint) Andre's St. Joseph Oratory. We found the vibration of God in these and many other places of worship powerful and uplifting.

For inspiration on the spiritual roots of the making of a nation, we had the opportunity of taking in the sites of: Mt. Rushmore; the Little Big Horn; Houston Space Center; Forts Sumpter and Polaski; Colonial Williamsburg; the Jamestown and Yorktown battlefields; Monticello and Mount Vernon; Washington DC, the Smithsonian Museums, the Capitol Building, Lincoln Memorial and the Washington Monument; Pennsylvania's Gettysburg; Massachusetts' Concord, and Connecticut's Mystic Seaport.

I am filled with such gratitude that Carla and I had the opportunity to take this pilgrimage around this great continent and to take you with us in spirit and through these writings. Of course, for all the places we went, there are so many more that could be explored, but these are the places that God took us to, and they are, therefore, perfect. Arriving back on Camano Island came in the natural course of our travels, but we both felt we could continue the life of nomadic pilgrims, always enjoying the starting of the engine after a stay somewhere, feeling the awakened interest: what will come in the course of our travels today? However, "To everything, there is a season, and a time to every purpose under heaven." A time for pilgrimage, its completion, and a time for home.

Upon arriving, we are once again in the saddle of service, a meeting in person with all those in our "virtual office," and with those helping with putting Mother's talks and transcripts into usable form and eventual books. Jerry and Lois are hosting a welcome home Service and potluck on Sunday, and on Monday, we will say goodbye to our dear friend W. at a graveside service, then spend time with K. and family, and we will enjoy hot fudge sundaes on the same day as a full solar eclipse (the last one was on my birthday in 1979 when Larry and I went to Eastern Washington to get a full-view experience of it). Then, there is getting caught up on correspondence, the business of life, and spending time with Mother's words, preparing them for publishing, and whatever else God has slated—as I know, He will fill the days and nights not only with His Divine Presence but seva (service) to Him in all forms.

In any transition, there are many things to do, sometimes there is a "grinding of gears" while shifting from one mode to another. It is good to be mindful of transitions in life, both small and big.

Leaving, or arriving, home from work is a transition, going on vacation (there are many circumstances of those going on vacations, getting sick, as if they can let down, and somehow that translates into the immune system letting down as well), there are those larger-life transitions, like sickness and death that cause even greater ripples, and sometimes tsunamis, in life. Through it all: to breathe, to be mindful, and to stay connected with God so that we are ever anchored in our true Self, not swept away in the many changes that life is constantly offering us. If we are very mindful, we will notice that even the tide of breath from in to out, and out to in, is a transition. May we move into life's new situations with a calm, knowing oneness with our Heavenly Father, Divine Mother ever with us, guiding us, and giving us inner assurance that no matter the changes, all is well, all is well.

Yogacharya David and Carla at Glacier National Park.

August 27

MARRIAGE: THE GREAT FULFILLMENT

Ram and Sita: one of the
great love stories of all time.**

arriage is one of the great foundational structures in society that serves many purposes. Marriage fulfills our desire for a loving partnership between husband and wife; it provides a nurturing home for children; it has both shared and divided tasks by husband, wife, and extended family that make life easier and bring balance; it is a way to build prosperity and endure adversity when it comes. There are so many benefits that come with a working marriage.

However, all this must be tempered with the reality of a life lived together. As a mediator, I worked with many couples; most were in trouble. We have all grown up with the children's stories that end with, "And then, they lived happily ever after." And so ends the fairy tale after strife, struggle, and overcoming great odds, the two come together. If this is part of the anticipation in a marriage that coming together as man and wife is the end of difficulties and a vague "happily ever after" vision, then there will be great disappointment on the horizon.

It is oftentimes assumed that a married couple, once they have confirmed their vows, should know how to be married. However, what experience shows is that marriage holds all the pleasure and all the pain that all life brings to us. Knowing how to maintain intimacy, handle financial challenges, the stresses of work, raising children, keeping a home and cars, and all the business of life requires a great learning curve. Marriage unfolds as we grow older, and rarely is it everything one—or both—in a couple thinks it will be. For some, it seems a betrayal that differences come into play, that there is anxiousness around money, intimacy, children, remaining monogamous, and more—these all seem to separate husband and wife, not support them.

One of the themes that I see repeated in struggling marriages is the inability to hold respect for one another. It is easy to vent stress upon a partner, the one closest to you. Having traveled to campgrounds with RVs, it is interesting to observe couples managing to back a trailer or motorhome into a campsite. For many, it is not a familiar or comfortable situation, and communication can quickly devolve into anger and blame when it is not going well. For some, raising a voice and finding fault comes as a matter of habit. I have thought that if some were to be videotaped during such interactions, one or both would be embarrassed to hear how they sound, their tone of voice, and words used like weapons: all responses meant to hurt and do damage.

Finding a place of respect for one another is one of the great secrets of a successful marriage. I love to hear one partner speaking in praise of another when the other is not in the room. To be over-familiar, discounting, and constantly blaming, poisons the atmosphere. Master once told the story of when he went back to India. One of his cousins had married a woman that Master's family had arranged for him (for Master). She treated her husband terribly, verbally abusing him while in his presence and when he was not in the room. Master took her aside and said that since they had once been intended for each other, he felt he could tell her that the way she treated her husband was not correct. That if she wanted happiness, she must change.

What is perhaps the strongest bond in a marriage, and represents the greatest potential, is the spiritual bond that goes beyond personality, situation, or worldly pressures. One key is a mutual understanding that God has brought you together, faith that you are meant to be a couple, and by remaining spiritually aligned, God can work out the kinks and make things even better between you; knowing that your attunement with God brings out more love, tolerance, patience, and the ability to see the divinity in one another (what greater intimacy is there than that!). When a couple seeks to serve God in one another, there are no limits to the fulfillment that can come about as a result.

Marriage cannot be a simple "Happily ever after," but that does not mean it cannot be the most meaningful and loving relationship you can have on a human basis. It is the working out of life that can either draw you closer together to solve the many problems faced or it can tear you apart. To be connected to God within, letting Him guide you, awaken love in you, and give you the courage to open yourself fully in the presence of another, is the greatest ally you have in bringing out the best in a marriage. In the end, marriage is your practice ground for your oneness with the Infinite Beloved, and being one with Him in all of what life brings to your doorstep, "For better, for worse, to love and to cherish, in sickness and in health, in prosperity and in adversity." Amen!

August 31

MARRIAGE WITH GOD

Hanuman shows that only
Ram and Sita are in his heart.**

Traditions around the world speak of a deepening relation-ship with God—a marriage with God. This feeling for God as your all and all, your Beloved, is dual in nature: of being lover and beloved; it also holds out a promise for the complete merging of two who become one.

Human love of one for another has so very many variations, but a romance includes physical chemistry and deep emotions of the heart. One of the great challenges of human love is to separate chemistry (lust) from real love. Chemistry can be a powerful imitator of love, at least in the beginning. Chemistry can make you feel that you cannot live without another, that you can only think of another, and, in intimate moments, that you are merging into another. However, chemistry can be had with someone with whom you are not compatible on any other level. When the chemistry subsides, as it always does, and there is no friendship, no alignment of interests or purpose, then there is a sense of betrayal of "love."

Real love endures and is based on respect and friendship—it is a feeling that resembles the patina of wood. Patina is created through years of usage, and even those things that are not good for the finish, such as sunlight, dust, and scuffs, all add to the patina that gives it a rich glow that cannot be created in any other way except through time and usage. There are times when love has to endure much, but in the end, it creates a deepening glow that shines all the more with kindness, care, and usage.

This human love, whether in romance, friendship, work, or familial relationships, is all preparation for our marriage with God. God is the consummate lover, ever attentive, giving, and keen for your welfare. However, even as God gives all, so does He demand all. The principle of, "As you give, so shall you receive," is never truer than with God. A human tendency is to withhold from another when hurt and disappointed. This tendency must be overcome, not only in human relationships (this is part of the preparation for the Divine Romance), but most especially, you must learn not to withhold from God. There is a mathematical preciseness—exactly the way you withhold equals blocking out the flow of God; not because God is withholding from you, but because you have built a barrier through your withholding.

When you learn to surrender, to give your all, then the floodgates open and you receive the infinite nature of God—unending love, ever-new bliss, life, wisdom thoughts, expansive consciousness, and unending gifts of Spirit. Now, as you receive, so you give. You give all that God gives to you back to God, God as Spirit, God as creation. The more you give, the more you receive; the more you receive, the more you give. The patina of Spirit grows and glows, and you are infinitely enriched as God gives to God. You give without thought of what you will receive, only knowing that it is God giving through you, and you giving back to God in whatever way He directs.

In that direct relationship with God, both giver and receiver merge and are ultimately consumed, one into another. One becomes two, and two become One, a play of Spirit, not to create separation, but to enjoy the giving and receiving in its unending variations. Think what a dismal life of playing it alone results in when compared to the wonder and beauty of being God's expression and beloved. God, being the senior partner, is not unmindful of the wishes of His beloved; however, His will is far-reaching, wise beyond counting, and takes into account the good of all. Therefore, God is not going to cater to every wish of His beloved, but He definitely compensates for every lash that may be received for His Name's sake.

To enter into this Divine Romance, you begin with giving, sur-rendering, serving, and loving. If you cannot find it in you to know how to do these things, then pray to your Infinite Beloved to show you how. If you stand back in indifference or fear, then you are withholding—with predictable results. Love can only be known through free-will; love can never be compulsory. We ever stand on the threshold of a new beginning, and, even now, you may enrich the patina of your Divine Romance and explore the infinite nature of your Beloved by stepping through that doorway.

September 3

IN THE GRIP OF GOD

All is in God's hands.**

I am in God's Grip, and there is no other place I would rather be. From my late teens, God prodded me towards Him and away from the world. I did not know it was He at the time; in fact, I had no faith in any concept of God that I knew of then. I only knew that I was restless and definitely not content with what I saw in the world. That restlessness grew into a deep spiritual pain, and finally, in my extreme state, I turned to God, and He lifted my pain, though later, it came back—the shepherd's dog nipping at me without respite.

Then began the long journey of sadhana in which I had further glimpses of God's Light and bliss—a training of the mind to stay focused on Him through using the techniques my Gurudev taught. Those creaky doors yielded, a bit at a time, opening, then closing tight, then opening again, always with the shepherd's dog driving me on when I would have rather gone back to sleep. I even resented the shepherd's dog, thinking why could I not be happy as others seemed to find happiness in this world? Thankfully, sadhana drove me on, for what I sometimes thought of as a curse, I now see as my greatest blessing.

And many a time I fell; many a time, I made mistakes and suffered the consequences. Unfortunately, not only did I suffer, but those around me suffered as well. Even through the Dark Night of my Soul, through many mistakes and missteps, Grace found a way through my ignorance, my vanity, my lower human desires, and my indifference. What endless patience God and Guru gave, never giving up on me, transforming the base metal of humanness into the gold of Spirit—God and Guru being alchemists extraordinaire.

With many missteps on my part, I never wavered in my desire for God, and gradually that transformation took shape; a new being was born, something far beyond my ability to enact. So, while I was an active participant in the process, I was increasingly very much witness to the extraordinary forces at work in me. God experience went from very occasional glimpses, then, to a most-of-the-time Reality, culminating in an every-moment state of being.

Now I live in His grip, God's power and intelligence flowing through me, and I am witness to what He does in and around me. And I am more humbled than ever before, for the witness in me is in awe of what He is about. There is no life more fully lived than when in Him; His bliss, His grace, is ever at work. And what He has shown me, what I most definitely know, is that same spark of Divinity, that same seed of Grace that has grown into a tree, is in every living soul that walks the earth.

Not all will awaken to this transformed life in this lifetime, but there are those destined to live in Him and shed His qualities to all the earth. As one or two awaken, so that quickens the lives of others, and one or two awaken over there, then there, and on and on, it spreads as the world is lifted into greater heights. When a significant minority transform—not that large of a percentage, actually—the transformation will spread all over this earth. Suddenly, it will not be about money, power, and fame, but about recognizing the Light in one another and in the world itself. Even though the world may be of no great support to those living a spiritual life at this present time, there is no greater opportunity to be in the vanguard of what is to come—to help lead the way through your own example. For I can tell you from my own experience, there is no greater way to live this life than to be in the grip of God.

September 8

REAL HAPPINESS IS SEEKING YOU

Wisdom of Rumi.**

This weekend, we are taking the time to come to the Loon Lake Retreat for an intensive study of the liberating methods of Self-realization. For all those who come, there are many more who would like to be there, but we may all share something of our time together in satsang through our connection in Spirit.

There is much written by saints and realized masters as to the goal of spiritual practice; however, no matter how perfect the words are for its description, there is no replacing actual God-contact and having direct experience of those realized states of consciousness.

To live in divine consciousness is the greatest accomplishment of a lifetime because it does the greatest good for the individual, and it has the most powerful uplifting effect upon all creation. If someone is starving, they must of course have food, and if someone is in excruciating pain, they should have some relief. But in meeting such immediate needs, a temporary solution is given for a temporary problem. No matter how great the need is in the moment and how good it is to be able to offer relief, the deeper, longer-lasting suffering of humanity is found in the mind and soul. Identifying this suffering is the first step in the recovery of the consciousness that leads to long-term happiness.

After identifying that the cause of this suffering is separation from divine consciousness, we must discover how to get relief from this mental and spiritual pain. Deep analysis shows that much suffering comes about due to the attachment we have to the things and situations of this world. Attachment makes us think that our happiness is dependent upon having certain situations or objects, and if we do not have them, then we are miserable (or if we have them, and they are taken away, then we are unhappy). Real happiness is to be found within and is not dependent upon these outer conditions. If happiness is thought to stem from something that is temporary, and what in this world is not temporary, then happiness will always be followed by pain when that temporary situation changes.

This understanding makes us know that only by finding an unshakable source of happiness within, one that transcends the things of time and space, will we find a solution to suffering. Great saints and spiritual masters who have gone into the laboratories of their own deepened experience tell us that there is an eternal fount of joy and bliss to be found within. This fount does not run dry, is not dependent upon outer conditions, and makes us know the truth of who and what we truly are. This truth is known through direct experience—it is portable, going with us wherever we go, and it transcends the limited human mind.

One might well ask, "If this is true, why is the whole world not running after unending happiness?" And really, that is a most poignant question, but the answer is in what was said earlier about attachment: it acts as a screen that hides this simple truth. A child has a toy, then sees another child with another toy. At first, the child is happy with his or her own toy, but when seeing the other child with a different toy, cries such tears at the thought of not having the other toy. We must give up attachment first, then the truth is revealed, but we do not like to give up our attachments, having come to believe that our happiness lies in having certain things or situations.

However, when we have a ready and simple faith, we find that the truth is not far away. Having the willingness to open our heart and mind to the radiant Presence already existing within, reveals the doorway to this most wonder-filled and exciting experience that can be had by all. We do not need to build complicated creeds and beliefs; in fact, that is contrary to the prime simplicity that gets you entry. Let go of all thoughts that happiness lies out there somewhere and let us open our mind and heart to the divine revelation that is seeking out an opportunity for awakening us now. Let us join together; if not in person, then in spirit, and seek out this omniscient Presence that is also seeking us.

September 15

LOON LAKE AND LAHIRI BABA

Lahiri Mahasaya.

O nce again, we entered the breach and took the plunge into deeper sadhana during our time at Loon Lake. Our topic was a meditation upon Lahiri Mahasaya, the Father of Kriya Yoga for our Modern Age. Kriya Yoga has been part of the yoga tradition from time immemorial, spoken of in the Mahabharata and other ancient spiritual texts. Clearly, such techniques were part of the early Christian Church, such as when St. Paul wrote, "I die daily" (I Corinthians 15:31). Certainly, he did not die in the ordinary sense of the word; rather, he entered into the same breathless state as do meditating yogis in Samadhi, or in Christ Consciousness. Common knowledge of these meditation techniques had fallen into disuse down through the centuries. Babaji revived this yogic science back into use through his beloved disciple Lahiri Mahasaya and through Jesus. Babaji then orchestrated its introduction into the West through that powerful spiritual engine, Paramhansa Yogananda, and for us, then, through our own Prem-Avatar, Mother Hamilton.

Our time together was spent going deeper into the Hong Sau, the Light and Sound meditation practices, as well as the Clearing and Charging Exercises Babaji taught me. Then, we took incidents from the master's life as launching pads for exploring his experiences and relating them to our own. One of the great things about saints and realized masters is that their divinized lives become allegories for realization: blueprints surcharged with divine consciousness for those who meditate deeply upon them. So, Lahiri Baba's own life and experiences become a gateway to the Infinite—such is the grace of a great spiritual master.

Besides our time delving into the master's life, we also chanted at every opportunity—led by Cate and Carla on the harmonium. We took walks in the scenic woodlands surrounding Loon Lake; some even took dips in the mountain lake and paddled on the mirror-like surface in kayaks. The spiritual charge from such gatherings helps propel us to the Goal of goals; it lifts our spirits as well as those attuning themselves to our gathering even at great distances—even from an ICU hospital bed.

Special thanks to Carla for all her work in organizing these retreats, to Karim and staff for their beautiful service to us during our stays and working with Carla in between, and to those beautiful souls who have sponsored others, including Carla and I, in attending the retreat. Jai Gurus! Jai Lahiri Mahasaya!

September 17

Promise of a New Day

Pathway to the Light.**

The constant rehearsing of problems that might happen, or that have happened, creates an underlying anxiety that drains our energy—what is this all about?

Being prepared for when things go wrong is a prudent thing to do—having a filled pantry, working flashlights, and first-aid bandages, all are good things to have around, just in case. However, the conscious and unconscious mind can take this to an exaggerated degree and make warning sounds in our bodies and heads 24/7. Far from being useful, this becomes destructive as it produces false warnings, skews our judgment, can make us over-function or withdraw from life, and burn up life-energy without benefit—wearing us out and robbing us of joy!

As I have often said, "It has been a rough couple of thousand years!" Our history is filled with starvation, war with its pain and misery, lack of justice and stability, extremely difficult working conditions, little medical care, and limited opportunities—it has not been uniformly bad, but a large share of the world's population has had it very difficult. While there are definitely difficult lives in the world today, there are also great advancements on so many fronts, and increasingly, a great number of lives are so much better off, statistically better than ever before. However, the echoes of traumatic experiences can resound even when we are surrounded by relative peace and prosperity.

I worked with a psychiatrist who was making a study of WWII holocaust survivors and their children. The survivors of these death camps oftentimes got about their lives, not talking about or seemingly devastated by past experiences. However, their children and children's children exhibited post-traumatic stress, seemingly for no apparent reason—until you've considered the ungrieved horrors that the parents and grandparents went through were passed down to their progeny. Their holocaust-surviving parents did not have the time or energy to grieve for their devastating losses; they simply had to get on with their lives to build something better for themselves and their children. But, the emotional charges from those losses were passed down to new generations, waiting for the day that they could be worked out.

We have all come from "tough stock," and the many losses and difficulties of those previous generations can be passed down through families—it can explain much in what may seem unexplainable symptoms. Then, add on the layers of past lifetimes a soul has experienced during this dark Kali Yuga; for example, the emotional charges of past life experiences lurking deep in the subconscious mind—all building. This complex weave of the psyche reveals why unexpected challenges can seem to occur from thin air, as well as unexplainable strengths and talents we simply come with, fully intact, from birth.

Some can look at that list of atrocities and problems and think, "How can there be a God?" Others can look at that same list, see how well we all do in general, how much kindness and caring there is in the world, how much healing happens daily, and think, "It is only by the Grace of God that decency is as prevalent as it is!" I, of course, come down on the side that God's Grace—always active and present—makes us yearn for a better world and desire growth. Along with Grace is human free will, which can choose horrible actions, creating a daily testing field for right action for every individual and group. Family history, past lifetimes, and of course the environment we live in interlace their influences, both positively angelic all the way to the demonic. Like the immune system fighting off toxins, germs, and viruses that threaten our health from within and without, so we need a superb mental and spiritual "immune system" to create and maintain total health and happiness.

Although we may strive to maintain a positive environment to live in, we may freely admit that there are many things outside of our control and acknowledge that if those negative things beyond our influence are given preeminence in our mind, they can bring us low. The greatest boost to our physical, mental, and spiritual immune systems is God remembrance. Through God remembrance, the first thing that happens is that we take our mind off the merry-go-round that makes us feel overwhelmed or powerless and align with the supreme power and divine intelligence of God. God is positivity itself: hope, faith, and a doorway to all things possible. Remembering the attributes of God: "Oh Lord, You are all-powerful, wisdom, and light itself, You are peace and love without limit—You are my all, and all in all." Chanting God's name, meditating upon Him, listening to inspiring talks and music, elevates our mood, changes our thinking, stimulates smooth life-energy, and purifies the mind—both our conscious and sub-conscious minds are uplifted through our contact with the super-conscious mind.

Of course, we may have legitimate concerns in our life, but we no longer turn these into a worry machine. Now, we see those possible problems in the light of God. He is working out His will through us, His willing instrument—in fact, it is for this purpose that we have taken incarnation and there is no place we would rather be than here and now—because this is where He has placed us.

Recently, a devotee went through a serious operation. She said that while in recovery, she felt that she was in the hospi-tal for some greater reason—she had deep conversations there with a young man with addiction problems, visited many on the ward, and was a bright light, and in fact, the nurses gravitated to her room due to her calm and positive manner. When I was in the hospital, I too felt that this was my opportunity to pray for all those there, including the caregivers. With the mind so busily engaged in bringing the Light of God to a situation, there was no time for worry!

This world is on an evolutionary climb out of the Dark Ages, and, yes, there are challenges; however, with God in our heart, this is a new day, a bright day full of promise and glory. God is on the move, and whether the world around us reflects that or not, it is certainly true for us as we lead the way into the path of joy, light, and abundance—Grace operating within, without, and all about.

Put your mind on God, put your mind on God, put your mind on God and your life is chang-ing already—feel the peace and joy of His ever-abiding

Presence right in your own heart and soul. Learn what it
is to live a life without fear, always aware of His ever-abiding Grace residing in your heart, mind, and soul. Be it so!

September 20

UNSHAKABLE FOUNDATION

Calm amidst the storm.**

There has been an extraordinary call for prayers in the last little while, indicating that the world is going through a transition. Even as this world goes through seasons of the year, and today, we stand on the cusp of the fall equinox, so, too, there are times in life when there are intense changes and transitions that affect us all.

To the sensitive yogi, Master said that there are four times of transition each day. Of course, we are all familiar with sunrise, sunset, noon, and midnight as common markers of the day. However, the meditating yogi will notice special times of the day that are propitious for going within, 4–6 a.m., 11 a.m.–noon, 5–6 p.m., and 10–midnight. One can take advantage of these subtle but powerful tides of energy by using these times for prayer and meditation.

I was so charmed when traveling in Islamic countries when the call to prayer came at different times of the day. Around sunset with the sinking sun radiating deep orange was one such time; the very warm day cooling a bit, the call to prayer coming from different towers around the city, shop owners retiring to the rear of their stores and bowing to the Creator of us all on their magic prayer rugs, the whole city becoming quiet for some minutes while the world acknowledged the One who makes it all possible. Such a lovely feeling.

Other transitions may not make it so easy to find peace, for there are times in life when health, prosperity, work conditions, family life, and friendships can all go through transitions, sometimes going our way and other times not. And yet, finding peace, inner assurance, and a solid foundation in a constantly changing world is at the heart of our spiritual practice. Even Mother said she could have an initial shock when something first happened. We too may feel, at first, an initial disturbance, but like a compass needle that always finds north, so our minds go directly to God. Other times, we may find no disturbance at all when something untoward happens; we simply feel the great divine peace from start to finish.

Naturally, from a human standpoint, we like to have things go easy. For some, when a transition takes something away and makes life more challenging, we can feel betrayed. Somewhere inside, we feel that if we are making spiritual effort, then everything should go perfectly smoothly in this world. However, we do live in a world of duality, and the alternating currents will always be at work, bringing both (from a human standpoint) good and bad situations. While it is true that leading a spiritual life will avoid many a painful trap in life, no one can avoid all difficulties, and at times, hardships seem to come bundled up and delivered all at once.

To find lasting happiness, we must rise above this world of duality, for this world will never be able to deliver happiness. There is a Source of serenity and joy within that cannot be eclipsed by dualism. Avatar Buddha said that life is suffering, then he gave the formulae for transcending it. Attachment to the things of this world makes us blind to this innate Source, so we must remove our full attention from this world, and through deepened meditation, become established in the ever-abiding Presence within—Nirvana.

Being established in such peace, we now have an unshakable foundation for entering into any and all circumstances of life, and the things of this world do not make us over-glad, or, over-sad—they simply are. Our real source of joy comes from our oneness with the Infinite Beloved—Sat, Chid, Ananda—eternal existence, consciousness, and bliss. As the great Lahiri Mahasaya said, make acquaintance with God in the springtime, for elsewise, you may find Him elusive in the winter of life. Seek Him out daily, and learn to make the Divine Presence the unmovable core of your being.

September 24

GOD: PERSONAL AND IMPERSONAL

Mother Hamilton at Sunday Service, Seattle, Washington, 1977.

The ferry glides upon the almost perfect blue water; islands near and far with their scattered trees make the scene so charming. A perfect day. We are making our way to Victoria to see devotees. With pilgrimage and hospital stays in this past couple of years—it has been a long time since making this journey.

I am reminded of times past, going back thirty-seven, thirty-eight years, and making this same trip, with a group of us following Mother Hamilton when she came to Victoria to see devotees. Being on the ferry with Mother, then staying with devotees, Sunday Service at the YMCA chapel, brunch with all of us (the Seattle and Victoria group) and Mother at a beautiful Atrium restaurant, then making our way back on the ferry. It is hard to describe how compact life was, and how much experience was packed into such occasions. Actual talk with Mother was very little; it was just being with her, being part of her journey—it was everything for us in the moment.

Of course, Mother had very different kinds of relationships with each disciple. With some, she was very personal, staying at their homes, spending social time with them. Then, for many of us, it was very sporadic to have time just with Mother outside of Sunday and Wednesday Service, very rarely one-on-one. While Mother was everything to me, she was far more impersonal in our relationship. There seemed to be an inner circle of devotees, and then the rest of us. I sometimes wondered what it would be like to be part of the inner circle, but I was secure in knowing that what I had with Mother transcended social circles or the proximity of being in person with her. I was content with what I had.

It is interesting now, because it has proven true over time, that many who were part of that "inner circle" did not stay with Mother; however, there were those of us on the "outer circle" who have stayed true to a bond formed with the guru so long ago. Mother said that those who were more physically distant from her often made more spiritual progress than those close; such is the mystery of discipleship. Jesus said, "Many are called, few are chosen" (Matthew 22:24); and, Krishna said: "Of many thousands, one here and there seek Him out, and of those, a rare one rises up to know Him truly as He is" (Gita 7:3, adapted); the path of realization is indeed inscrutable.

Such are my thoughts in the early morning hours while being here with devotees. Now, I find God in this form, is different with each one, some brought in closer, some kept more at a distance. However, what is equal is the love that God expresses through me for each one. For God is both personal and impersonal: the personal shows distinction, the impersonal none. God has His play, His lila, and He enjoys it. God is also unqualified Spirit, without separation, limitation—beyond time, space, and form. As He is in Himself in Spirit, and also the creative Hand manifesting as all nature—so His seemingly dual nature is within all souls—the microcosm in the macrocosm. In Spirit, He is one, whole, complete; and in creation, He joyfully expresses Himself as varied forms in the ebb and flow of life—with all of its dramas.

Being made in His likeness (unqualified Spirit) and in His image (expressive form), each soul has both completeness and dynamism deep within the soul. However, many have forgotten their heritage of perfect Spirit within, and seek to find their happiness in the constantly changing images of creation—a vain task never to be completed. For, only in Spirit is wholeness experienced, and with that realization comes the experience that it is the same Spirit being expressed as multifarious creation—the same oneness, known in the deepest meditation, reveals the deep underlying oneness in all forms (this oneness in creation is Christ-awareness—the only begotten Son of God).

Mother acted impeccably with each soul, perfect for what each one needed for his or her spiritual evolution. With me, she kept an impersonal distance that made me seek Her out in Spirit, not becoming overly familiar with Her outer form. It was perfect for me and made me know Her in Her Divinity first and foremost. Others, She swept up in Her lila, and that was perfect for them. Inner attunement stands the world on its head in terms of who is in the "inner circle" and who is part of the "outer circle."

In my current life, God has become far more impersonal in Spirit. He is a strict taskmaster, and when I venture too much into His play, He is quick to draw me back to Him. *My God is a jealous God*—speaks to His instant inner direction that brooks no insubordination of too much focus on this world, even when I think it is a task done for Him! And when He flows through me as form, He does so joyfully and easily. But usually, I am mostly in

Him. One of the interesting things about this is that, when I am deep in Him and He makes me think of someone or some situation, I feel such intimate contact in Spirit with that one—a complete knowing oneness. There is an inscrutability to His divine design, belying the human logic that tells us physical contact is the only means of feeling close to another; however, this other form of wisdom is at once knowable through intuition.

Oh, in my humanness, how I would love to ride on that ferry with Mother once again, basking in her physical presence—even for just a moment! To be the littlest one in her retinue—what joy there is in that thought! Yet, as I think of Her, Mother's shining presence glows in and around me, a treasure beyond all treasures! Such is the play of the Guru—God within, God without.

September 26

LAHIRI MAHASAYA: PERFECT JOY EVER AFTER

Lahiri Mahasaya Samadhi Temple at Keshashram, Haridwar, India.

O n this mahasamadhi anniversary date of the great spiritual master, Lahiri Mahasaya, we reflect on the life of this most humble and joy-filled spiritual personality to whom we owe so much for our spiritual path. As I think on his form, I am filled with such joy—the bliss he emanates is contagious; it overflows the cup of the little soul and merges into an infinite expanse—atma into paramatma.

In the *Autobiography of a Yogi*, we read:

> At my guru's home I found many disciples assembled. For hours that day the master expounded the Gita; then he addressed us simply. "I am going home." Sobs of anguish

broke out like an irresistible torrent. "Be comforted; I shall rise again." After this utterance Lahiri Mahasaya thrice turned his body around in a circle, faced the north in his lotus posture, and gloriously entered the final maha-samadhi. Lahiri Mahasaya's beautiful body, so dear to the devotees, was cremated with solemn householder rites at Manikarnika Ghat by the holy Ganges . . .[32]

With what simplicity, what grace for this most perfect master to leave!

How are we to explain such a flawless transition? For spiritually illumined masters such as Lahiri and Babaji, who have been making such ascensions daily for many years, merging into Divine Consciousness is a long-practiced entrance that comes naturally. As St. Paul said, "I die daily," leaving of the body in what yogis call samadhi; Christians call it Christ; it is entering into the supreme consciousness through the ajna or the Christ Center.

In the beginning, when attaining samadhi, the body becomes fixed, and the breath is still—what can appear to be a death state—however, the soul has never been more fully alive. As purification continues, the aspirant may remain in God-consciousness while moving the body; however, there are times of having this unbroken consciousness and other times of feeling separation. Ultimately, the soul, through deepened communion, is able to go about its business in the world without a break—ever one with the Divine nature of the Soul. What could be easier or more natural than to enter into this state? Only when it comes to what we call death, it is done for the last time and through God's direction without any intention of returning to the earthly vessel—maha-samadhi—the last or great entrance into divine union or yoga.

---

32   (p. 331).

While there will certainly be sorrow for those remaining behind, for the master, there is a blissful release and the certain knowledge that he or she has fulfilled this earthly mission. Through our focus upon such ascended masters, we attune ourselves to their divine consciousness and thus their grace may impart a blessing upon us. May Lahiri Mahasaya bless us all and lift us up to the same beautiful state of consciousness he enjoyed in his life, and ever after.

September 30

HAPPY BIRTHDAY, LAHIRI BABAJI

Happy Birthday to dear Lahiri Babaji.

t was on this holy day, in 1828, that our dear Lahiri Baba was born in the Ghurni village in Bengal. Babaji watched over the great master as a child, patiently waiting over 30 years before they should meet in the Himalayas. The grace of these two exceptional masters continues to flow to us, as we honor the life of Lahiri Mahasaya.

Health Update: The surgery on my arm was Thursday. I am home with orders to keep my arm elevated for the next two weeks.

The five-inch incision removed an area with melanoma, unrelated to the past melanoma in the internal organs. I will give a talk for Sunday Service.

October 4

HEALTH CHECK

Good exercise: Yogacharya David with
his bike in the Banff Canadian Rockies.

I have completed the health tests for this current round, and they
have come out with positive results. Yesterday, I had a consul-
tation with my oncological naturopath; he has played a central
role in my healthcare these past two years and contributed to the
clean health reports with his recommendations for supplements
based on blood tests and his knowledge about how cancer cells
proliferate. These plant-based prescriptions have been targeted
to support the body by strengthening the immune system, robbing tumors of what they need to grow (i.e., zinc interferes with
the delivery of copper which cancer cells require), and supplements that have shown cancer-fighting ability (specifically for melanoma that, in the past, grew in my internal organs). Cause and

effect are not always easy to determine; however, this is the only medical treatment I have been receiving—allopathic doctors have had nothing to offer without tumors being present.

There are things I can do on my own as well. For instance, I have had weight gain, and that is not only hard on my overall system but can be an aid to tumor growth. Being overweight affects cancer risk factors, such as the insulin growth factor, and it can result in chronic low-level inflammation. Fat cells produce estrogen and affect cell regulation which is an additional risk factor; of course, being overweight can affect general health and quality of life as well.

With that in mind, I have set some goals for myself—if this is an issue for you, this is a time when we can all join together to attain our ideal weight. The doctor suggested I set a goal of losing 2 pounds a month, which seems extremely doable. I will see him in six months, and I will have trimmed 10 percent of the weight off and looked to increase lean muscle. With good intentions only, and no specific goals, it is too easy to continue on as I have, so I will check in weekly with the scale for feedback on how I am doing.

My method will be to take advantage of "low-hanging fruit" for common sense weight loss: no desserts, baked goods, or chips. Eat healthy vegetables and go easy on fruit and grains. For me, limiting or eliminating snacking. When traveling, my biggest offense was snacking on chips; those days are over. I have a good sense of what foods trigger cravings; no more of those. I have been successful in the past in losing weight when I set my mind to it; however, I know others who have greatly benefited from programs such as Weight Watchers, which offers a good structure and support.

At the end of six months, I will assess how I feel with 10 percent weight loss to see if it should be more. When I am happy with the results, I will spend the next six months maintaining my weight without gaining any back. After that, I will regularly check in with the scale, the truth-teller for trends, to maintain what I have set out to weigh. This long-term follow-up is essential, for in the past I have lost the weight, but the slippery slope leads to gaining it back over time.

If this is a goal for you as well, I would love for you to join me on this journey. Weight is a big issue in our prosperous times, learning how to manage our eating and activities to produce the maximum health benefits is one of our great challenges as machines do more work for us, and high-calorie foods are so easily and cheaply available. Bon Appetit and good health to you at your right weight!

October 8

BEHOLD: THE DIVINE GOAL

Lamp of Divine Love.**

A

ll humans strive for happiness; this is a commonality amongst everyone. Even for those who have self-destructive behavior, if you go deeply enough into their motivations, you will see that there is some anticipated payoff. In a very real way, this world is an experimental laboratory in which every person is testing each one's theory on what will produce the greatest amount of happiness.

Even for one who is ruled by fear, you might say he or she is miserable, and that would be true—however, the need to guard against some perceived threat is thought to be preferable to living a life free of fear. The masochist gets perverse pleasure from his or her own suffering, the sadist from the suffering of others. All seek happiness in one form or another.

Those of us who seek out God-experience have come to the conclusion that there is nothing in this world that can give complete happiness, for anything that is born must die—death, being the end of things, must necessarily take happiness with it. Therefore, only that which is eternal can give fulfillment to one's heart's desire. But eternality alone is not enough, for life without abiding joy is hell; so, ongoing bliss must be part of the equation. The other required element that may seem self-evident, but is also necessary, is that one must be a conscious participant in this experience of eternal bliss. The combination of an eternal self, consciousness, and bliss—Sat, Chid, Ananda—must all be present for real and lasting happiness. There are other elements, of course, such as truth—no one would be satisfied with a life based on lies—expansiveness, purity, openness, the happiness of others, connectivity, and more.

Happily, these elements or qualities are all met in our conception of a Divine Life, or God–fulfilled happiness, which is a reality when all of these aspects are realized in one's life. Be inspired by saints and realized beings around the world, and enter into the experimental laboratory of spiritual practice. We meditate and pray, we chant and sing to the Infinite, we serve others, and we indeed get a taste of happiness. In the beginning, as we deepen our spiritual practice, we may discover a honeymoon phase in which happiness comes easily, but like all honeymoons, this is a stage, not the mature fulfillment.

This is because we are not one hundred percent of one mind. A part of us seeks God; other parts are ruled by passions and fears. Like adding green wood to a fire, if the heat is not intense enough, the green wood can dampen the fire. I have watched green wood stream water out of one end of the log furthest from the intense flame. If the fire is too weak, the green wood will only smolder and even kill the flame. Therefore, the fire of spiritual practice must burn brightly in order to consume all the "green wood" of conflicting desires.

Association with realized souls and those aspirants with burning zeal adds to the flame of enthusiasm and makes us burn bright. Reading or hearing inspired wisdom adds dry, seasoned wood. Making God-contact in deepened meditation, and singing His name throughout the day, inflames the soul and makes it mad for God. Love for God radiates Divine Light in us and helps others to burn brightly. The ego-mind of separation is consumed in this flame and the Divine Goal of Satchidananda—the eternal Self, full-consciousness, and bliss are now enjoyed, fulfilling our deepest heart's desire. The experiment is proven—we now know from our own experience that realizing God alone is the source of true and lasting happiness!

Since God has not arranged for me to give a talk this Sunday, I wish all Canadians a very happy Thanksgiving. I am also including this most perfect song/poem from *The Gospel of Sri Ramakrishna*, a song that Bhupati sang for the great master and his devotees when Ramakrishna was suffering from advanced throat cancer.

> Hallowed be Brahman, the Absolute, the Infinite, the Fathomless!
> Higher than the highest, deeper than the deepest depths!
> Thou are the Light of Truth, the Fount of Love, the Home of Bliss!
> This universe with all its manifold and blessed modes
> Is but the enchanting poem of Thine inexhaustible thought;
> Its beauty overflows on every side.

O Thou Poet, great and primal, in the rhythm of Thy thought
The sun and moon arise and move toward their setting;
The stars, shining like bits of gems, are the fair characters
In which Thy song is written across the blue expanse of sky;
The year, with its six seasons, in tune with the happy earth,
Proclaims Thy glory to the end of time.

The colours of the flowers reveal Thy sovereign Beauty,
The waters in their stillness, Thy deep Serenity;
The thunder-clap unveils to us the terror of Thy law.
Deep is Thine Essence, truly; how can a foolish mind
perceive it?
Wondering, it meditates on Thee from yuga to yuga's end;
Millions upon millions of suns and moons and stars
Bow down to Thee, O Lord, in rapturous awe!

Beholding Thy creation, men and women weep for joy;
The gods and angels worship Thee, O All-pervading Presence!
O Thou, the Fount of Goodness, bestow on us Thy
Knowledge;
Bestow on us devotion, bestow pure love and perfect peace;
And grant us shelter at Thy hallowed feet.[33]

---

33 (pp. 433–434).

October 12

MY SECOND SPIRITUAL MOTHER

Swamiji asks me to read from *Stories as Told by Swami Ramdas* during Satsang, Anandashram, 2005.

Today, we mark the mahasamadhi of a great soul, Swami Satchidananda of Anandashram. Swamiji is my second "Spiritual Mother," being an indispensable help in my sadhana to realize God. His life is a shining example of perfect humility; he was a dedicated and loving disciple of Papa Ramdas and Mother Krishnabai, and a tireless servant of God.

So many thoughts of him flood into me, each memory a thread that by itself is wonderful—and making a woven fabric that is far more than the sum of its parts and past description. So, the puny human mind can only take up a strand at a time and sense its quality—it is all that it can do, and it is so inadequate for the task of knowing the greatness of his beloved Soul.

When I first went to Anandashram in 1998, I was there to do deepened spiritual practice. After two months of pilgrimage around India, I was exhausted from travel and looking forward to being at the ashram for the next four months. I had thought that I would have my room, chant at the mandir, and practice meditation while there. However, I was to discover there was a hidden treasure at the ashram. Daily, I came into contact with Swamiji, his inner worth slowly making itself clear to me.

Somehow, I made my way into his room one evening; the door was open, and I came in and sat on the matted floor, my back against the wall across the room from Swamiji. Swamiji, Gopi (later Swami Muktananda), Anantraman, and a small group of his intimates carried on the business of the ashram: answering letters and attending to endless details. I pronamed on the floor across from him when I came in, sat for an hour, then pronamed, silently rose, and left. Someone came to know that I was doing this and told me no one was allowed in Swamiji's room at that time! I wondered if I was doing something wrong, but Swamiji gave me a nod when I came in, and another nod when I left—at the ashram, inmates (the term for individuals who live at the ashram) are not shy about telling you if you sit in the wrong place; I continued my nocturnal sittings.

One evening, I did not attend Swamiji; I was not feeling well. The next night, he asked about my not coming; it was only then that my mind was completely settled. I was not an unwelcome intruder! One night, I entered and Swamiji immediately said, "Close the door and lock it," to one of the attendants. This was new, totally unexpected—what was happening? "Tonight, we are going to show David how to wear a dhoti," a single cloth that wraps around the waist and hangs to the feet. After giving me a cloth and showing me how to fold it at the waist, Swamiji gave me his own belt for keeping it secure. Swamiji said, "Papa said it is 'dangerous' for Westerners to wear dhotis!" That night, I discovered that I managed very well without the training wheels of a belt and wore the dhoti quite comfortably for most of my time at the ashram after that.

Another time, Swamiji presented a wooden carving of Ganesha to me, such a lovely and unexpected gift. He told me about a statue of Ganesh in India that drinks milk when milk is presented to its trunk. He then called for a glass of milk and a spoon; they were soon brought to his room. So childlike, so innocently, he took a spoonful to the wooden statue's trunk; we both watched in expectation, but alas, no milk disappeared. Finally, without any self-consciousness, Swamiji said, "He is not taking today." Swamiji's role was that of a CEO of a large ashram, responsible, conscientious, and well in command of the ship he navigated, yet standing there together, watching the trunk and spoon full of milk, we were two divine children looking to see what God might do. It left a deep impression on my soul.

We returned to the ashram every few years, and Swamiji and the ashram treated us with such love and solicitude. Swamiji was holding satsang outdoors after his walk. A chair was brought out for him under the banyan tree that Papa had sat under years before. I sat on the ground; mats would appear as if by magic for everyone to sit on. Swamiji called for another chair; all wondered who the visiting dignitary was. Then Swamiji asked me to come and sit on the chair next to him! He reached over and took my hand, and we sat hand in hand for the rest of the satsang; this was repeated at each satsang thereafter. Oh, what treasured moments, my heart fairly bursting its banks, wordlessly singing in awe and gratitude; no thought could intrude upon this feeling of upliftment from this remarkable God-man—my second spiritual Mother.

The next memory thread comes at the end of my last darshan with Swamiji. I ask him for permission to leave. He says, "No, I want you to stay always." I am touched and surprised by this response, but I will not leave without his permission. Suddenly, my mind has to consider living at the ashram only—is this what God is willing for me? Then, after a few minutes, he says that he knows that I must go. "Swamiji, will I see you again?" "Not likely." These simple words wrench my heart, and tears brim in my eyes. I am aswim in grief at the prospect of not having Swamiji living here on earth. Cruel master time is pushing us to make our departure. I bow at his feet. I take a few steps back and bow to the floor again. With all the ashram in attendance on either side, I bow again after a few more steps. During the recession from the long room, seven times I take a few steps and bow to the floor. It feels like tearing my own skin off to leave, but God has ordained the moment.

Once, Swamiji said, "Whenever you think of being here, you are." It was his blessing for me, and it has proven to be true. And when I think of being with him, I am—not just in memory or thought, but in living spirit. These memory-threads are pulled out of my heart and shared with you with all love and reverence. May you taste his spirit, feel his quiet, and know who he is in God—for he was, and continues to be, a great blessing for one and for all.

October 15

Removing Mountains of Worry

Yogacharya David at Glacier National Park, Montana, 2016.**

A nd Jesus said unto them, "Because of your unbelief: for verily I say unto you, If ye have faith as a grain of mustard seed, ye shall say unto this mountain, Remove hence to yonder place; and it shall remove, and nothing shall be impossible unto you" (Matthew 17:20).

Faith is such an interesting word, especially as it pertains to our spiritual understanding. The dictionary tells us faith is complete trust or confidence in someone or something. Jesus often relates faith to spontaneous healing of a remarkable nature. Faith in God, faith in yourself, faith in the goodness of life—so many elements to such a deep word.

You start by mastering the ABCs of spiritual living, and faith is a basic foundation block. Your basic attitude about life tells a lot about your real inner life. Faith in God means you shift the burden onto Him—God is the operator; you are the machine. Your part is to sensitively attune yourself to the Operator of the machine, and be an extension of His will, intelligence, and power.

When acting in perfect concert with Divine Consciousness, you are free of fear and doubt. Perfect faith means absolute comprehension that God is in control. I have had numerous medical tests and procedures and it has surprised me how much fear is exhibited by patients. You can understand concern, and a natural desire not to have to be there, but health hits very close to home, to our attachment to this body; hence, imagination can run rampant and add worry upon worry.

There are, of course, other challenges to faith. Money problems can be a great strain, not having enough, being in debt, and feeling the pressure that you should have more, and it reflects who you are if you do not have enough. Faith in God is knowing who you are, independently of outer circumstances; faith is knowing that God is your supply, and through active attunement with Him, He will lead you toward the prosperity that is exactly right for you.

Another area is relationships: having that perfect someone in your life, children who behave correctly, or problems with parents, friends, or workmates. Faith in God means that He is your primary relationship in life. Through your attunement with Him, you feel His love, and His companionship; you are a friend to others, and in time, draw good associates to you, and He is your protection in difficult relationships.

Faith runs through every part of your life, and each day you can assess your progress in the development of perfect faith. With faith, you have peace, inner assurance, and a true knowing that God is guiding and protecting you. Faith is a true basis for your spiritual life.

October 21

SPEAKING TRUTH

Speakers of Truth: Papa, Mother, Mataji,
portraits in Bhajan Hall, Anandashram.

Years ago, I took a solemn vow to God: *always speak the truth.* There are many disciplines one can take up, but this is one of the most stringent. You may think, "Well, I generally speak the truth," but *generally* won't do—it must be every word.

When I was young, I would tell a lie to avoid getting into trouble. It was based on fear; so, truth and courage must go hand in hand. Even into my adult years, I might have said something that was untrue, even if it was shading a thing to make myself look better. So, to speak the truth means you are simple, open—without guile or pretense—like an innocent child.

There is one essential component that must accompany truth for it to be complete, and that is love; the intention for what is said must be for the highest good of all. I have seen so-called truth used like a bludgeon; a cruel stroke not meant to heal but to hurt and dominate. This is not truth, for the intention behind the revelation comes with a crooked purpose—it is based on a lie. In the Mahabharata, Krishna works to mediate a solution with Duryodhana before the great war, but the egotistical king is spoiling for a fight and refuses to budge.

After the war, Duryodhana angrily berates Krishna for causing the war, and relates a number of events when blaming him—as the reader, we know that what Duryodhana is saying is factually true. Krishna tells Duryodhana that all he says is a lie! To understand Krishna's response, we must go behind the scenes and understand that the Lord is not responding to the outward facts, but to Duryodhana's premise that the war was Krishna's fault—in reality, it was Duryodhana who pushed the world into cataclysm. A series of facts alone does not alone determine truth.

I have seen an individual tell all the worst things about himself at a first meeting in a social situation. On the surface, it may seem he is a humble person. But looking a little deeper, rather than self-abnegation being the reason he is "truthful," he is actually trying to preserve his ego. It is an attempt to inoculate himself, "If the worst is said by me, then you will not criticize me, for I have already done that, and even exaggerated my faults." So, you see, it is not the truth because, one, it is an exaggeration, and two, the motivation is not humility, but egotism—the socially intended purpose is a falsehood.

Once when I was crossing the border into Canada, the guard asked me a question—I went on to add information to my answer. He very curtly cut me off and said that I should only answer the question asked! I took this to heart. Always speaking the truth does not mean we must say everything we know; we only need to know that what we say is true. To make sure this is not a "sin of omission," we need to know our purpose in choosing our words. If by not saying something, someone is harmed, then we should carefully consider our action—we must be clear whether it is the falsehood of fear or desire nature that was driving our words.

There are many tests in everyday circumstances for us to speak and know the truth. Some people have the tendency to see the worst in everything. Listening to the news can make the world seem like a terrible place. However, the news is very one-sided; almost all of it is bad news. Little is said about the vast, vast majority who did not suffer trauma on a particular day—because there is a lack of balance, it is not the truth. On the other hand, there are those who do not want to face a truth because it makes them uncomfortable, or it is painful; this is lopsided in the other direction. And, some will watch a show about an extremely bad situation, and say, "Now, that is **real** life!" But whose real life is it? Does that mean that all those who are not drug addicts, victims of abuse, or are murdered do not have real lives? And then, there are those who become livid at what they hear about a public figure—yet, how are we to know the inner person and the whole situation from what is reported? Truth means we do not distort the reality—truth goes to the heart of the matter with clarity; truth should not be swayed by emotion or bias.

When truth and love go together, it does not diminish the clarity of truth. There are some very hard realities about life, and people commit acts of evil that should not be swept under the rug. However, as a member of this world, and that world includes the evil which is done, if our outrage for wrong action disconnects us from God and the universal vision, then our emotional reaction cannot be said to represent the whole truth. If a group has suffered some trauma in this life, then they see someone else suffer a similar fate, and in response, they see red and are consumed with hatred at the action; then, this can mean that they are not dealing with the whole truth, but with a painful reaction to their own past projected upon the present. Those committing terrible acts must be stopped and stopping them is a loving act for the villain as well as the victim, because although the victimizer may be jailed and face consequences for those actions, the villain is prohibited from further heinous actions which would continue to further darken his or her soul.

To know the truth in its totality, you must have a calm mind. By meditating deeply, you pierce the veil of separation and realize the all-pervasive Spirit—you know truth as God knows it, and through the universal vision, you realize that you cannot be separate from any part of creation. To perceive truth on this level entails more than speaking the truth—however, speaking the truth is a pre-requisite to attaining and becoming established in this higher plane of consciousness. Those who lie and try to cover things up and then go on to say that they represent the highest truth cannot be what they say they are.

Let us explore together the practice of speaking the truth—it is one of the great disciplines we may engage in. As we go even further into it, let us then be focused on realizing the supreme Truth at its highest level. How do we know we have come into knowing this higher truth? The great master, Jesus, said that when you know the truth, it sets you free—no truer words have ever been spoken.

October 30

A TRUE SEXUAL REVOLUTION

Shiva with Parvati: perfect balance
of male and female energy.**

Periodically, we read about the public downfall of men and women due to sexual misbehavior. However, while these cases are portrayed as spectacular, sexual energy is very much with us and is highly influential in all of our everyday lives. It can be innocently "making yourself look nice," or two available people flirting. Then it can take a dark turn, to the extremes of predatory deviancy and sexual violence—and everything in between. To find the high road of sexual energy is the task of all incarnated souls—this is especially true for those treading the path of spiritual practice who require a keen awareness of its benefits and pitfalls.

God designed human bodies to represent sexual opposites: male and female. It has been said that in the higher yugas, in more enlightened times, a couple could produce a baby without sexual contact, through the power of thought or a touch of the hand. However, for most humanity today, coming together as man and woman is the typical means. What has been the most successful formula around the world is for a man and woman to form a bond of committed marriage, then to raise children as a family.

However, sexual energy does not simply run through straight lines of husband and wife. We must learn the wisdom of what it can do for us, and how it can lead to our downfall. There is no doubt that Western society has become highly sexualized, with advertising, film, television, and print media all capitalizing upon the power of sex energy to sell products and ideas. There is precious little in this media to support the beauty of a committed relationship, the sacrifice of love, and the benefits of transmuting sexual energy into creativity and spiritual realization. The efforts to liberate the sexual repression of the past all too often result in debasing relationships such as serial affairs, and the blatant use of sex to sell anything and everything; as well, it is used as the means to gain and exploit power.

Those of us following a spiritual path must come to a right understanding of the role of sexual energy, finding in this most powerful human drive the very means for unleashing its spiritual potential. We know, through our own experience, how potent a force sexual energy is. From childhood to getting on in years, it plays a part in our lives. In religious traditions, sex is many times demonized for the downfall of humankind—and there is truth in this, but that teaching must be properly understood.

The preexistent soul is free of desire nature and common human needs—it is of pure light and consciousness. When soul consciousness mingles with earthly expression, it can be done with a light touch—producing no binding attachments. However, the soul can also become focused on the object of the senses, creating a desire for more and more. This desire nature creates a split of the human self from the real Self. Now, instead of being a pure Soul-expression, awareness is driven by desire nature. Sex, survival instinct, and the desire for power are incredible allurements that are occasionally satisfied, but always call for more. Consciousness, controlled by these forces, falling from its original state of freedom, is now at the beck and call of lower impulses. Sexual energy being so powerful, and having such a drawing power, becomes binding when unregulated in human affairs—it literally and symbolically is the counter-opposite of spiritual freedom.

For animals, sexual energy is powerful but regulated by nature. Certain mammals mate only a few times in life, going years without reproducing. Higher human evolution loses connection with natural regulation; many times, the higher the intelligence, the more cunning and dominant sexual desire can be. To recognize how powerful, pervasive, and destructive sexual energy can be is not to say it is all-powerful, but it is critical to recognize its importance and how demanding a task it is to purify and transmute it. You can think of our mission as twofold: one is to purify sexual energy on a human level, and the second is to raise and transmute it into a wholly new paradigm—the super fuel for Divine Consciousness.

In addition to transmuting sexual energy for spiritual advancement, we also know from history that many great artists and writers have been abstinent during times of intense creativity. The uprush of compelling creative energy draws upon transmuted sexual energy; that is why there is no interest in the sexual act when the energy is flowing up the spine to creative centers. This transformed energy takes away any urge for procreative activity—this is not in any way repressing the energy but giving it creative expression.

Purifying sexual energy on a human level means finding beauty in complementary relationships between the sexes, the ability to transmute it into a creative force, and appreciating its sacred power to bring about new life—a truly remarkable miracle. Mother Hamilton is perhaps unique in spiritual annals, particularly in the West, for teaching about the uplifting beauty in relationships between men and women. Anything from the tasteful use of makeup by ladies to gentlemanly behavior by men, she sought to bring out the best of behavior and consciousness between the sexes—not for the exaltation of base drives, but for coming to know the real expression of Soul through the body. During the infancy of the sexual revolution of the 1960s, Mother had a mature vision for finding the higher road for sexual energy. She delighted in being a woman; she deeply appreciated the role of men; she was for "equal pay for equal work," but also knew that men and women have some great and good differences. I have never known anyone, man or woman, so perfectly balanced in male and female energy, yet she was always the perfect expression of a woman.

Even with this great example before them, there were many who followed Mother's teachings that were tripped up by sexual energy in their path toward God-realization. Every aspirant knows that sexual desire is one of the great oppositional forces in their sadhana. In addition to this general battle, there is also a particular time when entering into spiritual experiences that the full power of sexual energy emerges and seeks to reassert its dominance. Whatever latent desire nature is present, it is now given high-octane fuel from the serpent or kundalini force. Given the powerful role sexual energy plays from the beginning to the end of our spiritual journey, we must know its proper role and be its good and faithful steward.

Keeping the utmost integrity in thought, word, and deed is your greatest ally as a devotee. When feeling sex-energy stimulated (outside of marriage), avoid the situation, and go deeper into prayer and communion with your infinite Beloved. Surrender this impulse at the feet of the Lord and visualize the energy flowing up from the base of the spine into the higher centers of the heart, the ajna (the third eye), and the sahaswara (the crown of the head). This shifts your spiritual practice from any sort of crude form of repression to that of the transmuted energy. Teach yourself to appreciate the superior experience of spiritual purity and freedom. Instruct the mind and desire nature, "Oh mind, observe, see how the energy flowing up the spine leads to bliss, expansiveness, and freedom. Contrast that to how confining, demanding, and ultimately unfulfilling it is when I give into it." Sexual energy is like a snowball at the top of the hill; if you stop it immediately at its beginning, you can more easily master it. But, if you give into it, it starts rolling down the hill, and when you try stopping it after it has become as big as a house, you will be hard-pressed to change it—however, a strong determination, backed by divine will, can move mountains and change the course of a runaway snowball!

Spiritual freedom and purity are vastly superior to anything the five senses can offer. The body uses divine power and directs it through the nerves; when it is channeled through the senses, you are experiencing pure spiritual energy indirectly, and much diluted. However, when you have God-experience, you tap directly into the Source of the intelligence and power that is creating this entire universe. You may think of the yogis sitting in their caves in deep meditation as the ones who are doing without—sitting all alone and nothing interesting happens. In reality, they are united with the kingdom of heaven that is all bliss, fulfillment, and knowledge of God—they are monarchs not of this earth, but of infinite Spirit. By comparison, this earth, in a carnal sense, will seem grubby, shabby, and low-grade.

Husband and wife who, through time and experience, deepen their relationship and spiritual attunement, can successfully transmute all experiences into spiritual awareness. Through divine prompting, there may be a physical union that plays a part in their lives which elevates the sexual experience into spiritual union. The after-effect is merging into an ocean of Infinite expanse. On a human level, there will always be differences between two people, but in Spirit, there is a perfect joining of two souls into One. Mother said that such a union is the highest experience on a human level.

When raised, transmuted sexual energy becomes the very fuel for total spiritual union with God. The sex force that plagues aspirants in their sadhana as an oppositional force and proves to be the downfall of many, now becomes his or her greatest ally. That is why the downward-facing serpent in Genesis is later changed, and in the teachings of Moses and Jesus, the serpent force becomes upward-facing and leads to spiritual illumination.[34]

Through an intelligent application of will with a higher purpose, the aspirant realizes the full benefit of transmuted sexual energy. Creating a list of "do-nots," without understanding its tremendous positive potential, leads to perversion. However, with a clear awareness of all that sexual energy can do and the ways it is transformed into creative endeavors and spiritual upliftment, the aspirant discovers the real source of a truly liberating sexual revolution.

---

34   Elisabeth Haich speaks of this transmutation with great wisdom in her book, *Sexual Energy and Yoga*.

October 31

THE ROSE BLOOMS FROM THE BLOOD UPON THE CROSS

Rose entwined upon the cross.

This writing is dedicated to all those who follow the Way of the Cross and the Christ. It has been said that one should write with one's own blood, and this I do. For the Way of the Cross demands everything of who you are, and everything you wish to be. And what do you receive in return? Everything that is God becomes your own. You walk this path alone, even as Jesus was stripped of everything, even his dignity as he went the Way of the Cross. Blessings to all who strive to emulate our beloved Christ in every detail—in his crucifixion and in his resurrection.

The Rose Blooms from the Blood Upon the Cross

It is upon this cross that I am nailed. I have come but for this purpose. The past, my limitations, and my all are purged from this little cup of myself; for new wine cannot be poured into an old wineskin, lest the skin burst at its seams and the elixir is lost.

I cry out in my agony, I writhe and groan, for it is a heavy price that I pay. "I cannot do this," says my humanness, and yet, somehow, I do. It is Grace that has put me upon my cross; it keeps me there, and will not abandon me, ever. However, I am often more aware of my suffering than sweet Grace—that only wants my highest good.

I suffer not just for my soul's sake, but for all creation. For the lifting of one link of life's chain, lifts all. "Oh Lord, when will this end?" And Grace answers, "When every contaminant has been scoured from the cup, so that nothing of the three lower natures will sour My wine of pure Spirit." Thus am I nailed. In this way I suffer. But, it is the suffering to end all suffering. The bridge may groan under a tremendous load coming over it, but still, it stands. And if this body were to drop off when the work is done? What of it! I have an eternal reward that surpasses the life of this body in the way the sun's light is greater than the firefly.

My friends, be not afraid. Each cross is perfectly fitted to its wearer. Yours is perfect for you, even as mine has been for me. It is Love that sees you through; it is Love that makes all possible. Go boldly forward, knowing that all is in His sweet hands, shaping your soul into His likeness and image with the utmost care. For you are not different from He; He cares for you even as you love the Infinite Beloved. It is love that gives to love—and the rose blooms in the desert.

November 5

THE GREATEST TREASURE IMAGINABLE

Beautiful grounds but they lack depth without God.

Carla and I have wheels under us once again, this time moving south. After a wonderful stop in Ashland, where I met with aspirants and we had a potluck followed by a Service, we continued on our way, 1,200 miles, to Indio, California. It is here that my brother, who recently left the body, had an RV space at a deluxe park. Parked a few spaces away are motorhomes that are worth more than 2 million dollars each. As you might imagine, the grounds are most impressive—ponds and waterfalls, grassy stretches with bougainvillea, petunias, and roses in prolific bloom. We have come to stay here until the new owners take possession—meanwhile, we are cleaning and preparing the space; the summers leave a generous amount of dust and cobwebs to be hydro-washed, thoroughly swept, and polished.

It is interesting to meet the neighbors who come down for the winter months. A friendly, pleasant lot, each with kind condolences for my brother. After being here for a couple of days, it struck me this morning that there is a vibration of materialism here. People naturally thinking of keeping their lots and machines in good condition and repair, but more than that, the topics of conversation about their lives and the lives of their children and grandchildren, travel, etc. Fairly normal, and nothing offensive at all; however, I have been used to talking with those on the spiritual path, and while ordinary topics are part of the conversations with devotees, there is always a subtext of lives being primarily focused on realizing God.

And, what a difference that makes; it opens the world to something much larger, more meaningful than simple existence. It was interesting to hear how grandparents took their children and grandchildren to South Africa for a safari and touring—interesting to a point. Then, the interest wanes as there is nothing more, nothing for the spirit. Their joy at being with their grandchildren and enjoying their excitement is wonderful and meaningful—however, it does not go deep enough. It is a reminder of the vast difference in quality the spiritual journey makes in life.

The real change in leading a spiritual life is connected to an existence above this world. For the devotee, no matter what happens in duality, there is an unchanging supremacy of existence whose happiness and bliss are independent of ordinary life. This crucial difference is incorporated into the aspirant, woven into the fabric of his or her being, to enable the fulfillment of the greatest potential.

Spiritual practice keeps the devotee from falling into ordinary, humdrum existence. Meditation is the touchstone of this higher existence. Giving our life over to God transforms us into being a conscious participant of Divine unfoldment. Ultimately, through the continual focus of the mind on God, we become an expression of Divine Consciousness—knowing it is He alone who thinks, speaks, and acts through us—now the world stands revealed as made up of nothing but God-stuff.

However, on the way up to this exalted state of awareness, we stand with our feet in two worlds: one foot in material existence, the other in the awareness of God's Presence. In this sometimes tenuous, in-between state, we must demonstrate the utmost integrity—not slide into forgetfulness of Divine awareness. We live in this world, we fully participate in it, and we share our concern for its wellbeing, yet we never forget the core of who and what we are in God. That must come first, the world second. We know that in seeking out God first, it is also for the highest good of the world. However, the world oftentimes does not share that view; so, it makes its demands on us. In the process, we must choose—situation by situation; we are tested to put God first.

We are richly privileged to be living this spiritual life, with the highest teachings and the great examples of fully realized masters to guide our way. And in living this life, we are each day tested to see if we will put God first, to love Him most. Let us ever keep this lofty goal uppermost in mind, tread this path with firm steps, never wavering, or faltering. The greatest happiness and spiritual wealth are with us now—it is our greatest treasure imaginable.

November 9

BE A LIFE-LONG LEARNER

Arjuna seeks Truth from Lord Krishna, even though the
answer crushes his own desire—yet the truth sets him on
the right track. Painting, *Krishna Tells the Gita to Arjuna.***

A crucial decision you make in life is when you make a commitment to be a life-long learner. It is a theme you can,
and need to, commit to daily. Learning from experience
is the basis for all personal and spiritual growth. You must be
able to observe yourself and others accurately, then discriminate
between what works and does not work for your good, and, for
the highest good of all concerned—this is the way to learn from
experience.

Blame and shame are two mindsets or attitudes that inhibit
learning. I sometimes joke that to assign blame early and often is

a management tool. You see this with some personalities; their default is to blame others. An enormous consequence of doing this is that it engenders feelings of powerless; you (the blamer), are at the whim of what everyone else does. It also tends to make the mind bitter towards the world that is forever letting you down. Hearing a woman say that all men are such losers begs the question, is there a flaw in her analysis? First is an assessment of the truth: are all men losers? This is unlikely, or at least men are no more so than women. And the second ignored truth: is she unwilling to take responsibility for the men she chooses to get involved with and for her part in the unfolding disastrous relationships? With this blaming attitude, she is not going to learn from her experience—to be savvier and choose differently, as well as to go on and learn how to develop intimacy—something she may definitely want in her life.

Blaming others shows the fragile ego of someone that is aggressively finding fault in order to avoid personal accountability. In the prayer from Anandashram, it states: "Who is to blame is not important, only, how shall we set the situation right?" This is a tremendous statement, for blame is no longer a focal point; rather, the mind becomes intent on resolving an issue. Certainly, we must be able to analyze what went wrong, and that will make each person's actions clear; however, the focus is on how to set the situation right, not who did what.

The second attitude is shame. Shame can be an automatic feeling, with some, that no matter what happens, there is a deep feeling of exaggerated responsibility. Shame wants to hide, to put it all away. An overdeveloped sense of responsibility hampers individuals; they will not see the truth of a situation. Shame is something I came into this world with, for as a child, I did not want to be seen, and I felt a burning shame when things went wrong.

However, shame is a distortion of truth and is therefore false. Also, the desire to hide from facts stops our learning from experience in its tracks. Blame and shame are equally culpable for being villains in our desire to grow from every situation—they are two sides to the one ego coin and are, therefore, equally untrue. We must be able to overcome these tendencies of mind. When similar situations occur again and again, a pattern repeating itself, then we must see clearly without the prejudices of our familiar attitudes of blame and shame.

Detachment is your great ally in knowing the truth. Anger and fear—connected with blame and shame—can rule the mind. When detached, you can look at a situation coolly, without being overheated by anger and fear. You begin by watching your breath. As you observe yourself breathing, you then become aware of your body. Is it holding tension? Is fight, flight, or freeze running throughout your system? As you breathe with all of this, you do not judge, you are simply a witness to what is. You are also aware of your thoughts. Ask: are thoughts triggering panic or rage? Breathe, be aware of your thoughts. Through the observing-self, step back from pure identification with your thoughts, emotions, and physical sensations that had been demanding all the attention.

With detachment, you become quiet, still. In that still-quiet, your reasoning and intuitional mind are optimized. You open yourself to what the truth of a situation is: your thoughts slow down, your emotions are quieted, and your body relaxes—these are all signs that you are successfully detaching from the dominance of body and mind. In this state, you can open a connection to Divine Intelligence. What is the truth here? You set aside your ego-prejudice. You take the risk that truth may completely annihilate what your ego-mind would like, or who you judge to be at fault. Truth trumps opinion. This requires your surrender to something greater than yourself.

Truth may reveal itself instantly, or it can take time for it to unfold in your mind. There may be many lurking, closely-held opinions and emotions that polarize truth away. There have been questions I have had that simmered for months, even years, then one day, quite mysteriously, one came to the front burner, and in a flash, my question was answered. It can take time to step away from these deeply-held limiting beliefs—to be detached. When you are detached, when you are calm and simple, then truth will approach you—make itself known to you.

There is truth with a small "t"—what the truth of a particular situation is—then there is Truth with a capital "T," a direct revelation from the superconscious mind. To really be a life-long learner means that you seek out both levels of truth and Truth: this is the greatest quest in life. There are many scientists, philosophers, and people of all walks of life who interest themselves in what the truth of a particular situation is; but there are few who take the journey all the way to the Truth of what God is. The surprising thing? Truth may reveal itself through observing a flower, or it may come from the lips of a child. Both Truth and truth often come in prime simplicity, going directly to the heart of the matter. Be an explorer of truth and Truth—be forever a life-long learner.

November 12

SWAMI SATCHIDANANDA: A TITAN FOR PEACE

Beloved Pujya Swami Satchidanandaji.**

On November 11, the armistice for WWI was signed at 11 o'clock (11–11, at 11 a.m. in 1918). This ended the fighting in what was billed as the war to end all wars; we now know the fallacy of that hope. From the time Grog hit his neighbor over the head for an extra portion of mammoth, there has been conflict and violence amongst humankind. It is a sad commentary on human development and an enormous waste of lives and materials that could have been used to improve the lot of all. Instead, violence has been used in one way or another to beat each other over the head for much of our recorded history.

Violence and war do not truly serve humanity. When we look at the earth, there is more than enough food and materials for prosperity for all humankind; what is more, including leaving vast tracts of nature intact as natural habitats, when all is intelligently used. This last year, we drove around the North American continent; there were long miles of territory left just as nature made it—excluding the road we were driving on. With a dedication by all that ensures clean air and water, along with a commitment to treat nature as our essential partner and not just a product, we can have a very nice lifestyle and a healthy environment that will satisfy our Creator, showing that we have been wise in our use of His gifts.

A very positive thing today is that the casualties of war have dropped. Measuring by this past decade, and comparing it to the Cold War era, the number of deaths from war is now three times lower, and by WWII numbers, it is now one hundred times lower; that, with a much larger population today. Each life is precious, and each person is a child of God, so one is too many to lose to senseless violence. In addition to the violence of war, there continues to be slavery, violence in homes, and on the streets, and a lack of justice for many in this wide world. However, even with these problems that affect humanity's dear brothers and sisters, we may take joy in the fact that war casualties are so reduced.

From Buddha and Jesus, we have examples of loving compassion as a hallmark of their lives and teachings. Looking at the world through their eyes, we see all humanity, nay, all creation, as intimately connected with our own existence; their welfare is not separate from ours. Papa Ramdas embodied this universal vision, and Master and Mother gave the love of God to one and all. Surely, the world has had teachings and examples enough for us to know what is right and wrong, yet human nature periodically wants to exert itself to dominate over its brothers and sisters—to not lift them up.

In the face of so much of what we see and hear of selfish disregard for others, what are we to think? What are we to do? The most basic teaching is one that can be understood by all; it is called the Golden Rule: Do to others what you would have done to you—in other words, treat others exactly the way you want to be treated. There it is, a little thoughtfulness about what that means to each of us would make this world a heaven on earth. To start the ball rolling, let us start by embodying this principle in our own life from this day out—be kind, considerate, truthful, and compassionate.

While sitting at the feet of one of India's greatest God-men, Swami Satchidananda, I was privileged to see and hear him offer his wisdom to those who came to him. In one instance, Swamiji was proactive in influencing an all-India situation that could have resulted in a war. There was a movement urging Hindus to travel to Ayodhya to tear down a Mosque built on Hindu holy ground 500 hundred years before. Even though there were those of Islam offering to move the Mosque, these firebrands were determined to have a show of force. Swamiji offered to give the leader of this movement time to speak at the ashram. It was in Hindi, so I did not attend. Several of the Ashramites walked away from his talk, saying they could not understand his logic.

After the man's talk, Swamiji met with him privately to reason with him, noting that his actions would lead to violence—but to no avail. Tens of thousands boarded trains for Ayodhya and a firebomb landed on a train car, killing over 40 people. A tragedy that lit a match in a tinder box of sentiment. An incident Swamiji had tried to avoid. It reminded me of Krishna mediating between the Kurus and Pandavas, hoping to avoid a tremendous war, and Rama who sent emissaries to Ravana to negotiate a resolution that would have made the ensuing war unnecessary. Even though these incidents did not avoid conflict, they are examples for us to follow in our work for peace.

Time and again, I witnessed Swami Satchidanandaji counsel loving action in the face of difficulties. If someone in the family was misbehaving, then to serve that one with love was the proffered advice. It was sometimes a different approach than I would have thought of at the time, but always consistent with loving compassion as the highest principle. Today, we celebrate Swamiji's birthday (Nov. 12) and the two themes of peace in the world and Swamiji's life of dedicated service towards finding peace within, peace in families, communities, and the world fit together perfectly.

One must not think that Swamiji lived in some "bubble," insulated from life's difficulties because he spent his years in an ashram. All the world's problems came through the gates of the ashram; he dealt with every sort of human trouble. In fact, in his early days at the ashram, he thought he should live in isolation because he could not serve at the ashram with perfect equanimity in the face of what he saw. God had other plans for him, however, and after a time in which he lived in a hut next to the Ganges, he was called back to seva for Papa, and would never leave again.

Those of us who live in families with challenges, in workplaces that disturb our peace, or those who are made uneasy by world situations can take a page (even a whole book!) out of Swamiji's life and strive for compassionate peace in all situations. Although he was quiet, he was courageous in standing up for principle in the service of peace. Swamiji was definitely a titan member of the Golden Rule Club, and each one of us may add our part to solving war and conflicts through our working for peace within and peace without, even as he so beautifully did throughout his life.

November 16

Do It Now

Swami Satchidananda and Swami Chidananda
with Yogacharya David, Anandashram, India, 1999.

I listened to a recording of Mother talking one-on-one with a devotee from many years ago. It is an interesting glimpse into her teaching someone one-to-one. In it, she tells this man that his spiritual approach has been mental only, that he meditates but it is only out of curiosity, dry of devotion. On the other hand, he is extremely critical of those who are around him. As a result, Mother was feeling the effect of his actions in her own being very greatly, making for an experience that was very tough for her to handle.

In her conversation, she told this man he must develop love. That Mother only gave love, and if one does not, then there are

karmic consequences. That every action has an equal and opposite reaction. She emphasized again, an **opposite** reaction—we
pay the price in body, mind, and soul for the choices we make.
Mother went on in this conversation with this individual to talk
about many things, but this part of her conversation struck me
because of something that happened afterward.

I met with this same man some thirty years later. What had
he done with Mother's exhortation that he cultivate love and
not a mind that criticizes and finds fault with others? When I
met with him, he was married to the woman he had been in love
with since high school. He was, however, disappointed with her,
making remarks that were dismissive and expressing his disappointment. In the privacy of his den, he told me that he thought
that there was a conspiracy in which Jews controlled the reins of
power in this country, and globally. He was also bitter about what
happened to his son, who had a mental illness.

Now, I reflected upon these things. Mother giving this man all
the love of God, working with him to love God, to give love for
hate, and to love at all times. What I experienced thirty years
later was a man filled with bitterness about many things. I did
not find him filled with joy, light, love of God, and humanity. No, I
found him living in a type of mental and emotional prison.

To generalize from this particular situation, we must, each of
us, really analyze ourselves: Is our circle of love growing? Is our
heart softer and more open? What is the trend of our mind—do
I know God, and experience Him more and more? What is the
use of saying we follow a spiritual path if our thoughts and actions
do not increasingly manifest the truth we have been taught?

I have seen firsthand the principles Mother taught about karma.
She quoted the great Newton and his third law of motion: For
every action, there is an equal and opposite reaction; she emphasized the word opposite. That is due to the fact that what you
do comes back to you. Oftentimes, your mind is the instrument

of your own torture when you cultivate a negative attitude. You may be certain that an individual who harshly criticizes others will slice and dice himself or herself when a quiet moment comes; that one cannot possibly feel close to God.

Time slips by so easily. Certainly, there can be situations in which time seems to creep, but then we come to a point when we look back and suddenly so many years have gone by; things we had thought to do have not been done.

On my first pilgrimage to India, I met a famous swami at Anandashram, Swami Chidananda. He had a saying, "Do it now, DIN!" When it is the right thing to do, then DIN, do it now. We must take ourselves in hand and really make the effort if we are to fulfill what our deepest Soul yearns to accomplish in this life.

Whether it is to make health changes, to be more loving in relationships, a change in attitude, getting up earlier, meditating longer, expanding our circle of love, or total surrender to God—DIN, do it now! Do not ignore the call to dive deeper, soar higher; do not live with regret for a single day wasted. We are not here to lead a half-dead, zombie life, sleepwalking through old habits that no longer serve us. Rather, we are here to live a dynamic life filled with love, light, and wisdom—a God-realized life.

November 19

AM I MY BROTHER AND MY SISTER'S KEEPER?

Ram and Sita, after rescuing Sita from the bestial Ravana. Lakshman,
Ram's brother (standing on the right), always looked at his sister-in-law,
the lovely Sita, as his mother, even though they traveled long years
together in the wilderness—always the perfect gentleman.**

There has been much in the news about men in high posi-
tions who have abused their power by taking advantage of
women, anywhere from exercising poor judgment about
sexual advancements to criminal molestation and rape. It is as if
the stars have taken a turn and what has occurred behind closed
doors has now come into the open.

After Cain murdered his brother, Abel, he infamously said to God when he was asked about Abel, "Am I my brother's keeper?" (Genesis 4:9). The answer is, "Yes, of course, you are!" Not only do you not murder your brother out of jealousy, but you are here to positively love and care for him. And the one who parses words may ask, "Who is my brother?" The same question was put to Jesus when he was asked, "Who is my neighbor?" The master answered that question by relating a story about the good Samaritan. The hero in the story, a man from Samaria, stopped to help a hurt man on the side of the road after a priest and Levite had passed him by (both were considered holy men by birth). Remembering that Samaritans were considered untouchable by those in Jesus' audience, it was just such an unlikely fellow who rendered assistance to the stranger. The moral of the story: all of humanity are our neighbors and our brothers and sisters (Luke 10:29–37).

This applies to our sisters, as well. Mother Hamilton loved the differences between the sexes, and she emphasized to us the proper relationship between the two. Some thought Mother was not with the times; however, great principles prove themselves to be timeless. We collectively suffer when true principles are trampled; we are all affected when any one of our sisters is treated with disrespect—her inner qualities not seen or even looked for.

I am sure many of us have had moments when we were not at our best in how we have treated one another. However, let us learn from our mistakes and strive to do better. Remember, nothing is done in secret that will not be shouted from the rooftops! Let us be our brother's and our sister's keepers and support one another, bring out the best in one another. Our time here is short, but we are accountable for what we do, so let us do right at all times and in all places; and more than that, see all others in their true essence—as beings of Divine origins, and to be respected as such.

November 22

THANKSGIVING: GRATITUDE IN ACTION

Portraits of Mother Hamilton and Paramhansa Yogananda.

My Guru-lineage and realized Masters the world over, to whom I bow in humble gratitude.

Thursday, November 23: A National Day of Thanksgiving.

An observation I have made through the years: when feeling close to God, gratitude comes naturally; and whenever I am mindful of feeling gratitude, it lifts my mood and makes me feel closer to God—gratitude and God are definitely closely linked. A prescription I make when someone is feeling depressed: for a minimum of 30 days, make a list of at least three things you are grateful for at the end of the day. Believe it or not, someone who is feeling very down has a hard time coming up with even three things. However, paying attention to three gratitudes daily makes the difference; it lifts the mood and zeroes the attention in on looking for what is good, instead of only seeing what is wrong.

There are many reasons why individuals become discouraged about life, some personal, some global. A negative-tamasic mood robs one of joy and draws a curtain between the soul and the true Self. We must have perspective in life. Knowing that the Light perpetually shines in the darkness is the greatest reason for optimism, at all times and in all places. Everything works for the ultimate good, and through intense focus on God, the soul is lifted out of duality and is established in bliss. For spiritually aspiring sadhakas, this is the ultimate for which to feel gratitude: to know that you have the Goal of goals in mind (a remarkable purpose), and the capacity to achieve this Goal in this lifetime is cause for great celebration and joy—a true day of thanksgiving.

What a wonderful thing to have a day dedicated to Thanksgiving. But, do not limit giving thanks to just one day—but for all days. Start a conversation with God that lasts throughout your waking hours. Look for micro-events that you might normally take for granted, and then express your gratitude to your Creator for it. I think of those whose legs do not work, and then my ability to stand up and walk from here to there—an action many take completely for granted; yet, how wonderful to be able to do just that—to simply get up and walk. Or, to look out on the day with two eyes that see, to breathe freely, to move a hand, even to have a thought—especially a thought of our infinite Beloved. Notice micro-events all through the day, then say, "Lord, what a wonderful thing to be able to do: to look at the sky, breathe the air, give someone a smile, strive for a goal; this life is a miracle in action, a joy to behold! Even the things that dissatisfy me, You have put them into my mind so that life can be better, so that I can work for improvement; for that inspiration to improve, I give thanks."

If you are realistic, from a human standpoint, there are many more things you do not have control over than what you do. And, in your daily life, you must choose to focus your mind on certain things, and not on others. That is efficiency. When something requires your attention, you screen out of the conscious mind that which is not essential to the moment. In that way, you can concentrate your energies on what is needed. Through habit, many focus on what is, or can, go wrong—not on what is going smoothly. An airline pilot told me that his primary job is to anticipate what can go wrong, such as a lightning storm ahead, and then to avoid it. This is putting looking for problems to positive use. However, most who focus on what they do not like, or are afraid of, are not using their time and energy to good effect. They simply repeat frightful or repugnant thoughts over and again, without any purpose, except to wear themselves out and cause great unhappiness.

You must use wise discernment in choosing your thoughts. Ask yourself: What is the practical effect of this thought? Does this thought keep me safer, make me more productive and happier? Or, does this thought sap my life-energy, rob me of joy, and bring me to a standstill? Your thoughts steer your life—are you skillfully navigating toward positive goals? Or, are you getting stranded on the shoals of indecision, or mindlessly headed into storms of chaotic living? Your thoughts are the one thing you can definitely choose; with practice, you become master of what you focus your powerful mind upon: aim to bring about only the highest-minded results.

I do not know why in modern culture there is such a cynical dismissiveness of the lessons that the story *Pollyanna* teaches. You will hear, "Oh, don't be Pollyannaish," said with complete ridicule. But let us look at the story. A little girl is living with her missionary parents in a far-off country, and she really wants a doll for Christmas. Instead, what comes by way of donations are crutches. She is so disappointed. Her father knows her deflated feeling and kindly suggests that she play *The Glad Game*. Think of all the things she is glad for; that is the game. Isn't she glad she doesn't need crutches? She tries it, and she feels better. Then, she makes *The Glad Game* her habit. Her parents subsequently die, and the little girl is sent to live with a relative who does not want or like her. But, she continues her *Glad Game*, and she is so infectious about it that she changes the people around her for the better—eventually, even her bitter aunt opens up. *The Glad Game* her father taught her not only helped her survive psychologically, but it attracted people to her and even changed the lives of a community. What would critics have you tell her? To face reality. She had a load full of hard reality in her life she could scarcely avoid! She survived and even thrived through terribly difficult circumstances by looking for the good when it seemed that life gave her nothing but hard knocks. Sounds like a lesson we could all draw inspiration from, not deride from some superior tower of ridicule.

So, play your own *Glad Game* with God—bring to mind the micro-reasons for gratitude in your daily life: when you have enough money for food and shelter, it is no small thing; to have the power to walk, talk, and carry on in your life is a miraculous blessing; daily, you have an enormous opportunity to fill your life with gratitude. And most of all, you have been taught the truth by the greatest of spiritual masters; you are on the path to becoming a spiritual master yourself, and you have spiritual brothers and sisters to help you on your way—these are the greatest blessings, and more than ample reason to have gratitude every moment of every day. Cultivate your gratitude conversation with God until it is the most natural thing in the world, and you will find that life is, perhaps, made up of a very few big events that many people look for to validate something to be grateful for, but, easily, there are unending micro-events in everyday existence that the gratitude habit makes you aware of, and brings to you joy and true happiness for yourself and those around you. A very happy day of Thanksgiving to you and to all.

A devotee just sent this link for a University of Washington medical article, quoting scientific studies that confirm that gratitude is healthy for: a stronger sense of well-being, a healthier heart, love of job, better sleep, ability to cope with stress, and more. I am glad that science is catching up![35]

---

35   https://rightasrain.uwmedicine.org/mind/
well-being/5-surprising-health-benefits-gratitude

November 26

BUILDING YOUR TEMPLE

Dome of the Rock Shrine, Jerusalem:
where Muhammad ascended to Heaven.**

Spiritual progress does not mean development only in one aspect of a human being. His emotional, intellectual, and dynamic nature should evolve simultaneously. Karma is the foundation, Jnana the upper structure, and the dome at the top is Bhakti.[36]

—SWAMI RAMDAS

Papa (Swami Ramdas,) says so much in words that are easily understood by sincere aspirants—it is a gift of his spiritual genius. However, we may benefit from contemplating what

---

36   Anandashram, *Thought for the Day.* www.anandashram.org

Papa states and expanding on how we can apply it in daily life.

Great masters, such as Swami Ramdas, like us to live a balanced life. Papa and others, such as the Buddha, experienced intense sadhana, or spiritual practice, in order to realize the great Truth. Upon attaining the supreme state of realization, they are then in a position to say what was essential in their journey, and what was either not essential to their attaining realization, or is not universally necessary for all aspirants, and, therefore, need not be duplicated. Buddha articulated the "Middle Path," which was not what he practiced, but it was what he prescribed to all who followed his teachings to attain Nirvana. Papa also went through extreme practices, but after he attained Sahaja Samadhi, he said that others need not be so austere.

Papa goes on to verbally paint a picture in the above teaching. He states that Karma Yoga is the foundation for spiritual living. Karma means action: it is what you physically do in life. You are to live a life of purity, starting with eating healthy foods in moderation—not with avarice; you work, and do all actions in the spirit of service to God in others—not for greed; and, all that you speak, is in concert with the highest truth you know—do not lie. In your spiritual quest, you build the foundation of your spiritual life with actions that match what you know to be the highest light.

When Papa says the intellectual (Jnana) builds the upper structure of spiritual practice, he is not speaking here of gaining additional facts, reading books for knowledge, or any other type of, what you would normally think of as, intellectual endeavors; Jnana means wisdom, and more specifically, discrimination. In your spiritual practice, you must make choices along the way, and the higher up you go on the spiritual ladder of consciousness, the more discernment you need.

Krishna stated that extra-ordinary powers are pitfalls for real aspirants. Mother taught, "Keep your mind on God." A statement so plain that you may not comprehend its full significance until you are well along the path.

Keeping your mind on God translates into **not** getting seduced by sex, greed, power, name or fame, and the many other traps that present themselves to you as you ascend the spinal stairway. Discernment is absolutely necessary as you build a life upwards—knowing that you must have a solid foundation and well-constructed upper stories to prepare yourself to succeed in the great quest.

Bhakti, intense love, and attraction for attaining the supreme state of God-realization, makes the dome for your temple of spiritual practice—that which caps the spiritual life with success. The drawing power of love is required for the kind of complete self-surrender that is necessary to be assumed in Divine Consciousness.

There is no greater power in all of creation than love; it makes you want to be absorbed in your Beloved and lose yourself in Him. Physical activity done in service and the practice of wise discernment, by themselves, are not enough to take you all the way. When lifted into the highest centers of consciousness, you focus on one thing, the Goal of goals—consummation in samadhi by ultimate Love. Divine Union is the consequence of this total surrender and leaves behind all spiritual practices when lover and Beloved merge and become One.

Building your spiritual temple by constructing a solid foundation, intelligently designed frames for the upper structure, and a brilliantly radiating dome in your daily life is a wonderful thing; it shows you what is needed in order to realize God. But knowing the way and being immersed in the supreme Reality is not the same thing. Be inspired by these beautiful teachings from Papa: take the complete plunge into spiritual life with total enthusiasm—be absorbed into the Infinite Beloved who dwells beyond time and space and all form—realize the Truth even as the Buddha, Papa, and Mother so fully immersed themselves in the highest Reality, and then help others to build their own temples of spiritual practice with nothing but the very finest materials.

December 1

WE ARE ALL RENTERS—NOT BUYERS!

Yogacharya David at Udayagiri Caves, India, 2013.**

t is a natural thing when coming into this world without a conscious awareness of your larger existence, to feel that this body
and this world are your all and all. However, this becomes a
problem since everything here is temporary. The basis for your
existence is quick and flows through an hourglass. This can only
provoke anxiety on some deep, existential level, especially as you
see the sand running out for yourself or others.

The question then must be asked, "Is there no alternative?" This
question has been the prodding for spiritual quests since humans
have walked the earth; from looking up at the stars while beside a
warming fire to using an electron microscope when exploring the
atomic building blocks of creation.

Through the Renaissance and the Age of Reason, science gained a much-deserved credibility for answering questions as to the nature of this universe. However, when questions regarding the nature of the soul, the "why" of life, become the topic, you are summarily sent to the philosophy department. Quite often in the philosophy department, you are shown the structure of a valid argument (is your argument properly formulated?) but not much to satisfy a questing soul. This deeper yearning is considered by the philosophical to be the province of emotional religionism and held at arm's length by the "logical" as stemming from a magical brew of illogic. And when you turn your attention to much of what religion is today, you find it formulated on faith, "Here is the creed, accept the creed—the real answers for the soul will be found when life is up." Ah, what to do for a questing soul who does not have faith in the creed?

In my case, as with many of us, my interest took me to those who spoke of having actual experiences, of experiencing states of consciousness that positively described what, at my core, my soul needed to know. Beyond being interesting to hear about, these experiences made my soul say, "Yes!" These are mystical experiences; that is, experiences that reach beyond the five senses and are not the product of logic, but they hold up to logical scrutiny when you accept the premise of the experience. They also have the added virtue that they are not formulaic, nor are they in need of accepting a creed, but they are based on those seeking out and having their own experience. If science, philosophy, or the acceptance of a creed satisfies a soul, then that is sufficient. However, I needed something more—I needed to touch Truth and to experience it in such a way that my soul found complete satisfaction in the here and now.

A product of this exploration for me not only emphasized the temporary nature of life in a body, nothing great in that obvious deduction, but also, it gave me experiences in what transcends transitory nature: the ever-existent Soul. During these particular experiences, I was lifted above the imprisoning limitations of normal ego-bounds and I saw and knew that "I" was never created, for I was without beginning, or end—this "knowing" was liberating beyond belief. I saw that I existed before taking incarnation in this body and I knew that I would continue to exist after this body has returned to its natural elements. I experienced that I have always been and will always be. I found this awareness to be sublime; it filled me with an inner assurance and satisfied my soul's quest.

Today, the exploration continues; however, knowing the truth of the existence of a transcendent Soul is a definite foundation upon which to build. It is a reminder that for this body or for the possession of any material thing: having a position in life, membership in a family, or in any other relative connection to creation, I am a renter, not a buyer—everything created comes with an expiry date.

There is the story of the manager of an estate. The owner was rarely seen, so the manager alone was responsible for its smooth functioning. After some time, the estate manager became arrogant in his position. One day, the owner arrived with a new plan for the estate that did not include the need for the manager. The manager was sent packing, with nothing but a few personal possessions. Likewise, we should all be proper managers of what God has given us, knowing that one day, we too will be sent packing with nothing but our self, the quality of our being, to recommend us. We will then report to the supreme Creator, who is no respecter of title, money, or position—all stand equally before the all-knowing One. Only one thing will count: the quality of our inner self—built with a lifetime of what we think, say, and do—our consciousness that exudes from our innermost being. That is what lasts, and that is what counts.

December 3

Right Relationship With Power

The lilies of the field, "Even Solomon in all his glory
was not arrayed like one of these" (Matthew 6:29).**

Think of the power of a seed growing into a great tree, a supernova collapsing into a black hole that swallows everything that comes near it, including light, and the power that creates this fantastical universe we live in. Now, consider this same power exists in you as a Son-of-God in Christ Consciousness. The great master said that when you have faith the size of a mustard seed, you can move mountains—think of it! (Matthew 17:20).

However, it is a very good thing that we are not conscious of this vast potential for remarkable powers when we are still working to properly manage what power we have been given. Each of us has power, whether we think of it in that way or not. We have the power of thought, movement, speech, and the ability to make plans and carry them out—we could call these everyday powers. As we move into a broadening world of power, it may bring us parental authority, being a manager or business owner, a political position, or being in the public eye—making us accountable for the increasing influence we have.

Each one of us is to be a beneficial steward of what we have been given in this life. Taking the attitude of being a servant of the Most-High, no matter the position we hold, puts us into right relationship with power. When a position of authority is in our purview, then working for the highest good of all keeps us on the path of right action. Again, the master said that according to what we are given, whether it is money, position, or authority, according to how we use that power, we may be given more, or, if it is misused—that which we have will be taken away (Matthew 25:14–40). So, whether we are a janitor or the head of the company, we are equally accountable when standing before our Heavenly Father.

When 36 years old, Mother Teresa of Calcutta moved to the streets to serve the poorest of the poor—not a typical path to a high worldly position. Yet, her name endures; she has become an iconic personality symbolizing selfless service. No one would have guessed this would be the result when she started out, leaving her comfortable teaching position for an uncertain life on the streets—as she felt prompted to do by her beloved Christ. However, she endured with uncommon integrity and humility; as a result, she was given more worldly power. Throughout it all, she kept her spiritual bearings clearly in sight. When name and fame pursued her from nook and cranny around the world, she kept God and service to those who needed it most to the fore, both for herself and those who followed in her footsteps. She began with so little, and it grew into a worldwide phenomenon.

When undergoing spiritual transformation, I was taken through a time when spiritual powers naturally came to me; among these powers was knowing future events, desires materialized, and the ability to read the minds of others. As this occurred, I had Mother's teachings in the forefront of my mind, and Krishna's exhortation from the *Bhagavad Gita*—such powers are considered an impediment to realization by aspiring yogis. I was also aware of a deep-down attraction I felt for these powers, and that concerned me. So, I asked God to take all such power away from me—and He did.

Another power in which I had pride was intellect. Through the experiences God gave me, He periodically took away my intellect. I came to know that intellect is but an extension of consciousness, but not essential to it. In fact, the most brilliant experiences I have been given have not been derived from intellect—proving to me its inferiority. In addition to intellect, the powers of movement and speech have also been taken away at various times, showing how little I am in control of those, and how easily they can all be taken away—in reality, all are gifts from the Divine. This teaches me deep humility and gives me a natural outpouring of gratitude for what is given at any particular moment. These *everyday powers* can easily be taken for granted, but I know without a doubt that God is the Source of every power that flows through this and every form. Having right relationship with power enables me to be in right relationship with my Creator. Power, like so many attributes of God, is then taken off the altar of false gods to be worshiped—bringing lasting peace and harmony to the Soul.

December 8

RIGHT RELATIONSHIP WITH GOD AND TITHING

Buddha statue with money offerings.**

Dear _____,

It is wonderful to hear from you, so glad these discourses are of value to you; this is a perfect way to stay in contact when we are at distant places from one another.

You have brought up the subject of tithing: it is a relationship between the soul and God. Yes, there are practical aspects on both sides, as it provides us money for the work we do for God and Gurus, and of course, there is only the rare person who could not use more money for personal use. However, tithing touches on parts of life that go beyond practicalities.

Carla and I tithe 10 percent for every dollar of our personal income. When I do, it sets up a relationship between God and me. Giving the "first fruits" to God puts me in mind of gratitude for what is received. It acknowledges that God is the Source of all good, including prosperity on a material level, and it puts me in right relationship with my Creator.

When we receive tithes, we put them on the altar under Master's picture (when we are on Camano). We offer it to God and Gurus in gratitude, then we have an account that is for the tithes and use those funds for the work we do for God and Gurus.

I understand that money can be tight; I have been in that situation a time or two myself! I also think it is wonderful that you are in a position to help others. I had the blessing to adopt a child and have been a support to others at various times, so I know how important it is for the one receiving that support, as well as how it feels to fulfill God's will when giving it. Blessings to you, and blessings for this young man—that he may receive what is being offered and thrive.

I do not ask for anything for what I do for God and Gurus; in fact, I took a vow before Mother not to do so. So, I truly have no expectation that anyone should give anything. Many a time, the ones I have given the most to do not reciprocate. While others I have not spent much time and effort with on a personal basis are faithful to a fault in supporting this work. Such is the way of God; He has made it so that we have never been without shelter or food, and we have had funds to do what is necessary for Mother's work.

So, it comes down to right relationship between the soul and God. What can practically be tithed, and what feels right? Go inside and ask God, "What is the right thing here so that You and I are straight with each other?" For many years, I did not think of tithing that much. When I saw Mother, I would put some money in the bowl on the way out. Later, I was sorry for my casual attitude—not really thinking of what Mother might need, and perhaps even more, of my own immaturity. And not because Mother thought the less of me, for many of those years I was a student and not flush with funds, but because I was not mindful. Mother was the most important person in my life; she meant everything to me, but I was not conscious of how that should have translated into tithing. Surely, any extra money would have helped her, but it really reflected my own lack of thoughtfulness.

Later, I stepped forward at a time when Mother needed it and was able to give substantial support. For that, I feel such gratitude. Even when I was supporting a family and not having extra, God gave me the ability to do something that made me feel good and right with God and was of practical help to Mother.

I do not purport to say what is right for each person; I only know what my own journey is, and has been, on this point. Even though you hesitated in bringing it up, I think it is a topic we all live with, and it is important. So, I am glad you have given me an opportunity to tell you something of my thoughts; and that by bringing it up with me, you are bringing it out into the light. At the end of the day, you want to feel that you are in right relationship with God and Gurus—that you may stand easy and breathe the fresh air of openness and truth.

With all love and blessings,
David

December 17

O Holy Night

Holy Night Nativity.**

Early morning reveries reveal much about the imagery that embodies the holy night of Jesus' birth. Deep in my meditative mind, the sound of Aum/Amen resounds like a symphony of angels emanating from the heavens. Multifarious sounds ring in constancy; expanding consciousness can lift you from worldly clinging and announce the birth of something new, something rare in this world—Divinity incarnating into this world as all is quiet of worldly sounds and reverberates with heavenly song.

Innocent and peaceful sheep (good tendencies) are in the fields, and shepherds (those watchful of good tendencies and desire for Self-realization) are awake for the holy night. Heavenly forces are at work; the night sky shines with portents of shimmering light seen in meditative watchfulness. Inner illumination announces a sacred birth. Individuals can cultivate a desire to be a good and faithful servant of God, but it is only by Grace being born into the world of the individual that spiritual realization can really come into its own. An Inner light is calling to awaken the shepherds—something special is coming; the fulfillment of a promise made at the foundation of creation—the birth of a God-man, a God-woman!

Mary (feeling-nature purified into surrender to intuition) and Joseph (reason in proud obedience to God's will) are the parents of this new-born awareness. The wise (those who have given the gold of material desires and possessions, the frankincense of heavenly worship, and the myrrh of the bitter disappointments in life), lay at the feet of God their gifts of all they have, and all that they are. What a gathering—what a perfect attunement to God's most perfect gift to the world!

It is both a fulfillment of a promise and only a beginning; there is much more to go through; the Christ-child is only now born and must suffer the glorious Way. King Herod, filled with great passions, rises up in murderous rage with the desire to kill sacredness. These Herod-passions are steered clear of by the sincere, and the child is secreted away into the land of Egypt, preserved in safekeeping until the time is right for inborn Divinity to make its way up the circuit (of spinal consciousness) in Galilee.

So, the story of God-incarnate unfolds. And it all begins in humble and wondrous beginnings on that holy night that promises so much. Be watchful for those portents that come to the surrendered and the humble. Listen for the celestial sounds of sacred watches; look for the blessed star that announces a new life in God; feel those powerful forces in motion in heaven and on earth; and be among the faithful looking to their Lord of Christly Divine Intelligence that guides them into union with the Holy Ghost (Divine Mother) and their Heavenly Father through the awakened Son of God within.

December 18

SURRENDER GIVES BIRTH TO THE CHRIST

The Holy Family.**

M ary is feeling-nature purified into surrender to intuition. As the story goes, Mary receives a visitation from an angel, a communication from the Infinite, that she is to bear a child. From the human perspective, she must reflect on the fact that she is unmarried and has not been with a man; this pregnancy will destroy her reputation, ruin her betrothal with Joseph, and leave her with an uncertain and difficult future—she will be publicly shamed, with a high probability that she will be stoned to death. Even with all of this, Mary replies, "Behold the handmaid of the Lord, be it unto me according to thy word." And the angel departed from her (Luke 1:38). Such perfect surrender to a life-changing and difficult task from God.

Joseph goes through his own trial when he hears from Mary the disappointing news of her pregnancy. He makes a decision that he will not publicly humiliate her and thus avoid a stoning of Mary, and he will, somehow, privately annul their engagement and put her away. While he is taking the time to think this through, he has a dream. Joseph is told that the child is a product of a Divine act and that he should take Mary to be his wife. He is a thoughtful man. He turns it over in his mind, and, in the end—he surrenders.

Mary represents feeling-nature, even as Eve from the Garden of Eden. Eve succumbs to temptation, and then Adam follows. Adam represents reason. We all know Adam and Eve from our own inner struggles. Eve is feeling, which is feeling-nature of the senses and emotions—both closely tied together. The senses and emotions get triggered by someone or something tempting us. Even though we know it is wrong, the feeling nature is so strong that reason will work itself around the temptation to where it thinks wrong is right; or perhaps it tells itself, "I don't care what the consequences are; this is what I want!" Eventually, we do care about the consequences, especially after the magnetic draw of allurement wears off.

Thus, in her surrender, Mary redeems Eve, even as Joseph saves Adam. These acts of submission to God pave the way for the birth of the Christ-child—the only begotten Son of God born in man—not just in one person—anyone who completely surrenders heart and mind to God may become a Son of God. In talking about this with C. after Service, he added something that came to him from God. Adam and Eve have two children: Abel and Cain. Abel is the good son; Cain is the bad seed. Abel and Cain represent duality, so when Adam and Eve (reason and feeling) go against the will of God, the dual forces of good and bad are born.

This part I had been shown by God before, and I have related it in my talks. However, C. then pointed out that Mary and Joseph had only one child, a Christ-child. Christ Consciousness is the one that rises above duality and is in union with God. In Christ Consciousness, there continues to be a dual nature—in the sense that there is the Father and there is the Son. However, this is not the same as the positive and negative poles of Abel and Cain, as is further represented by the two thieves on either side of the Christ during the crucifixion. Christ is not a negative pole to God but is one with the Father—in this case, duality is the thin veil separating the two. Christ Consciousness resurrects union with God beyond the duality of good and evil.

Going against God's will brings duality which separates us from God. The negative pole of Cain murders what is good inside Abel. However, good cannot be completely destroyed, even in the most evil person. For God says to Cain, "What hast thou done? The voice of thy brother's blood crieth unto me from the ground" (Genesis 4:10). Goodness cannot be completely eradicated, for its blood, its essence, cries out from the ground, or the sub-conscious mind. No matter how bad someone is, the opposite of good remains buried, perhaps deeply buried, but it continues to cry out.

Total surrender to God's will brings about the birth of the Savior, the One who lifts you above good and evil, where the lion and the lamb lie together in peaceful harmony. This is a tremendous message, worthy of salutations from all humankind—a message that is truly a universal proclamation for the ultimate destiny of all.

December 24

A WONDERFUL TIME OF THE YEAR

Happy Birthday, Mother Hamilton! A Guru who knew how to have fun!

As with many, Christmas is a wonderful time of year for me. I love the message and the feeling of the real reason for the season as well as the decorative lights during, what is for us, the darkest time of year, the little traditions celebrated, and deepened meditation upon the personal and impersonal Christ. I knew that the special feeling that comes with our Christmas Service in Maple Ridge and on Camano Island was to be the heart of a spiritual and a social Christmas, and that afterward, it would be a time of growing inner focus. Carla also had elective surgery this last week, and so recovery time for her added to being home and more reclusive.

I realize that, for some, it is also a season that brings up those things that have been lost. I have definitely lived long enough to have people and situations that are no longer here. Christmas celebrations with my Guru come to mind, and how she brought such life and meaning to the season as well as to her birthday celebration on Christmas Day. However, I will say that a very definite virtue of a deepened communion with God is that it is the sole relationship that continues to deepen, glow, and provide life, inspiration, renewal, and ever-new joy to devotees; it never fades with time. In God-consciousness, all people, past and present, feel near and dear. So, while I may miss certain interactions from the past, the sting of loss is replaced with a warm glow. When you use the feeling of loss to deepen the connection with your infinite Beloved, then wounds are healed and loss becomes gain.

It is the one thing about God—He is not a thing of the past, or a story that becomes staid, but a deep well of living waters that brings new birth and new openings to the most tremendous gift ever given to all God's children. The angels' universal sound is singing its song in my ears and beyond; the warm Christ-light is blazing as the leading star and it lights the Christmas tree of my spine and brain, and love is glowing from my heart, radiating out to all creation. These thought-feelings fill my heart, mind, and soul, and I share them with one and all—there is no limit, no aloneness, no feeling of loss possible in this ever-new birth. This is the gift I wish, hope, and pray for one and all—that you share in this God-experience. You will find it waiting for you to unwrap from under your tree-of-life, right within you. There are many wonderful things about this world, but none compares to the universal Christ-presence that has been sown throughout creation, and that is most definitely residing deeply in you.

P.S. Thank you so much for your cards and gifts; each one is received with love and gratitude. I want to share with you a list of some holiday movies we enjoy. All, I think, are family-friendly, though some may not appeal to little children—of course, you may not like all of them as much as I do, but, I think you will find there are many gems here, and hopefully, some you may not know and will come as delightful surprises—others simply reminders to see again.

It's a Wonderful Life (spoiler alert, Clarence gets his wings!); White Christmas (when young, I thought musicals were stupid; now, many are delightful!); How the Grinch Stole Christmas (Christmas does not come from a store, it is much, much more!); Elf (You are an angry elf!); Lost Christmas (Who would think Shiva would save Christmas?); The Santa Clause (I like the sequels as well); The Last Holiday (Queen Latifah to God: "You just mess'n with me now!"); Christmas with the Kranks (Botox scene makes me laugh every time); Christmas in Connecticut (A fun Classic); Jesus of Nazareth (Zeffirelli makes each scene look like a masterpiece painting—and James Earl Jones plays a wonderful wise man—you can watch it up to the birth of Jesus); A Christmas Carol (there are many versions, but Alastair Sim makes the most grumpy and then joyfully-redeemed Scrooge in this 1951 classic); Holiday Inn (You just have to love corny musicals, and Fred Astaire's dancing, of course); A Christmas Story (You'll shoot your eye out!); and Miracle on 34th Street (Edmund Gwenn makes the best Santa!).

December 27

After Christmas Glow

The deeds and miracles of Saint Nicholas.**

The St. Nicholas tradition tells us that St. Nicholas used his family's wealth to help those without means. In one case, he dropped gold coins into the drying socks of three young sisters who had no money for dowries—without which, they would eventually be driven to live on the streets by any means they could.

Not that it is so rare in this world, but I am privy to knowing of many acts of kindness that are done quietly and without a need to be known to the world. In years past, prior to Christmas celebrations, I have done something to be of help to another—given some gifts to those who could not afford them, or food or clothing to those in need—I would do it in the name of someone for whom I would ordinarily buy a gift (but did not really need another thing). This deed may have been done openly in the name of someone, or anonymously; either way, in my mind, it was done in the person's name for whom this gift was intended—the story of that deed was their gift.

This past Christmas Season, I have seen devotees giving from their hearts, and it has come as special gifts to me. In the late-night hours tonight (or is it early morning?), just as I was ready to say goodnight, God gave me the inspiration to tell you a few of the good deeds done—as a gift for you. So, I have turned the Christmas tree lights back on, and in their glow, I write to you. Devotees of God are natural givers, and I think these will warm your heart, just as they have mine.

Gift number one unwrapped: A couple who have raised their own children came to know of a teenager who was without a home. They offered this young person their home and their love to provide a stable base and a caring family from which to have a chance to begin a new life. Within a short amount of time, he went from very poor grades in school, when living in chaos, to getting As and Bs after joining this new family. It was quite a commitment by this couple, but what a change and opportunity being given to this young person.

Gift number two to set your heart aglow: A few devotees have banded together to send money to a family that is known to them in Africa. There has been ongoing support for this far-away family by a devotee-couple after getting to know them while on a trip there. And then, in celebration of this holy season, a small group got together to send special funds for Christmas to this family who work hard, but opportunities do not allow for even some basic needs. So, willing, caring hands have joined together to make Christmas special for a family halfway around the world.

Gift number three is all about giving hearts and faith in God: One yogi-couple with a family came to know of another nearby family who were having a difficult time. The father was not able to work due to an injury, the mother works two jobs, and the three children (two of whom have full faith and confidence in Santa) were without any gifts for Christmas—while they waited for some funds to come that had not yet materialized. This spiritual family gave their travel money to the family-in-need without hesitation, travel money they had saved over time and intended for going to see their own family for the holidays. They trusted that God would see to their own needs, and they felt completely right in giving this money—just days before Christmas. And, indeed, God did take care of them; meanwhile, the family-in-need had money to brighten their Christmas for the whole family.

I am the constant recipient of random acts of kindness, gifts of loving service that are saturated with love. Just a few stocking stuffers from God's busy little elves: A devotee said he wanted to stop by. He brought his guru and Carlaji a beautiful meal, a generous gift of money as a tithe to God, and a year's worth of small gifts of inspiration to be opened throughout the coming year on specified dates. Another devotee made a large number of meals for Carla-ma and me to eat after Carla's operation that she had just before Christmas. And then, there are those who quietly give support for this Work we do for God and Gurus, without fanfare, or need to be broadcasted. It is a staggering fact; there are numberless acts of kindness and devotion that come my way—each one making my heart glow.

Through the news, we can come to believe this world is completely lacking in goodness and selflessness. My own experience is quite the opposite. I know that the vast majority of people are fundamentally good, and that there are shining soul-stars, such as those just mentioned, that light the darkness for us all. I think of all these luminous lights in the firmament of Spirit, and it makes me smile—most definitely, it gives me a warm after-Christmas glow. May your heart also be lit from within by these inspiring examples.

December 30

Spaciousness: You Are
a Citizen of the Stars

You are a citizen of the stars.**

M any people live lives that are too cramped, with a consciousness that is too small and too crowded. In this tight space, tension reigns supreme—it all feels like life is too much, that you are not big enough. This is in contradiction to the fact that you are truly made up of an infinite nature, being made in the likeness and image of God.

To counteract this cramped living style, you must move into spaciousness—where your consciousness easily accommodates expansiveness. Attuning yourself to your greater Self, you grow larger than your limited situation; you feel God-consciousness expand in you, making you know that all God is, is also available to you.

Those things that work against this roominess of Spirit include: when you are in pain or struggling with a physical condition, limited money, and prosperity in the moment; unhappy relationships and social situations; an unsatisfying work situation; and, a lack of balance in your life. These things can press in on you, making you feel small, and these situations feel very big. This oppressiveness puts you under tremendous pressure. This is not the way you are meant to live.

In truth, your life is an expression of infinite nature; you are meant to live in freedom, joy, love, and light. To tune into this greater Source, you must rise above your determined beliefs that you are small, and your problems are big. It is true that on a human level, many things can come at you, and challenges can really stretch you, but you are not a human-self only. You must remember that you are a child of the Infinite, and in remembering this, you claim access to the realms of your greater Self.

When meditating, bring to mind your expansiveness. Feel that you are not limited to one little human body, rather, you know yourself to be a citizen of the stars, that there is no limit to consciousness. When done with meditation time and you reenter into the world, continue your connection with your greater Self—that you are a living instrument of limitless thought, energy, and abundance. Your life is "right-sized" for you; you need only open yourself to all that God wishes to manifest through you. Let go of fear, resentment, limiting beliefs, and know that your infinite Beloved is, even right now, actively manifesting all that you need to be in His likeness and in His image.

No two lives are identical, so do not compare yourself to any other, for that would deny the uniqueness of how God chooses to be in you as a co-creator with Him. So, any time you are feeling too cramped in your living space, feeling the pressure of life, and that you are too small for the shoes you are wearing, then, instantly, recall who and what you truly are—a child of the Infinite—as such, you expand to be larger than the problems and challenges you face; you walk amongst the stars and vast resources are streaming to you in order for you to live your life exactly as it has been ordered from above. In that spaciousness, breathe freedom and know that God is the solution to every problem and that His ingenuity for solving problems is even greater than yours for creating them! There is plenty of room for you to breathe, live your life, and be exactly who God designed you to be.

December 31

A NEW YEAR ALIGNMENT

Reaching the pinnacle of your life.**

As we enter into a new year, it is a propitious time to reflect on our lives, with a summary of this past year and a projection into the next. Sometimes, day-to-day living makes life full of details: moving from one place to the next, one situation to another, and through all the busyness of life, we lose touch with the bigger picture. A new year is a wonderful time to focus on the themes that truly matter.

We come into this life with missions to accomplish. We need only look at those recurring themes in our life for hints as to what we have come to do: for some, it is education and learning, having and raising a family, a profession and trade, a passion for a sport, hobby, or craft, and having a loyal group of friends—all can be a big part of our lives. Some of these can seem rather pedestrian; others are vital. However, what is important to one may hold absolutely no meaning for another—the fact you hold it as valuable is what makes it important.

There are everyday actions that are the **mechanics of life**, things that we do that have value, but don't rank as very memorable, such as household chores, maintaining the car, and paying the bills. These are the things that take up so much of our time. They also produce major problems if they are not attended to, but are not the kinds of things that come to mind if we are asked, "What did you accomplish in your life?"

And yet, especially if we struggle with some of the mechanics of life, they can become a big part of what we have come to learn. A theme of learning for me has been organizing and simplifying things in my life. I find that being better organized helps me to accomplish the more important goals. There is a lady from Japan, Marie Kondo, who has made an entire profession of helping people organize their stuff. She wrote a bestselling book that I like very much, *The Life-Changing Magic of Tidying Up*. I fully intend this coming year to once again make a total sweep of all the things in my care and use her method for keeping only those things that bring me joy.

In addition to the daily mechanics of life, there are those things that are really **important**: such as a safe and loving home for children and family, financial security, professional goals, being a loving and supportive presence for friends, and maintaining a healthy body and environment. These important goals are closer to home, the things that speak more deeply to our souls and have a lasting impact on our lives. Many of the repetitive activities that make up the mechanics of life only exist in order to support these important things. Sometimes, we get a sudden reminder of how important these things are when we have a health challenge or a financial trial.

These past couple of years, keeping this body healthy took on a new focus of importance after being diagnosed with tumors. Subsequently, I have been working with a naturopath and getting scans and tests done several times a year—including taking supplements prescribed by the naturopath and working on healthy habits. Of course, I had been eating healthy before, but as I say, this has made healthiness even a deeper focus. All continues well in this regard as I enjoy perfect health—for that I thank our ever-gracious God and Gurus, your thoughts and prayers, dedicated health professionals, and health insurance workers who have helped make this possible. This new year will definitely entail making perfect health an ongoing reality.

In addition to the mechanics of life and attending to those important aspects, there are those **essential** elements in life that are must-dos. Like a pyramid, the mechanics of life form the foundation for achieving what is above it—the things that qualify as important—and then moving up to the pinnacle of the pyramid to that which is essential, the crown of your life. For example, for my father, it was clear that he came into this life with a keen desire to run his own business, and he spent a great deal of his life doing so in a dharmic way, filled with honest right-action. If he had not done this, he would have definitely felt that his life was not complete—this was essential for him. What is essential for me is not the running of a business; my purpose took a turn from my father's to that of a spiritual quest for Self-realization.

In my adult years, everything in my life—education, profession, family—has all been in support of this one overarching goal. But, there have been times in my life when my actions seemed to betray this **essential goal**. And this is what is vastly important here: when the pyramid of the foundational mechanics of my life does not support my important goals, which in turn do not enable me to realize the crowning essential summit of life, then I am out of sync with the very purpose of my coming—and this, being out of sync, leads to great suffering. Confusion and suffering occur when incarnating souls do not remember why they have come. Knowing God and serving Him in all souls in accordance with His inner direction has been, and continues to be, the real purpose of my life.

Every life has a unique set of circumstances for what a soul has come to learn. It is incumbent upon you to be clear as to what is essential for you to learn and to become. You must be fully aware of what is important to you, and align the mechanics of your life to support those important and essential goals. Through this alignment, you may rightfully enjoy peace and an absolutely fulfilled life.

Starting a new year is a wonderful time to calibrate all three of these parts of your life—the mechanics of daily activities with achieving those goals that are important and never losing sight of what is essential. Missing, or misaligning, any one of these three parts will lead to suffering, while having all three in sync makes you know that you are on track with why you are here; it also makes you know that with your sincere efforts and God's Grace, all success is open to you for the fulfillment of your purpose, just as God has designed it for you. In the thought of your per- fect alignment with your true purpose, I wish you a very happy New Year and the flawless fulfillment of all that you have come to accomplish.

Conclusion

From Sense-Drunk Life, Back to the Sea

I am but a human, frail and dark

Of foibles and errors do I possess,

But one gift appearing above all those earthly treasures

Stands my desire for Thee Alone.

Minor fiefdoms strive to conquer soul,

Petty princes try to grasp the whole

But no reach can circumference that Kingdom

Shining as my Eternal Abode.

Some day, the Rightful Ruler of old

Will again stand preeminent above it all

And reclaim rebellious land.

Standing upon truth and peace, we will hear its echo.

Like a pied piper of old will my soul call

To out-of-control, scattered mice, sense-drunk life,

And those pesky critters

Back to the sea that is One for us all.

Now I stand upon that crown of glory,

Freedom at last reigns in the soul

Order restored, with mind, sense, and desire

Brought back into the fold of One.

So, to all brethren do I call:

"Shy from error and cling unto truth

Let go of all that holds in bondage.

To our Infinite Reach, let us be away!"[37]

—YOGACHARYA DAVID

OM TAT SAT AUM

Mount Temple, Alberta, Canada, painting by Dennis Brown.

---

37   *Climbing the Sacred Mountain: Poems and Prayers of a Western Yogi* (p. 103).

References

Arnold, Edwin, Sir. (1905). *The Song Celestial or Bhagavad-Gita.* London, England: Dryden House.

Emerson, Ralph Waldo. (1847). *Poems.* London, England: Chapman Brothers.

Gupta, Mahendranath (Recorder). Swami Nikhilananda (Translator). (1942). *The Gospel of Sri Ramakrishna.* New York: Ramakrishna-Vivekananda Center.

Haich, Elisabeth. (1975). *Sexual Energy and Yoga.* New York: ASI Publishers.

Hickenbottom, Yogacharya David. (2023). *Discourses Vol. One: 2013–14: Living a Spiritually Rich Life.* Camano Island, WA.: The Cross and The Lotus Publishing.

Hickenbottom, Yogacharya David. (2022). *Silence: Entering the Cosmic Sea of Consciousness.* Camano Island, WA.: The Cross and The Lotus Publishing.

Hickenbottom, Yogacharya David. (2021). *Climbing the Sacred Mountain: Poems and Prayers of a Western Yogi.* Camano Island, WA.: The Cross and The Lotus Publishing.

Hickenbottom, Yogacharya David. (2019). *My Spiritual India.* Camano Island, WA.: The Cross and The Lotus Publishing.

Kondo, Marie. (2014). *The Life-Changing Magic of Tidying Up.* Berkeley, CA.: Ten Speed Press.

Paramhansa Yogananda. (2004). *The Second Coming of Christ, Vol. I–II.* Los Angeles, CA.: Self-Realization Fellowship.

Paramhansa Yogananda. (1995). *God Talks with Arjuna: Bhagavad Gita*. Los Angeles, CA.: Self-Realization Fellowship.

Paramhansa Yogananda. (1979). *The Second Coming of Christ, Vol. I–III*. Dallas, TX.: Amrita Foundation.

Paramhansa Yogananda. (1946). *Autobiography of a Yogi*. New York: The Philosophical Library.

Paramhansa Yogananda. (1929). *Whispers from Eternity*. Los Angeles, CA.: Self-Realization Fellowship.

Porter, Eleanor H. (1913). *Pollyanna*. Boston, MD.: L.C. Page and Company.

Seton, Elizabeth Bayley. Edited by Regina M. Bechtle and Judith Metz. (2000). *Collected Writings, Volume 1, 1774–1808*. Hyde Park, NY: New City Press.

Gupta, Mahendranath (Recorder). Swami Nikhilananda (Translator). (1942). *The Gospel of Sri Ramakrishna*. New York: Ramakrishna-Vivekananda Center.

Swami Ramdas. (1925). *In Quest of God*. Kerala, India: Anandashram.

Swami Ramdas. (1947). *The Pathless Path*. Kerala, India: Anandashram.

Swami Ramdas. (1957). *Stories as Told by Swami Ramdas*. Kerala, India: Anandashram.

Film References

A Christmas Carol. (1951). George Minter Productions. Directed by Brian Desmond Hurst.

A Christmas Story. (1983). Metro-Goldwyn-Mayer. Directed by Bob Clark.

Awake: The Life of Yogananda. (2014). Self-Realization Fellowship. Counterpoint Films. Filmmakers Paola di Florio, Lisa Leeman, and Peter Radar.

Christmas in Connecticut. (1945). Warner Bros. Directed by Peter Godfrey.

Christmas with the Kranks. (2004). Columbia Pictures. Directed by Joe Roth.

Elf. (2003). New Line Cinema. Directed by Jon Favreau.

Holiday Inn. (1942). Paramount Pictures. Directed by Mark Sandrich.

How the Grinch Stole Christmas. (2000). Imagine Entertainment. Directed by Ron Howard.

It's a Wonderful Life. (1946). Liberty Films. Directed by Frank Capra.

Jesus of Nazareth. (1977). ITC Entertainment, RAI. Directed by Franco Zeffirelli.

Lost Christmas. (2011). Impact Film & TV. Directed by John Hay.

Miracle on 34th Street. (1947). 20th Century Fox. Directed by George Seaton.

Mother Hamilton: A Divine Life. (2004). DVD. The Cross and The Lotus Publishing.

Somewhere in Time. (1980). Rastar. Universal Pictures. Directed by Jeanot Szwarc.

The Last Holiday. (2006). Paramount Pictures. Directed by Wayne Wang.

The Santa Clause. (1994). Walt Disney Pictures, Hollywood Pictures, Outlaw Productions. Directed by John Pasquin.

White Christmas. (1954). Paramount Pictures. Directed by Michael Curtiz.

Bible References

King James Bible Online: https//www.kingjamesbibleonline.org

Website References

Talks and Publications by Yogacharya David and Yogacharya Mother Hamilton: www.crossandlotus.com.

Mother Hamilton's quote reference: The Cross and The Lotus: www.crossandlotus.com

Anandashram reference: www.anandashram.org

Swami Ramdas: www.anandashram.org

George Washington quotes: www.mountvernon.org

Lincoln Inaugural Address and John Adams quote: www.nps.gov

Thoreau quote: www.thoreau-online.org

Declaration of Independence. https://www.archives.gov.declaration

University of Washington. https://rightasrain.uwmedicine.org/mind/well-being/5-surprising-health-benefits-gratitude

Image Attribution

With the exception of those listed below, all images are used courtesy of the David and Carla Hickenbottom portfolio. Photos were taken by David and Carla Hickenbottom or gifted with permission by friends, family, and devotees. Attribution for images from these sources has not been included here. Images of devotees or written submissions from devotees are all included after receiving consent for this book series. Images are either paid for or for free use under public domain, Creative Commons licensing, or from other sources as noted.

January 5. Paramhansa Yogananda. Cover of *Autobiography of a Yogi*. (1946 edition.) Commons.wikimedia.org. Public domain.

January 22. *Indian Goddess Durga Maa* by krhm73 on Shutterstock.com. License purchased.

February 5. Swami Sri Yukteswar and Paramhansa Yogananda in Calcutta, 1935. *Autobiography of a Yogi*, p. 458. Commons.wikimedia.org. Public domain.

February 22. *Sunset Desert Caravan* by Rene Rauschenberger from Pixabay.com. Free use under the Pixabay license.

March 7. Paramhansa Yogananda, 1952. Picture commonly known as "The Last Smile" by Arthur Say. Commons.wikimedia.org. Public domain.

March 12. *Mission San Xavier Del Bac* by Anza Trail NPS on Flickr.com. Licensed under Creative Commons CC-BY-NC 2.0.

April 2. Swami Ramdas, Anandashram, India, c. 1930s. Anandashram.org

May 18. *The Indian God Ganesha* wall relief carving, jigsaw style. Photo by Jannarong on Shutterstock.com. License purchased.

June 4. *Sacred Lotus Nelumbo Nucifera* by T. Voekler. Licensed under Creative Commons CC-BY-SA 3.0. Commons.wikimedia.org.

June 11. Sri Ramakrishna in samadhi during a kirtan at Keshab Sen's house, 1879. *The Gospel of Sri Ramakrishna*, pp. 676–677. Commons.wikimedia.org. Public domain.

June 11. *George Washington at Verplanck's Point*, 1790. Painting by John Trumbull. Commons.wikimedia.org. Public domain.

June 24. *Elizabeth Ann Seton* portrait by Amabilia Filicchi, 1888. Commons.wikimedia.org. Public domain.

June 29. *Imagine: Lancaster County Amish 03* by Utente: The Cad Expert is licensed under Creative Commons CC-BY-SA 3.0 and Gnu Free Documentation License. Wikipedia.org.

July 2. Swami Ramdas at Panch Pandav Cave, Mangalore, India, 1920s. Anandashram.org

July 2. Ralph Waldo Emerson, 1857 by Josiah Johnson Hawes, print from 1880. Commons.wikimedia.org. Public domain.

July 9. *Tree Silhouette and the Moon* by Oriontrail on Dreamstime. com. License purchased.

July 24. *Mahavatar Babaji* by Sananda Lal Ghosh. *Autobiography of a Yogi*, p. 293. Commons.wikimedia.org. Public domain.

August 27. *Sita with Rama* from *Adhyatma Ramayan*, Gita Press, Gorakpur. Commons.wikimedia.org. Public domain.

August 31. *Bhaktha Hanuman* by Ravi Varma Press, 1930. Commons.wikimedia.org. Public domain.

September 3. *Hands Holding World* by Stephen Denness on Dreamstime.com. License purchased.

September 8. *Tulip macro with Rumi quote* by snap 713 on Flickr. Licensed under Creative Commons CC-BY-NC-ND 2.0.

September 15. Lahiri Mahasaya. *Autobiography of a Yogi*, p. 317. Commons.wikimedia.org. Public domain.

September 17. *Road in Forest* by Ysbrand on Dreamstime.com. License purchased.

September 20. *Ocean Waves Crashing Near the Lighthouse* by Ray Bilcliff. Free use on Pexels.com.

October 8. *Fire Person Holding Lighted Oil Lamp Flame* on Photostockeditor.com 82909. Public domain.

October 30. *Ardhanarishvara*. 1940s India Bazaar Art. Commons. wikimedia.org. Public domain.

October 31. *Watercolor Roses on a Grey Stone Cross* by Abbie on Shutterstock.com. License purchased.

November 9. *Krishna Tells (the) Gita to Arjuna* by Mahavir Prasad Mishra. Mahabharata: Tej Kumar Book Depot. Commons. wikimedia.org. Public domain.

November 19. *Rama, Sita, Lakshmana* Lithograph c. 1880–1900. Commons.wikimedia.org. Public domain.

November 26. *Dome of the Rock, Jerusalem, Israel* by Thales Botelho de Sousa on Unsplash.com. Free use under the Unsplash license.

December 3. *Red Lilies* on Pixnio.com. Public domain.

December 8. *Low Light View Gold Buddha Statue* by Aerawan Srichai on Dreamstime.com. License purchased.

December 17. *Nativity of Jesus Scene with the Holy Family* by Romolo Tavani on Dreamstime.com. License purchased.

December 27. *Saint Nicholas,* 15th century icon from Owczary Historic Museum in Sanok, Poland. Commons.wikimedia.org. Public domain.

December 30. *Universe Filled Stars, Nebula and Galaxy* by Evgenii Puzanov on Dreamstime.com. License purchased.

December 31. *Giza Pyramid* by Alphaspirit on Dreamstime.com. License purchased.

Conclusion: *Mount Temple*, Alberta, Canada. Painting by Dennis Brown. With permission.

Acknowledgments

Yogacharya David has a unique ability to share spiritual teachings and soul-enhancing reflections in a most accessible manner—he can reach us in our day-to-day ways of being as we strive to live a purposeful life. He guides us, and, even as he laughs at himself, he still seriously advocates for a wake-up process.

It is a privilege to form what we call Team-David, a dedicated team of aspirants who willingly devote time and expertise to ensuring that Yogacharya David's legacy of teachings reaches those who long for a deeper, broader, and disciplined-yet-freeing approach to life's journey.

Carla Hickenbottom, David's wife and senior disciple, has been a major support throughout the preparation and publication process. Her loving oversight and her diligence as director of The Cross and The Lotus Publishing support us each step of the way.

Rebecca Harvey has been a major ongoing link to data collection and historical document searches. She seems to know just where to find more information on most everything we need. Her keen eye also provides an astute read that catches the forever-escaping grammatical challenges. Mira Lutz, our other Team-David member for the Discourses, has an excellent knowledge of grammar. It is a gift of Grace to have such a fine team working to prepare and publish Yogacharya David's series of six Discourse volumes.

Our team also includes my editor, Zia Cole, for all of the Discourse volumes—our gratitude to her for her astute eye and professional expertise.

Jan Westendorp of Kato Design and Photo brings her artistic and professional book-design expertise forward when working on our manuscripts. She provides us with elegant page layouts and image-refinement support, and in so many other ways, she has helped us create a beautiful series of six volumes.

Team-David feels that Yogacharya David would be delighted to know that his unique writings and teachings are available in book form for all who seek a deeper, sacred understanding of the human condition.

About the Author

Yogacharya David Hickenbottom (1954–2019) met his guru Yogacharya Mother Hamilton, a disciple of Paramhansa Yogananda, when he was a youth of 20. Yogacharya David became a Reverend in 1984, and Mother Hamilton bestowed the Yogacharya title to David in 1989.

The great Kriya Yoga lineage of India that came through Jesus, Babaji, Lahiri Mahasaya, and Sri Yukteswar to Yogananda, and then to Mother Hamilton, provides pathways to: an appreciation of, and a faith in, the everyday sacred, an understanding of higher dimensional wisdom, an integral intuitive knowing of spiritual truths, and the vibratory realms that permeate all that is, was, and will be.

Yogacharya David says: "An inner pain brought me to the path most unwillingly, and this inner pain kept me on the path. I put my shoulder to the wheel." He faced the crux of the spiritual dilemma—how to shift from the ego-driven lower or smaller human nature to a larger and luminous existence, intuitively attuned to our deeper and broader—vast—spiritual nature, thereby discovering the Living Truth. With this intense striving for Truth and Bliss, and with his Guru's Grace, Yogacharya David was carried through many years of Mystical Crucifixion spiritual experiences. His year in silence (2000–2001) established an inner state of stillness that never left him—and finally led him to his full Self-realization.

Also by Yogacharya David

2013–2019 Discourse Series:

- *Discourses—Volume One: 2013–14: Living a Spiritually Rich Life*

- *Discourses—Volume Two: 2015: Re-Union of Soul and Spirit*

- *Discourses—Volume Three: 2016: A True New Birth*

- *Discourses—Volume Four: 2017: Gateway to the Infinite*

- *Discourses—Volume Five: 2018: Standing on the Threshold of Eternity*

- *Discourses—Volume Six: 2019: Writing in the Book of Life*

Hickenbottom, Yogacharya David. (2022). *Touching the Supreme Spirit*: Infinite Calendar. Camano Island, WA.: The Cross and The Lotus Publishing.

Hickenbottom, Yogacharya David. (2022). *Silence: Entering the Cosmic Sea of Consciousness*. Camano Island, WA.: The Cross and The Lotus Publishing.

Hickenbottom, Yogacharya David. (2022). *Notes to Sadhakas*. Camano Island, WA.: The Cross and The Lotus Publishing.

Hickenbottom, Yogacharya David. (2021). *Climbing the Sacred Mountain: Poems and Prayers of a Western Yogi*. Camano Island, WA.: The Cross and The Lotus Publishing.

Hickenbottom, Yogacharya David. (2019). *My Spiritual India*. Camano Island, WA.: The Cross and The Lotus Publishing.

www.ingramcontent.com/pod-product-compliance
Lightning Source LLC
Chambersburg PA
CBHW070901120626
46546CB00001B/87